the empathy advantage

ARMINLEAR

Library of Congress Control Number: 2020012606

ISBN (peperback): 978-1-956450-10-1

Armin Lear Press Inc
215 W Riverside Drive, #4362
Estes Park, CO 80517

the empathy advantage

coaching children to be kind, respectful, and successful

Lynne Azarchi
with Larry Hanover

ARMINLEAR

Contents

preface
COVID-19, racism, and empathy

a s this book was going to print, both COVID-19 and many African Americans' deaths were *drastically* changing our world in ways that we could never have imagined.

COVID-19 and Empathy

We had to stay six feet apart. Everything closed, including businesses, governments, schools, and the Kidsbridge Tolerance Center. We endured "social distancing," quarantine, and isolation—the antithesis of empathy.

In the midst of the crisis, it seemed the word *empathy* was mentioned every day on TV and in the news. What's more, I witnessed acts of empathy popping up everywhere. Wearing a mask is a true act of empathy. Wearing one doesn't necessarily prevent the *wearer* from getting ill; it protects *others* from catching the virus. Other empathetic acts that we must honor were those of selfless, altruistic first responders and all the other heroes on the front lines, most risking their lives, to do what was noble and right for the society as a whole.

Those families who spent more face-to-face time with each other discovered how, in good times and bad, practicing empathy could lead to closeness, bonding, and cultivating deeper, more meaningful relationships.

In new roles, parents/caregivers substituting as teachers, and scrambling to be instant educators, learned how hard it is to teach. Many confided in me that both working from home and teaching were arduous challenges. To address this need, Kidsbridge created Kidsbridge@Home in March 2020, providing free online empathetic activities for parents/caregivers to do with their children and for teachers to send home to families.

Amid dramatic increases in anxiety, tension, depression, and even abuse because of COVID-19, empathy can come to the rescue by providing emotional support, caring, respect, and kindness. Empathy can also be used as a tool to reduce stress, conflict, and trauma.

For our kids, these times demand a paradigm shift away from the "old normal" of an emphasis on academics and testing for youth and a pivot to "teaching our children well" (i.e., self-compassion and empathy for others). Now more than ever, it is time for all of us to focus on creating and coaching empathic human beings. Even after the virus retreats, the need for teaching empathy and building a more compassionate society will be greater than ever.

Racism and Empathy

The deaths of George Floyd, Ahmaud Arbery, Breonna Taylor, and far too many others can be our impetus as parents, caregivers, and educators to work toward a future of racial acceptance, diversity appreciation, and equal protection under the law. Eliminating bias, discrimination, and hate is hard work for individuals and families, and it is even more challenging for entire communities. But it is the existential work necessary for our nation if we are to increase kindness and respect and achieve greater social justice and equity.

I believe that in order to move society forward in the years and decades ahead, we must ensure and prioritize that our children are more actively taught both empathy and empathetic action. This is one of the reasons I wrote this book. In order to understand racism, diversity, and inequities in the aftermath of these deaths and protests, we need to teach *all* of our children at younger ages and more consistently.

Racism is learned early; by the age of three, children accept racism and prejudice around them, even if they don't understand what those concepts mean. As parents/caregivers and teachers, we must actively engage our children in age-appropriate conversations about racism, stereotypes, and discrimination *earlier and more consistently.* All these harmful and injurious societal norms can be ameliorated if we have the courage and the tools to have honest conversations with our kids and each other about race. We won't have all the answers, and that's OK. But talking about bias and intolerance is far better than silence and superior to promulgating old myths and stereotypes through the complicity of avoidance and procrastination.

Hollow statements like "I don't see color" and "I am not a racist" don't eliminate racism, bias, and discrimination. These declarative statements don't encourage action and empowerment, nor do they advance social justice. Empathizing with the mothers and fathers of Black and brown children who tremble every time their kids leave the house is a first step to "walking in others' shoes." Further empathizing with a five-year-old "Black" child who is told that he or she cannot play because "their skin is too dark" is sadly something I hear about often. In addition to Black persons, institutionalized racism persists against Asian, indigenous, Jewish, Latinx, LGBT, and Muslim persons and other minorities.

Please discuss and acknowledge your child's feelings. Fear, confusion, and anger are normal, but guidance is needed to help children process those powerful emotions and the overwhelming images they are seeing on the media. Active listening is a great tool for you at this time. Please take this opportunity to educate yourself and your children with the books, articles, and activities recommended inside this book that teach diversity appreciation and acceptance so we can move our children beyond "tolerance" to a more inclusive society.

* * *

A door closes and a window opens—empathy provides a unique emotional springboard to do better than we have in the past. It is time for all of us to focus on creating and coaching empathetic human beings, both young and old. Teaching empathy is one of the greatest foundations and gifts that you can bestow upon your child. Let's change the world for the better—one child and one adult at a time. *The Empathy Advantage* is here to help you.

acknowledgments

there are so many people to thank. First, I'd like to thank all the wonderful, kind people who have helped with or contributed to the nonprofit Kidsbridge Tolerance Center for more than twenty years. I am surrounded night and day by selfless people and volunteers. They work long hours and make little money helping kids (many of them at risk), and they also energize adults to enhance empathy, self-compassion, and diversity appreciation, and teach kids to be UPstanders. They are rich with the joy of helping others.

I couldn't have helped so many kids, educators, and parents in New Jersey without the kind, thoughtful, and energetic help of the Kidsbridge staff, donors, and board of trustees, particularly Kidsbridge's Education Committee. I am indebted to Dr. Harlene Galen for reviewing the manuscript for educational pedagogy and accuracy. Others who inspired me in empathy acumen are Kidsbridge educator Rebecca Erickson; Professor Yonty Friesem of Columbia College Chicago; and polymath Maurice Elias, director of the Rutgers Social-Emotional and Character Development Lab.

I want to express my gratitude to my agent, Maryann Karinch. This book wouldn't exist were it not for her curiosity and desire to be convinced that empathy could be taught. With my Kidsbridge experience under my belt, I was able to do just that. In addition, gratitude goes out to Suzanne Staszak-Silva of Rowman & Littlefield for recognizing the value and urgency of helping adults improve both their parenting and their teaching skills to empower the next generation toward greater kindness and respect. Shout-out to illustrator Caroline Blodi for her creative, fun illustrations.

I would like to give a shout-out to writers who inspired me. First is my father. I discovered after he passed away that, unbeknownst to me, he had penned a treasure trove of radio plays, poetry, song lyrics, and even a letter to Tennessee Williams. My father aimed high, was an insufferable Type A, and never resisted the urge for creative expression. I think I owe him a debt for the insatiable passion I have to write, accomplish, and help others. Gratitude also to the first obsessed writer I met in college-Derf; I still have his brilliant journals and they inspire me. Kudos to my "writer friends" who have inspired me with publications of their own (Dr. Liza Gold) and others, dauntless to share numerous pithy diatribes and rants on current events and history.

I also would like to thank Larry Hanover for helping me write this parent guide and inspiring me to share the stories I lived and know. A shout-out goes to Robin Levinson for recommending Larry. Gratitude goes to my mother, Evelyn, for unconditional love. And last but not least, I'd like to thank both of my children, Rachel and Jake, my sister Karen, and particularly my husband, Steve, who supported my empathy quest, suffering my long hours over the years to research and write this book to help parents, caregivers, and teachers. By the way, Steve makes a mean pasta puttanesca.

one

why YOU should
care about empathy

You can only understand people if you feel them in yourself.
—John Steinbeck

When I teach schoolchildren about empathy, I can get a sense from the number of smiles and enthusiastic answers how the lesson went. But what I cannot sense is whether any of the children are hurting that day from being teased about their religion, a disability, their skin color, or something else. And I cannot sense whether one of them has actually bullied a classmate on the way to school or at recess. I cannot tell who has no friends or who has no support at home.

But after completing our program at the Kidsbridge Tolerance Center in New Jersey, we ask the kids to fill out surveys about what they have learned. Every so often, personal reflections and epiphanies emerge, and I feel a swell of sadness rising.

"A girl was picking on me because I am from Dubai," Jumana, a fifth grader, wrote after her class visited Kidsbridge, where we teach about empathy, empowering children to stand up to bullies, and more. "She called me 'Muslim Chick,' and soon everybody was calling me that name. . . . It hurts to be judged like that."

Jumana was by this time attending a different school than the one where she had been insulted for her religion. But the teasing had hurt her so deeply that the pain was following her months or even years later. My heart aches when I see children increasingly failing to understand the damage that words can cause. I often tear up because such stories confirm what I hear from teachers all the time: kids' ability to understand one another's feelings has been plunging.

But then one day I read the following response, and I turned emotional for a different reason. Because we'd had a win. It turned out Taquan, a third grader, realized he was guilty of being a bit of a bully himself and needed to change.

"Each activity [at Kidsbridge] shows why not to treat people bad or tease," he wrote. "So I stopped teasing people. That was a good lesson [because] when people tease me, I feel the same way."

Such epiphanies are why I wrote this book. Empathy is lacking in this world. Tolerance for those who are different is more absent than ever. But in these pages, I can help parents make this world change for the better, one child at a time.

Looking back, I guess I was always the Empathy Girl, who grew up into the Empathy Woman. It started with basic scary movies like *The Blob*—OK, even malicious Jell-O was enough to scare me in the early 1960s—and *Invaders from Mars*. If you looked for me in my seat, you wouldn't find me. You'd have to crane your neck and look under the seat, and *there* you'd find me, cowering underneath, fingers in my ears, praying the movie would be over soon.

My empathy could have gotten me into serious trouble as a kid when my uncle took me to a Yankees game in the Bronx. I was having fun until the crowd started to boo the opposing team. I asked my uncle why the crowd would do that. "There is no reason and it isn't nice!" I protested. His eyes widened and he gave me a funny look, at which point I realized I may have been just about the only Yankees fan with that line of thought. Fortunately, I didn't voice my concerns to anyone but my uncle, because other fans might have gone bonkers!

Then, in my twenties, the movie *Halloween* (1978) came out. I felt like I *was* those poor young female victims, and that was just from hearing about the movie from friends and seeing the trailers. A masked slasher hacking teenagers to death and dismembering them, with blood and gore everywhere? Why would anyone want to see such a film? I never did. That was way more than I could take.

This innate sense of reacting to what others feel and under-standing it in my bones isn't confined to the world of Hollywood make-believe or sporting events. When I get my morning *New York Times*, I rip out upsetting photos of children in distress and tearful victims of hurricanes and earthquakes so that I don't have to look at them more than once. I know it sounds like an overreaction, but that's how I am wired.

In 2017, I had the opportunity to go to Poland and visit the concentration camps, including Auschwitz-Birkenau. Many of my relatives were murdered there by the Nazis, so when I saw the rooms full of hair, thousands of spectacles and suitcases, and other personal items, I took it very personally. I had not expected to look like the photos of many of the female victims, and yet at Auschwitz-Birke-nau and all the other museums and exhibits, in my mind, I did. I was overwhelmed by visions of what bystanders could do to other people with wanton cruelty, sadism, and inhumaneness. For two months after I got home, I awoke in the middle of the night with my heart racing and my body shaking from dreams about my visit to a horrific time and place.

But please don't get the impression that being the Empathy Woman is all bad. Yes, it can be a curse in some instances, but it is also a blessing. It has made me who I am today, a person who volunteers for numerous organizations and is warmed by the glow that comes from helping others. No amount of money could buy all those smiles. Most significantly, it led me to become executive director of the Kidsbridge Tolerance Center outside Trenton, New Jersey, working full time on a labor of love: teaching children, youth, and educators about empathy and empowerment, respect, and kindness.

What is empathy? Simply, it is the ability to "walk in someone else's shoes." It is the ability to grasp the world from someone else's point of view. It is the ability to understand what others see and feel. Empathy requires respect for people different from ourselves.

How Is Lack of Empathy Manifesting in Our Youth?

- There has been an increase in bullying and cyberbullying.
- Teachers complain that their students do not know how to have a conversation.
- There have been increases in narcissism: extreme selfishness and self-centeredness.
- There has been a decline in face-to-face interpersonal skills with peers; kids don't know how to talk to one another and work out their problems.
- Screen time is out of control; many kids are on their smartphones and tablets more than they sleep. They are addicted.

Granted, I am living proof that people can be hyper hardwired for empathy. (There's even a technical term for my "condition"; it's called being an empath.) And yes, I accept that I'm a rarity. Simon Baron-Cohen, a professor of psychology and psychiatry at Cambridge University, suggests we place people on an empathy spectrum or quantitative scale. This empathy spectrum or scale would follow a bell curve (see figure 1.1), meaning that some people have a small amount, some a medium amount, and some a lot.[1] That's me—a lot.

Almost two decades ago, when I started this work, I read that empathy could not be taught. But I heartily object to that assertion: empathy *can* be taught. I am living proof that it can. I've taught it to more than thirty thousand youths and their educators at Kidsbridge, with an average of twenty-three hundred kids and two hundred educators coming through every year. Note the dashed line above the bell curve line in the figure; empathy can be increased at any level.

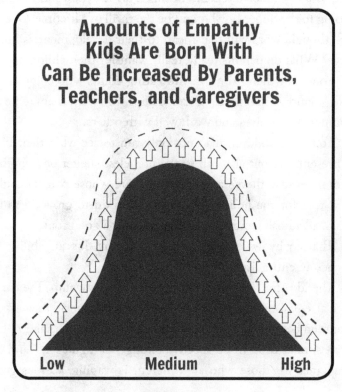

Figure 1.1

And parents, *I can teach you.*

In fact, you can teach empathy to your children, whether you spend just twenty minutes a week or two hours. No, this isn't a cure-all. But just a little effort, using proven and effective methods, with a dose of *fun*, can transform your child into a more sensitive, caring human being. I am an empty nester now; my children Rachel and Jake are both out on their own. But if I had known then what I know now, I would have tried to inspire them with empathy more often, more consistently, and more strategically. I would have closely followed the steps, tips, and strategies that you will read in this book. My kids would have more empathy and would have been better prepared for the future to function both as individuals and as part of a team.

Giving your children the gift of a new video game or smartphone may give them a little enjoyment in the short term—OK, "little" is a *big* understatement. Seeing a favorite pop star in concert or going to the Super Bowl might be the thrill of a lifetime. Over the years, though, what will that mean to their development as human beings? What do parents really, really want for their children?

You want them to grow into caring adults who enjoy lasting, loving relationships and close friendships. You want them to be able to support themselves and work well with others.

You want children who not only run to see what their birthday presents are but also run to the homeless shelter or a children's hospital because there's a child somewhere whose parents couldn't afford toys for the holiday. You want your kid to grow up to be a *mensch*, a Yiddish word for a good person or a good soul.

That's why we need to teach empathy. It's an ability that enriches an entire lifetime.

The idea for this book was not born in a vacuum. The current political environment has torn our American fabric in ways I've never seen before. Empathy is declining precipitously, hand in hand with a similar drop in perspective taking (see figures 1.2 and 1.3). Acceptance for those who are different is waning. Various groups feel targeted at one time or another, whether it's Jewish gravestones being overturned, a Muslim girl's hijab being yanked off her face, a Latinx boy being told to "go back to Mexico," or White persons from a midwestern factory town feeling like no one cares when the jobs dry up.

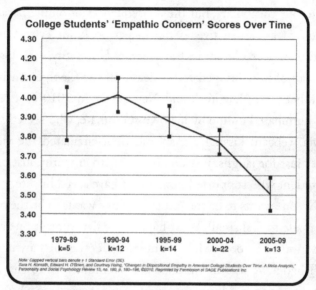

Figure 1.2

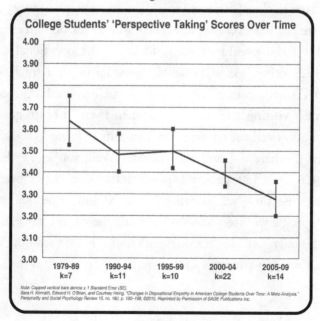

Figure 1.3

What people in general and the media are ignoring is how children are suffering. In my opinion, this is the crisis that no one talks about. Due to the recent cultural climate, bullying and cyberbullying have increased for children of color, Muslim children, LGBT youth, and many others. *Trolling* and *cyberbullying* are recent additions to our vocabulary, but the consequences of online harassment can be just as destructive as the in-person kind. Tyler Clementi, an eighteen-year-old student at Rutgers University with his entire life ahead of him, jumped to his death off the George Washington Bridge between New York and New Jersey in 2010 as a result of being humiliated online by his own roommate, who secretly filmed him via webcam kissing a man and then circulated the video on Twitter just for laughs. Just one person with empathy, just one college student who supported him, might have saved his life.

No one wants to be the "other." No one wants to be the outsider or be made to feel small. Yet it happens to everyone at one stage of life or another. It took awhile for me to suffer that first awful experience. I had a wonderful childhood in Trenton, with loving parents and terrific friends. Money was tight. Almost everyone who grew up in Trenton in the 1960s was fairly poor, so having no money meant you were just like everyone else. There was no reason to feel envy.

Yet I did eventually come to know the occasional pain of being the "other." As a Jewish kid growing up in a small, largely Italian-Catholic community in the city's Chambersburg section, I remember visiting a friend's house when I was in ninth grade and accidentally overhearing my friend's parents chatting in the kitchen. Out of nowhere, I heard the remark: "Well, you know the Jews killed Christ." I'd never been exposed to that thinking before. It was a shock that these adults, whom I valued and respected, thought Jewish people were responsible for killing their Lord. I instantly felt like a bit of an outsider in my friend's home. From then on, I was on alert for remarks wherever I went: in the supermarket, at the movies, in restaurants. It was disheartening—and a wakeup call. My family moved across the river to a town in Pennsylvania during the 1968 race riots. It, too, was a warm, wonderful place. But those around us had more money, so my identity was the "city girl," out of place, who couldn't quite fit in in the suburbs. Life was good, but that feeling of "otherness" lurked in the background, always hanging over me.

Empathy helps us transform "otherness" into inclusiveness. It creates better relationships, closer friendships, and stronger communities. It boosts children's social-emotional skills, strengthening them and their abilities to work and play with others.

Without empathy, we cannot understand diversity or people different from us. Without empathy, our focus and our children's focus are narrow. Children without empathy can grow up to be callous and fearful adults, what I call "bulls in a china shop." Without empathy, we only care about ourselves, to the exclusion of care and concern for others.

Recent research is alarming. It tells us empathy is dropping, narcissism is increasing, and in schools, social-emotional skill development is being sacrificed for grades and testing. Having a deficit in empathy and other social-emotional skills is distressing.

My background attuned me to the Jewish concept of *tikkun olam*, which literally translates as "repairing or healing the world." In practice, it means social justice. I participated in marches against the Vietnam War. I protested chemical spraying by crop dusters of farmworkers who harvested grapes and lettuce for a living, and I supported iconic union organizer Cesar Chavez, who sought better working conditions for migrant workers. I also helped raise money for Jews living in persecution in what was then the Soviet Union to escape to the United States.

My chance to put my empathy into practice came in 2002. It all happened out of sheer happenstance. The scene had been set on May 14, 2000, in Washington, D.C. I had ventured out with a girlfriend to participate in the Million Mom March against gun violence. She asked whether I would volunteer for a children's museum called Kidsbridge in downtown Trenton. It was a shell of an organization, barely hanging on and floundering financially. But having worked for four years for the Hayden Planetarium at the American Museum of Natural History in New York immersed in managing youth education and knowing its importance, I started volunteering at Kidsbridge.

In 2002, the executive director decided to quit. One of her last acts was to recruit me as her replacement because she thought I'd be great for the job. The place hooked me. Slowly, taking baby steps and then bigger ones, I taught myself about character education. What I found, though, was that what Kidsbridge could truly teach, and what truly resonated, was empathy.

It largely comes down to the Golden Rule: "Do unto others as you would have them do unto you." By understanding someone else's feelings, you find yourself able to treat others the way you would like to be treated. The Golden Rule, in short, is "Be empathetic! And be kind and respectful!" While there are many other important social-emotional skills, I find empathy to be the most important: the foundation and the first building block for other skills.

The Golden Rule

Did you know that *all* the major religions have a Golden Rule? When my staff members teach religious diversity at the Tolerance Center, we share various versions of the Golden Rule with the kids, and they have to match those versions to a world religion. It's hard and fun, because the versions are all so similar.

As adults, we are overwhelmed with parenting books and advice and don't know which attribute to focus on first. Is it grit? Angela Duckworth wrote a *New York Times* best seller on grit and its importance in childhood education. Is it resilience? Dr. Kenneth R. Ginsburg is the guru when it comes to teaching resilience to youth. But my money is on parents and teachers prioritizing coaching our youth to achieve a foundation of empathy (see figure 1.4).

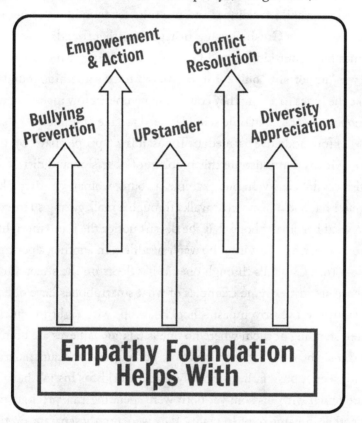

Figure 1.4

After establishing that foundation, we can then collect other building blocks—honesty, patience, respect, appreciation for diversity, and empowerment (aka empathetic action)—to create truly winning, sentient, and successful human beings.

Empathy is needed now more than ever. How can we have empathy if we are not interacting with one another? It's nearly impossible if we are focused on ourselves to the exclusion of others.

Yet just when we need empathy the most, it's on a downward spiral. One of the primary culprits is screens. Children aren't interacting with human faces if they are looking at screens, and if they think they are, they're kidding themselves. How many times have you called your child for dinner and five minutes found him or her still playing Candy Crush or using Instagram with a friend? How many times have your kids started Googling something at meals because it was "important," only for it to turn out to be something mundane like the lyrics to a song they couldn't remember? How many "urgent" phone calls does a middle schooler need to take at dinner?

How addictive is media? Thousands of people have by now seen videos that illustrate this problem of obsession and distraction with crystal clarity. In one example, a young woman wearing a knit winter hat and a heavy coat walks through a mall, gazing so intently down at her smartphone that she doesn't notice the fountain right in front of her. She falls into the water headfirst. In another, a person in New York City falls through open cellar doors on the street. Ouch! Those are just extreme examples of what smartphones have done to our society. I've driven past school bus stops with eight to ten children standing at them where no one is talking. All eyes are on their screens. There is no communication, no laughing, no camaraderie. I have seen a busy father who travels the world for his job having a rare lunch with his son; yet both were spending this precious time together in name only. In reality, they were utterly separate, on their own phones. They were in their own worlds, not interacting with one another. The skills of communication and teamwork of our youth have been diminished.

Signs of Diminishing Empathy

- The inordinate and increasing amount of time kids spend on media, resulting in addiction
- Losing face-to-face time, with interpersonal skills suffering
- The quality of media: violence, mean-spiritedness, backstabbing, bullying, name calling, reality shows
- Less time for character education in home and school
- Less time spent reading fiction and other books that create empathy
- "Fake news," with youth unable to distinguish what is real from what is fantasy and teachers having little time to dwell on these topics

Many people call for putting children on a "media diet" to not only increase their attention span but also reverse the effects of the sedentary lifestyle that screens can cause, which leads to obesity and psychological problems. A group called Wait Until 8th seeks to persuade parents to take a pledge that they will delay giving children a cell phone until at least eighth grade; if their children must have a phone earlier, they should get a basic phone (such as a flip phone) with just call and text service, no data plan.

Screens promote focusing only on oneself. Too much self-focus can balloon into an oversized ego. Whether social media is the cause or merely provides the outlet for narcissism to grow is a source of heated argument among researchers. But more than likely, it's an unhealthy combination of both in a vicious cycle. Best-selling author and psychologist Michele Borba writes that *narcissism*, defined by researchers as "self-centered, arrogant, and entitled," is increasing.[2] She says social media is widening its breadth as a true psychological problem, with children developing an unhealthy belief that they must compete online for social status. The consequences are stark.

Borba also states that there are five factors that squelch empathy:[3]

1. emotional unavailability of parents

2. absence of supportive fathers

3. cruel and mean-spirited media

4. raising children to mask their feelings

5. abuse, neglect, and stress in the first three years of life

Knowing this, parents can work to foster empathy by focusing early, creating a media diet, encouraging kids to express themselves, and being emotionally available as often as possible.

In the *2012 Report Card on the Ethics of American Youth* by the Josephson Institute, we can hear a cry for help to bring character education, respect, and kindness back to schools. A recent survey of high school youth revealed the following:[4]

- Fifty-seven percent agree with the statement "In the real world, successful people do what they have to do to win, even if others consider it cheating."

- Forty-two percent say they have used racial slurs or insults.

- Fifty-one percent say they have been bullied, teased, or taunted in a way that seriously upset them.

- Twenty-four percent agree with the statement "It's sometimes OK to hit or threaten a person who makes me very angry."

As educator and writer Paul Barnwell wrote in *The Atlantic*, "It's time for critical reflection about values our schools transmit to children by omission in our curriculum of the essential human challenges of character development, morality, and ethics." Echoing Barnwell's admonition about "broken moral compasses," a Denver high school teacher told writer William Anderson that far too often, "we're sacrificing the humanity of students for potential academic and intellectual gain."[5]

Empathy and the Nineteenth-Century Argument Against Slavery

Lucy Stone, the famous abolitionist, was having a hard time getting people, especially men, to support ending slavery. Brilliantly, she thought of a way to use empathy. She asked the naysayers, "Do you love your mother? Do you love your sisters?" Of course, the naysayers answered yes.

She explained to the naysayers that families were being broken up and separated. The naysayers swung to her side.

Throughout history, leaders and people have used empathy to make the world a better place. Empathy sustains us and nurtures not just the individual but an entire society, a country, a civilization.

As a parent, you can use your imagination and creativity to teach and model empathy. You can search for examples of people who have used empathy to accomplish great things and share them. Or ask your kids to think of their heroes or persons that they have noticed modeling empathy. Maybe they'll think of a brave woman from history like Harriet Tubman, or a religious figure like Mother Teresa, or even a sports hero like Pat Tillman, who gave up an NFL career and died serving in Afghanistan trying to make a distant country a better place. And let's not forget about kid heroes. Whomever they pick, a discussion or a book will take them to a place of empathy.

It's heartbreaking to realize that we are just scratching the surface of the reality of the harmful effects of lacking empathy. They go far beyond the interaction of one person speaking to another and not being in the moment. The consequences can have a domino effect that consigns a person, a family, a community, and perhaps a culture to long-term struggles that may have been avoidable:

- Many students lack social-emotional competencies and become less connected to school as they progress from elementary to middle to high school, and this lack of connection negatively affects their academic performance, behavior, and health.[6]

- In a national sample of almost 150,000 students, only 29 to 45 percent of middle and high school students reported that they had social competencies such as empathy, decision-making, and conflict resolution skills.[7]

- By high school, 40 to 60 percent of students become chronically disengaged from school.[8]

- Approximately 30 percent of high school students engage in multiple high-risk behaviors like substance abuse, sex, and violence that interfere with school performance and jeopardize their potential for life success. Many fall into depression and even attempt suicide.[9]

But please don't take this book as being only about sounding the alarm. There is hope because empathy can counteract these disturbing trends. Mark H. Davis, author of *Empathy: A Social Psychological Approach*, says increased empathy is associated with more tolerant attitudes, leading people to have fewer conflicts and resolve the ones they have more quickly.[10] As an added bonus, he points out that empathetic people can read each other's expressions more readily. That's good on its own and can even help people win prizes; Davis has demonstrated that people with empathy are better at face-to-face games, including the TV game show *Password*. That's because empathetic people have the ability to understand others' perspectives and are more skillful in sending and receiving clues, which is at the heart of *Password*. What's not to like about that?

It's critical for us to start a groundswell for empathy and character education right now. The No Child Left Behind Act, passed in 2001, had extraordinarily punitive consequences for schools whose students did not meet required standards for reading and math. School principals were fired, staff members were replaced, and schools faced other sanctions if they consistently failed to meet those required goals. Under the Obama administration, the consequences of this act were essentially waived out of existence, but the results of a dozen years under No Child Left Behind were dramatic. Schools were all about the test, and many remain so. Arts and music programs got axed or were scaled back.

And character education fell even further down the priority list. Social-emotional skills and the "whole child" are a poor third or fourth behind academics and sports. I witnessed a battle in my own school district near Princeton. Half of the parents lined up behind academics, and half lined up behind the "whole child." Bitter conversations, adults cyberbullying one another, angry complaints to the school board, and nasty letters to the editor of the local newspaper abounded. Many parents don't seem to understand the long-term advantages and benefits of kindness, cooperation, and respect.

James R. Doty published a fabulous book called *Into the Magic Shop: A Neurosurgeon's Quest to Discover the Mysteries of the Brain and the Secrets of the Heart* that addresses those advantages. In the book, he says that a common misperception about "survival of the fittest means the survival of the strongest and the most ruthless . . . [but it] is the survival of the kindest and most cooperative that ensures the survival of the species in the long-term. We evolved to cooperate, to nurture and raise our dependent young, and to thrive together for the benefit of all."[11]

Do you think Charles Darwin, to whom the idea of "survival of the fittest" is attributed, would agree? We will visit Darwin later, and he just might surprise you.

Instilling empathy over the long term inspires kids to become caring, nurturing adults, which is satisfying in and of itself. But empathy has even more to offer. In studying what makes good leaders, Daniel Goleman, Richard Boyatzis, and Annie McKee argue in *Primal Leadership* that empathy outweighs cognitive skills.[12]

They state that leaders who use empathy create the most energizing, top-performing cultures, including corporate cultures. Empathy shows up in leadership competence studies. When empathy is high, a leader is better at both persuading and inspiring teamwork and cooperation. What parent doesn't want his or her child to be a successful leader and contributor?

Look at the dysfunctional cultures of companies such as Yahoo!, Uber, Wells Fargo, and United Airlines (whose staff dragged a man off a plane), all of which have endured recent corporate PR crises. When you have a leader at the top who is not empathetic, the whole corporate culture collapses onto itself.

The rest of this book looks more deeply into empathy, showing that it can be taught, providing some basic science behind it as well as tips for teaching empathy to kids from toddlers to high school students and beyond. So be a leader yourself: learn how to teach your children about empathy. You'll create better people and do your part to make this world a little brighter place.

An Activity for You!

Now that I've told you my story and why I feel empathy is crucial for our children, I want you to try a little exercise. Think about the top nine things you want for your children out of life. They can be  anything you want. (I promise not to peek, so you can be completely honest!) Then put your answers aside for a little later. After you've read most of this book, you'll be referring back to this list to see whether your priorities have changed after a little coaching on the Empathy Advantage!

two
empathy CAN be taught

Dear Kidsbridge,

I am in fourth grade. I went to Kidsbridge
and wrote something disrespectful on the survey
[about kindness and respect]. I did it so my friends
would laugh. I realize what I wrote was wrong and
I'm sorry. I learned that I should not do something
bad to make other people laugh. So now I know to
always do the right thing. . . . I really feel bad and
angry at myself for what I did. I like to thank everyone for volunteering to teach us good things.

From,

Robert

I love aha! moments. I'm so grateful that Robert's letter demonstrates that he had one during his school's class at Kidsbridge. But
those aha! moments aren't like a solar eclipse, which we're lucky to

see once or twice in a lifetime. They are as common as the moon and the stars. I see them all the time. Class after class, we can actually see children's eyes widening at the very moment of understanding. We can witness the evidence in action that empathy *can* be taught.

Here is just a handful from the bounty of aha! moments I've seen in what children have written down after their lessons at Kidsbridge:

- I will always stand up for someone.
- I will try harder to help other people.
- I learned life tips to not make fun of people.
- I learned how to cheer up someone who is being bullied.
- I learned not to be a bystander but to help those in need.
- I learned to respect my dad and stepmom.

If you had read the research that was available when I was shifting Kidsbridge from having focus on character education to a focus on empathy, you would have assumed that such aha! moments were pure fantasy. Why? In 2002, when I started with Kidsbridge, pretty much everything I could get my hands on said *empathy couldn't be taught*. When I would have chats with education professors, they would tell me the same thing. It was a steady drumbeat of discouragement.

Carol M. Davis, in a 1990 journal article, leaned on the even older work of Edith Stein, who died in the Holocaust but whose writings were published decades later. Davis wrote, "What makes empathy unique, according to Stein, is that it happens to us, it is indirectly given to us. . . . When empathy occurs, we find ourselves experiencing it, rather than directly causing it to happen. This is the characteristic that makes the act of empathy unteachable."[1]

In other words, from Stein's (and Davis's) perspective, because I was called "Skinny Lynnie" as a child, I could empathize with others being teased about their weight because those hurt feelings from childhood would spontaneously emerge all over again. But that someone who had never been teased could never empathize? That I don't buy, just as I don't buy that empathy itself can't really be taught. Davis was one of the first naysayers I encountered in the research, but the statistical evidence gained through surveys conducted at the Tolerance Center demonstrate she was wrong.

Everyone knows what it is like to feel pain. We've all bled, felt chills from fever, felt the sting of accidentally being cut by a knife. Everyone knows what it is like to be teased. Maybe you were called skinny. Maybe you were called fat. Maybe you were called stupid or worthless. Maybe you weren't invited to that party or asked to dance. Whatever the case may be, you can be taught to link emotional experiences of your own that do match up to others in some meaningful way. You can be taught to relive that sadness or pain and "walk in the shoes" of another individual: a refugee, a battered woman, an injured animal, and so on.

Should empathy be felt spontaneously? Of course. But does a champion figure skater have to think about how to do a figure 8, a toe loop, or a lutz? No! After years of training, it comes naturally and without thought. Do basketball players think about arm position, height on their jump, and rotation on the ball as they go up to shoot a three-pointer? Not a chance! They may work on technique during practice, but the only way they can succeed on the floor is if everything flows naturally from practice.

Empathy can work the same way: through practice, but without the need to work up a sweat and head for the showers. One could say that building empathy is like building a muscle: it grows stronger and stronger the more it is used and exercised.

Thankfully, the view of empathy has seen a massive shift since I started in this field in the early 2000s. Now if you Googled "teaching empathy," you'd get more than 600,000 hits, and you'd be hard pressed to find many examples of the "Debbie Downers" whom I used to encounter. I'm grateful to see that viewpoint grow smaller and smaller in my rearview mirror.

That's not to say the naysayers have disappeared. You also have a small group that considers teaching empathy a mistake. That line of thought today is represented by Paul Bloom, whose book title sums up his perspective: *Against Empathy: The Case for Rational Compassion*. Bloom, a psychology professor from Yale University, argues that empathy is a "poor moral guide" regardless of whether we're looking at public policy, private charity, or interpersonal relationships. He says it can lead us to "parochialism and racism" and even spark war when our empathy has us favoring those close to us and wanting to retaliate against those in opposition. He argues that empathy "is part of the reason why governments and individuals care more about a little girl stuck in a well than about events that will affect millions."[2] Well, yes, millions turned on their TVs in 1987 to watch coverage of an eighteen-month-old girl known as Baby Jessica trapped in a well in Texas and to see her rescued, but I would say they were motivated not by empathy but by a combination of voyeurism and "I am sure glad that is not my child or grandchild." That's not what I would call empathy.

I just don't understand why anybody would want to go on record as a contrarian against empathy. What value can there be in being against respect, kindness, and compassion?

Aggravated and bewildered by the book title, I had to go to the library and read it. Actually, Bloom does make a distinction in his book. Bottom line, he thinks it is dangerous when governments and groups pretend to employ empathy, but the book did not really seem to be against teaching children empathy (Bloom has an open invitation to observe kids learning empathy at the Tolerance Center or in our mobile outreach programs in school classrooms).

Empathy must be the starting point, especially when you are teaching children or students and they are modeling you. It's true that people will rally around a little girl who falls into a well. It's also true that people are tribal. Yes, famine, disasters, poverty, wars, and disease can overwhelm us, especially when we are constantly bombarded by the media.

It should not surprise us, then, that psychology informs us that it is easier to feel emotion toward one person or a few, rather than toward hundreds or thousands. *New York Times* columnist Nicholas Kristof labeled this the "Darfur puppy" effect,[3] noting with tongue only partly in cheek that good, conscientious people who weren't moved by genocide in Sudan might be if the symbol were a single child or a suffering puppy with big eyes and floppy ears. But no good can arise if you don't have that empathy foundation.

We know what happens when leaders don't have empathy for their people. In Syria, a dictator has used mass slaughter and chemical warfare and made hundreds of thousands of people into refugees rather than having an iota of feelings for his own people. Empathy deficits do lead to parochialism and racism. If we don't start teaching and modeling empathy to the next generation soon, we will have the same dissonance, tribalism, and hatred in ten years that we, our children, and our students see around us every day.

When I came to Kidsbridge in 2002, I steered the center toward empathy because I realized it was job one. I also realized that the finger-wagging approach ("Don't do this! Don't do that!") was not working. Kids are no different from adults. Give them a lecture and their attention will drift. To be perfectly honest, assembly programs in schools are usually a waste of time as well. The children will start looking at the ceiling, fiddling with phones, texting, and passing notes—anything but listening. You can't just blurt out a list of reasons to be empathetic and call it a day. You've got to be strategic and be prepared to create "best practices": the most effective methods to accomplish the objective.

It was an instinctual feeling at first to figure out the empathy plan. I wasn't an educator by training. I had read about empathy, but there wasn't much available on how to teach it. Most of what I read at the time, in fact, was telling me what I *couldn't* do, and I had to dig through academic journals to find what I needed to know to get started.

The message at the beginning of this chapter from the fourth grader Robert, which arrived in my mailbox out of the blue, is just one of many examples of how empathy wins. Riding on a sea of guilt (as I discuss in later chapters, guilt can be good), he had to make it right, and a parent helped him find a way to do so through expressing himself in writing. But I knew that to succeed in this battle, we couldn't just trot out a bunch of anecdotal success stories and brochures with pictures of smiling children. I knew we would have to document our successes through a scientific approach. It took years of work and study, but we've been able to accomplish our goal. First, we created our own new activities, because there weren't a lot of effective programs out there. Second, we listened and observed. Third, we measured.

Following is an example of the first part of our strategy, an activity that we created and that is one of our "go to" lessons. It uses a simple chart made of felt that we have hanging up at the Kidsbridge Tolerance Center (expertly conceived and crafted by program manager Rebecca Erickson). The chart has a total of one hundred color-coded figures representing children and the choices they make. There are three groups: (a) orange figures representing "those who bully," (b) purple figures representing the "targets," and (c) the remainder of the group (using other colors), which I will describe in a moment.

There are thirteen orange figures, representing how many in an average group of one hundred would be among those who bully. They are the ones in charge of the culture of the group, the ones who push and shove smaller kids or tease them about their looks, their hair, how uncool they are . . . you name it. They do not have empathy for others.

There are fourteen purple figures representing the targets. They're the ones who bear the brunt of the bullying and go home brooding or even crying about the harassment they endure. When they go online at night, the harassment follows them and haunts them. They are the ones who need to develop not only empathy for themselves but also empowerment strategies. Targeted children need to realize not only that they're worthy of being treated with kindness and respect but also that they are capable of doing what needs to be done: asking an adult to intervene and stop the abuse.

Those parts of the chart are striking enough. But most important is the largest group of figures, totaling seventy-three. They are the bystanders. Some of them have empathy for the target and some do not, but the result is the same: they are watching and staying on the sidelines. Telling them not to be bystanders isn't good enough; they need to realize that doing nothing is actually the same as doing something wrong. They need to understand that, actually, they are the majority and have a responsibility to take charge. This Kidsbridge activity empowers students by having them learn what action to take: either contacting an adult or walking the bullied target away from the situation. Most important, we then practice this response together using skits and scenarios.

It's a powerful lesson because it applies to any group you can think of: a class, a school, a corporation, even a nation (think about what happened in Nazi Germany when too many bystanders did nothing until it was too late). Practically any time we teach this lesson, those aha! moments start bubbling up, including for adults. Many teachers and counselors focus attention on this lesson, realizing it is a tool for both kids and grownups.

> *I learned what I should do if a bully is making*
> *something to get you in trouble. Tell a teacher.*
> —Nikolai

The listening and observing in this activity entail *qualitative assessment*, which is the second piece of our strategy. We evaluate whether we are succeeding based on what the kids have learned and what they or teachers report. For example, we know that a child has attained more empathy when he or she says something like "I didn't realize I was a mean person and a bully until I visited your Center," or "Making fun of my friends is not a nice thing to do."

The third piece of our strategy, measurement, comes through *quantitative assessment*, which begins with rigorous data collection. We conduct surveys that measure attitudes about empathy, kindness, respect, the willingness to intervene, and other attributes. Surveys are administered to assess what attitudes students have both before and after the activity. The surveys and data workup are analyzed for statistically significant results by psychology undergraduate students from the College of New Jersey.

If the statistics demonstrated that the Kidsbridge curricula were not having measurable improvements in attitude shifts, we reviewed the activity scripts and reworked them, continually testing and reassessing until the program gave us the results we wanted. After all, why bother teaching a lesson if the kids aren't learning?

I am proud to state that the Tolerance Center has achieved "evidence-based" status. That means a majority of visiting students have demonstrated statistically significant improvements in social-emotional attitudes after spending just four hours at the center. Psychology professors and undergraduate lab students have found improvement in knowledge in not only empathy but also understanding in the following areas: (1) anti-bias, anti-racism, (2) religious diversity, (3) moral reasoning, (4) empowerment, (5) stereotype awareness, (6) respectful social media behavior, and (7) mindfulness.

As a parent, you should try to assess what you are doing, too. It's easier than you think (see final section of appendix A). In fact, the whole family should be involved in assessment. It makes for many wonderful and eye-opening discussions and is an empathy-generating experience.

Effective Programs

There's a wide variety of successful programs for teaching empathy out there and a wide array of practitioners offering them, such as children's museums and media labs. Here's a small sample as inspiration to propel you forward.

Historical empathy: Many American museums have found that one of the best ways to teach about history and make it come alive is pretending to travel back in time. *Walk in someone's shoes* from long ago and really experience or relive the challenges of those who came before us. Colonial Williamsburg in Virginia is built on this concept. Visitors can listen outside the old Capitol as Patrick Henry speaks about responding to British tyranny, see a Native American woman discuss her people's hardships, or watch an African American woman describe how ironic it is to see Whites fight for their freedom while her people remain enslaved. They can even participate in a court session and be selected to represent someone accused of stealing items from a store, watching eighteenth-century justice unfold. At Colonial Williamsburg, there are even stocks and a pillory outside for those who are "convicted."

Media labs: Around the United States, many schools and colleges have media labs in which students are taught how to create multimedia presentations. But some labs are set up with an "ulterior" motive; they want to foster empathy as the students put together new videos. Yonty Friesem is an assistant professor in the Communication Department at Columbia College Chicago and director of graduate studies for the department. He started as a videography instructor for the Together Project, using art to create empathy between Arab and Jewish children in Jaffa, Israel.[1] After receiving a special grant for the guidance of youth at risk, he decided to specialize in teaching media literacy with special populations such as students with learning disabilities, students with behavioral and emotional problems, mentally challenged students, gifted students, and youth at risk. At media literacy conferences, Professor Friesem and various schools and colleges report that they have successfully measured increases in empathy following video production.

Roots of Empathy: This program is targeted to preschoolers and kindergarteners in classrooms and brings in real babies.[2] Youngsters spend time with the babies and are asked how the infants are feeling. The children also observe loving relationships between the babies and their parents and see how the parents respond to the babies. This unique program teaches young children to experience human beings from a more empathetic perspective. The baby is the teacher! This Canadian-based program is offered in New York, California, Washington, D.C., and New Mexico. Fourteen years of independent research across three continents has shown that this program dramatically reduces aggression and increases social-emotional understanding among children.

Notes

1. For more information, see Yonty Friesem's website, http://digitalempathy.net/.

2. See https://rootsofempathy.org/ for more details.

Of course, I'm not the only one experiencing success. An article published in the *Journal of Counseling Psychology* in 2016 provided a "meta-analysis," meaning the authors took an overall view of a number of previously published randomized controlled trials on empathy. Most of these studies proved that empathy *can* be taught.[4]

I could cite additional research, but you get the point. Teaching empathy passes the test. You can see it in action. You can measure it in action.

At Kidsbridge, we start students on the path to empathy, and then it's up to educators and parents to take it from there with the post-program lessons and activities that we provide. The good news is that you don't need to travel to New Jersey to start down the path of kindness, civility, and respect. It's simple enough to do on your own—even for the busiest of families.

Now it's time for you to put empathy education in action!

In Europe, Empathy Education Is Already Working Wonders

We don't have to guess whether teaching empathy actually works. A look across the Atlantic Ocean shows us that Denmark has mandatory empathy training programs for young children, and they're working. Is it only coincidence that Denmark is consistently voted the happiest place in the world, with the Netherlands, which also mandates empathy training for preschoolers, close behind? I don't think so.

Children in the Danish school system participate in a national program called Step by Step as early as preschool. The children are shown photos of kids who are displaying different emotions such as sadness, fear, frustration, and happiness. The students talk about what they see and express what the other child is feeling. With this method, they learn empathy and how to read facial expressions. Facilitators and other observers are not judgmental, which makes the children very comfortable.[1]

Another increasingly popular program, CAT-kit, is aimed at improving emotional awareness and empathy. It uses such tools as picture cards of faces, measuring sticks to gauge intensity of emotions, and pictures of the body, on which participants can draw the physical aspects and location of emotions. The program allows children to describe experiences, thoughts, feelings, and senses.

In Denmark, most parents do not talk negatively about other children in front of their own children. They are always trying to find ways to get their children to understand another child's behavior without a negative label. If we remember that all children are fundamentally good, this helps us as parents role model the good in others.

In *The Danish Way of Parenting: What the Happiest People in the World Know about Raising Confident, Capable Kids*, well-known authors Jessica Alexander and Iben Dissing Sandahl offer three key suggestions for parents to encourage happy, well-adjusted children:

> Read all kinds of stories to children, not only happy ones. Talking about difficult emotions in books can be a fantastic way to build empathy. Many Danish children's books are shocking by American standards with the topics they cover, but studies have shown that reading about all emotions increases a child's ability to empathize. The original Little Mermaid, which is a Danish story, doesn't get the prince in the end, but rather dies of sadness and turns into sea foam. That opens up quite a different kind of discussion! Books are a great way to teach empathy.[2]

Notes

1. Jessica Alexander, "America's Insensitive Children?" *Atlantic*, August 9, 2016, https://www.theatlantic.com/education/archive/2016/08/the-us-empathy-gap/494975/.

2. Jessica Alexander and Iben Sandahl, *The Danish Way of Parenting: What the Happiest People in the World Know about Raising Confident, Capable Kids* (New York: TarcherPerigee, 2016).

three
the science and biology of empathy

Each species is a masterpiece, a creation assembled
with extreme care and genius.
—E. O. Wilson, biologist/author

for sixty years, Jane Goodall has inspired wonder with her discoveries about the intelligence of chimpanzees and her work in bringing them back from the edge of extinction. But while her discovery in 1960 that chimpanzees make and use tools is known as her groundbreaking achievement, her day-to-day interactions with these animals have enriched humanity beyond description. These interactions have produced heart-tugging moments that show us what we intuitively know just from our own pets: that empathy is real and alive in the animal kingdom.

One eighteen-second hug from Wounda is all you need to com-prehend that basic truth, leaving your eyes moist, your soul warmed, or a combination of the two. A YouTube video posted in 2014 shows Wounda, one of the more than 160 chimpanzees rescued and living at the Jane Goodall Institute's Tchimpounga Chimpanzee Rehabili-tation Center in the Republic of Congo. The chimpanzee had been near death, having lost much of her body weight from illness, but with the care received at the center, she was ready for release back into the wild.

Photo 9817060 © Ralph Paprzycki | Dreamstime.com

Wounda was let out of her cage, took a look around, and then, totally unsolicited, wrapped her arms around Goodall. The hug—a mutual gesture that is empathy's pure essence—reflected Wounda's gratitude for all the caring that Goodall provided. It was unmis-takable. It was, well, practically human. After eighteen seconds, Wounda finally let go and went off into the jungle to live her life.[1] I urge you to watch the video with your family.

The story of Wounda is no fluke. Researchers have witnessed the presence of empathy in animals and discovered there's a science behind the curtain of nature. Since humans are, in fact, animals, it stands to reason that other animals can be our gateway to truly understanding the hows and whys of empathy. From that starting point, this chapter explores what anthropologists have learned from studying our earliest evolutionary ancestors. Then it introduces a more traditional splash of science, things that can be seen and measured—in this case, the electrical signals traveling our body's neurological circuitry. I conclude with what scientists have learned from studying human behavior.

One of the best things in taking a look at animals for empathy clues is the realization that we are not alone in having this amazing trait. In fact, empathy is integral to species' survival. Read on and I'll tell you why.

Primates and Other Animals

There's a reason that kids are almost universally attracted to visiting the zoo, and in particular seem to love watching primates. Even children—perhaps more so in the case of children, actually—can see the similarities between us and our primate cousins. Their faces are so expressive! It's easy to observe the resemblance between them and us and to pick up on their feelings of sadness or happiness. Primates, including gorillas, orangutans, chimps, and gibbons, as well as humans use a wide-ranging toolbox of face-to-face interactions. These help to ensure the survival of the species.

How so? Well, for one thing, parents need to understand what their offspring are feeling if they are to be able to take care of their needs. They need an instinctive feel for whether their offspring need food and water, when they are ill, and when they are in danger. Second, empathy fosters cooperation. Cooperation includes things such as sharing food. What could be more important to the survival of a species than seeing to it that no member of the group goes hungry?[2]

In fact, research shows that chimpanzees cooperate first and think later. We learn a lot about chimpanzees by studying their psychology in rehabilitation centers and preserves. Research referenced here comes from Jane Goodall's Gombe Research Center in Tanzania. In the controlled environment there, it is possible to run behavior studies as we do for humans. One study looked at the willingness of forty chimpanzees to donate resources, help others, and punish a thief. Scientists concluded that chimpanzees had a bias toward cooperation over selfish choices, and the more social a chimpanzee was, the faster it was to choose cooperation.[3]

That sounds like a thought experiment we could do involving people, right? Let's consider the question of how well humans do in sharing food and keeping members of humankind from going hungry. If you've ever volunteered at a soup kitchen on Thanksgiving to feed the hungry, you've witnessed empathy of the highest order. Empathy's ultimate manifestation in my lifetime, I think, came in 1985 when celebrities gathered in Philadelphia and London for the transcontinental Live-Aid concert, spurred by images of people starving to death in Ethiopia, which raised millions of dollars. But humans also have the capacity to cause horrific famines and leave large populations to starve. The North Korean government's policies resulted in the deaths of hundreds of thousands in the 1990s. Soviet leader Josef Stalin starved millions of his people in the Ukraine. More recently, Sudan and Yemen are examples of places where famine was brought on by war and a lack of empathy for "the other."

Research shows that nonhuman primates are fully aboard the empathy train. They spend 45 percent of their time in social interaction, mostly on grooming,[4] in contrast to humans, who spend only approximately 20 percent of our time socializing.[5] As discussed in subsequent chapters, social interaction forms the foundation for empathy building, with much of it fitting the description of "quality time."

Primates are not the only animals that practice empathy. Nonprimate animals among which scientists have both observed and measured empathy include dolphins, orca whales, and elephants. Any of these animals can teach us a lot.

We can even learn from a rodent (relax, it's a cute little fella, hamster-sized and cuddly to the touch). The prairie vole is a critter living in the plains of the Midwest. Animal behavior researchers have found that these mammals, which are social and have just one mate for life, console one another when they are distressed. Consolation has been observed in animals like chimpanzees and elephants, but we never thought that small rodents could have concern for others, including those who are not their offspring.

"These voles are not smart, so this is not an intelligence thing," said Larry Young, a neuroscientist at Emory University who studies voles. "Some kind of gut instinct causes voles to respond intuitively to the stress of others. . . . As soon as voles see another distressed vole, somehow they detect it and they start licking and grooming it." In fact, the study showed, the unstressed partner matched the stressed partner as far as stress hormone response. Prairie voles don't go around consoling random other voles, Young said, noting that they only do it for siblings, partners, or individuals with which they live.[6]

There's a chemical culprit for this reaction. Oxytocin, which plays a key role in nurturing, works in part of the vole's brain to promote consolation. When oxytocin was blocked in the experiment by Young and his colleagues, so was the consolation response. The affected brain region, known as the anterior cingulate cortex, is the same one that's activated when one human encounters another in pain.[7]

Speaking of empathetic nonhuman mammals, let us consider one of the world's largest. The elephant never forgets, and it is also empathetic. There are many stories about how adults will not leave a dying adolescent or baby and how distress calls ring out when members of the herd are sick or ailing. Scientists have seen elephants assisting their injured brethren by plucking out tranquilizer darts and spraying dust on wounds. Animal behaviorists have even observed unrelated elephants helping each other.[8]

Scientists have noticed orca mothers and relatives in empathetic action such as grieving for dead baby orcas. One orca female in the Pacific Northwest was observed to have carried a dead calf for more than a week before finally relinquishing the attempt to resuscitate the dead baby.[9]

Neuroscientists' and evolutionary biologists' studies reveal that animal groups with the most empathetic and cooperative cultures tend to have better survival rates. We can also empathize with the mother orca whale. We'd do anything for our children.

The Power of Cuteness

Why are we endlessly attracted to photos of cute kittens and puppies? Empathy has an answer for us.

Did you know that the cuteness of our pint-sized furry friends may be a matter of survival? If they have features like a baby, we are instinctively attracted to them, according to scientists. As humans, we adore large eyes, chubby cheeks, big foreheads, and generally rounded features.

Oriana Aragon, a Yale psychologist, says this attraction may be a survival mechanism: "Our survival depends on us taking care of our young. It's part of our human species to respond to these physical features."[1]

Note

1. Photo 97234408 © Andreykuzmin | Dreamstime.com

Take turns saying what your favorite baby animal is  and why you think it's so cute. Challenge the family to think of wild animals on other continents. Buy some nature magazines and talk about those adorable eyes and cheeks and why they're just so doggone cute. Do we care about baby animals? Why? Do we care less about older animals? How come?

What Our Prehistoric Ancestors Teach Us

Could empathy have made a difference in the ultimate of Darwinian competitions: whether Homo sapiens or Neanderthals would survive to roam the earth. Many anthropologists have theorized about this. Of course, unless we count cave drawings, there's no record to tell the tale, and the archaeological record doesn't get us there, either. We're not even certain if the Neanderthals were a separate species or a subspecies of modern humans.

But scientists and evolutionary biologists have theories about empathy development. Gerald Hüther, author of *The Compassionate Brain*, not surprisingly echoes for humans what we've seen with nonhuman primates: The species that was best at learning and bonding would be the most successful in producing offspring. "Advancing socialization brings with it the formation of stable family groups," he wrote. "This is an essential prerequisite for the protection of offspring."[10] Hüther also says that close emotional bonding between two parents would ensure the success of the family unit and allow for further bonding with children. He writes that our ancestors could find greater success in maintaining and strengthening the bond between parents and children if they could figure out how to imprint cooperation on their offspring. In other words, the species with the greatest social and emotional capacity would outlive the other. See ya later, Neanderthals.

So, if empathy helps the family unit, it makes sense that empathy would help a larger group or a band of people, in other words, a bunch of families like a tribe or a clan. In that case, the somewhat selfish motive of taking care of one's own immediate relatives would be expanded into caring for the extended family and ultimately to those in the next closest circle. Caring for others without a selfish motive is altruism in a nutshell and could have been an evolutionary advantage for survival.

We cannot discuss the science of empathy without including one of the great experts on primates, Frans de Waal, director of Emory University's primate research center in Atlanta. In his book, *The Age of Empathy*, he agrees that we descended from "group-living primates" with a high degree of interdependence. Survival would require that group members rely on each other. De Waal says empathy "needs a face to work" and observes the very face-to-face interaction among chimpanzees that fuels Jane Goodall's life work. He also says, "No one is immune to others' emotions unless they are psychopaths."[11]

Exceptions to the Empathy Rule

According to the latest neuroscience research, 98 percent of people have the ability to empathize: the capacity to step into the shoes of others and understand their feelings and perspectives.[1] What about the other 2 percent? The exceptions to the rule are those with psychotic or psychopathic tendencies. Simon Baron-Cohen, a professor at Cambridge University and a renowned neuropsychologist (and a cousin of Sacha Baron Cohen, a comedic actor and fellow primate) has studied and researched psychopaths and sociopaths. He defines them with the very words of his book title: "Zero Degrees of Empathy." He lists narcissistic, borderline, and psychopathic personalities as people lacking "affective empathy," meaning their ability to self-regulate how they treat others is significantly compromised.[2]

Underlying his interest in primates is his passion to understand empathy, cruelty, and evil. "One of my motivations for writing . . . was to persuade you that empathy is one of the most valuable resources in the world," Baron-Cohen writes.[3]

Notes

1. Roman Krznaric, *Empathy: Why It Matters, and How to Get It* (New York: Penguin, 2014).

2. Carole Jahme, review of *Zero Degrees of Empathy* by Simon Baron-Cohen, *Guardian*, April 14, 2011, https://www.theguardian.com/science/blog/2011/apr/14/zero-degrees-empathy-baron-cohen.

3. Ibid.

Another researcher, NYU professor and psychologist Martin L. Hoffman, describes empathy as "uniquely well suited for bridging the gap between egoism and altruism since it can transform another person's misfortune into one's own distress, which in turn can usually best be alleviated by helping others."[12] That altruism (selflessness) trounced egoism (selfishness) was a huge advance for the first humans, one that would help the family unit or tribe be successful.

Before leaving this discussion, we need to hear from the brilliant E. O. Wilson, who has been called the father of sociobiology. We already know that empathy is declining, as measured by researchers in the United States, and expect that it is declining in other countries as well. In fairness, it can be challenging to care about others when your own survival is at stake. Wilson argues that empathy is such a high-level social skill that it has been shown even in the animal kingdom to outweigh fear and the instinct to turn inward. Gaining trust and alliances is critical to dealing with rivals, he argues, and was a precursor of apes evolving into humans.

"*Social* intelligence was therefore always at a high premium," he writes in *The Social Conquest of Earth*. "A sharp sense of empathy can make a huge difference. . . . Without doubt, a group of smart prehumans could defeat and displace a group of dumb, ignorant prehumans, as true then as it is today for armies, corporations, and football teams."[13]

So ultimately the most successful species do care about others and help each other. If science says empathy creates more love, nurturing, and care, then it is incumbent upon us as parents and teachers to model and teach it as early and consistently as possible.

In *The Compassionate Brain*, Hüther underscores our social evolution by saying that selecting a mate was no longer dependent solely on physical characteristics but on psychological ones as well. The combination better ensured survival in a hostile environment filled with animals competing for the same food and resources. "Now the greatest success in the propagation of their species *no longer automatically went to those who produced the greatest possible number of offspring*. It now went to those with who were the most talented at learning and at bonding."[14] Having a collection of parents who would have quality offspring, not just a large quantity, increased the survival chances of the whole clan.

Hardwired for Empathy

No discussion of the science of empathy would be complete without a quick journey into the brain and how we are hardwired for empathy. In fact, our brain's mirror neurons might aptly be renamed "empathy neurons." Neurons in general have the job of transmitting nerve impulses. (Picture yourself stepping barefoot on a Lego that a child has left on the floor. After a split second for those electrical signals to transmit to your brain, you feel the sensation of the most annoying pain possible and yell "Ouch!!!) Mirror neurons, which have been studied in humans as well as apes and monkeys, fire off when a person or animal acts—and when that action is observed in another. It can be more than just physical actions (monkey see, monkey do). For humans in particular, it can involve actions tied to emotions, pain, or stress as well. If mirror neurons mimic the other person's mind, this is the biological foundation of empathy.

Mirror neurons are located in the amygdala, the part of the brain involved with experiencing emotions. There is a neurological link between observing others and producing physiological reactions in ourselves. Mirror neurons continue to work as we grow older, but they even work among the littlest of us. In hospitals, babies cry when they hear another baby crying. Why do they do this? The biology of the mirror neuron suggests that babies are instinctually mirroring the emotions of other babies, which is why they copy the emotions they pick up through hearing.

Brains are built to care, compete, and cooperate. Empathy is innate in most humans and in primates and the other mammals discussed here. This is possible, says George Lakoff, director of the Center for the Neural Mind & Society at the University of California–Berkeley, because of mirror neurons: "When you have a certain emotion, it can show in your body, so if you are angry, you can see it in people's faces. People are happy, right? People are depressed, right? In many cases, you can see that because the muscles in the face and body reflect what someone is feeling. So, if you can see what someone else's muscles are doing, and if that connects to your muscles, to the neurons that control your muscles, you don't have to be doing the same thing . . . but that is going to be connected to your emotional system."[15]

New research by Dr. Helen Riess, associate professor of psychiatry at Harvard Medical School and author of *The Empathy Effect*, says that not only is each child born with neurons that generate an empathetic response, but there is also potential to build on these neurons, and early childhood experiences can help expand on this foundation. "Empathy is a mutable trait, it can be taught," Riess says.[16]

Last, I want to touch upon the "love hormone": oxytocin. This chemical, which I mentioned when discussing prairie voles, gets its nickname because it is released when people hug, kiss, and even play with their kids or pets. One small study found that individuals with high-functioning autism or Asperger's syndrome, who have difficulty with empathy, performed better in such tasks as looking into the eyes of another person after inhaling oxytocin.[17] Clearly, oxytocin will be a subject of extensive research for some time to come.

Walking in Someone Else's Shoes, Literally

Roman Krznaric can probably claim the title of empathy's biggest cheerleader without much disagreement. In *Empathy: A Handbook for Revolution*, he maintains that anyone can learn to develop this crucial personality trait and that empathy is as easy as learning to ride a bike or drive a car. Several years ago, he put his beliefs where his mouth is.

The Empathy Museum is his brainchild. It is a series of art projects in which visitors are active participants. It started in London in 2015 and, though it spends most of its time in the United Kingdom, has traveled to places ranging from New York to Brazil to Siberia.

The Empathy Museum has many exhibits, including one in which people of all ages can literally walk in other people's shoes. You can walk into a giant shoebox, which is where "A Mile in My Shoes" is housed, a collection of more than two hundred shoes and audio stories, including a British boxer fighting to stay in his country, an ex-convict saved by art, and more. The museum also has a Human Library, where instead of borrowing a book, you borrow a human to share his or her story. I recommend you go online to visit www.empathymuseum.com. Walk in others' shoes using the site and listen to the cool podcasts.

For another extraordinary exhibit, consider going to Dialogue in the Dark if it travels to your area. Blind and vision-impaired guides lead visitors in complete darkness for seventy-five minutes. Kids and adults get the chance to experience nature, a market, a busy pedestrian crossing, and other places as a blind person does, bringing them new understanding about what the disabled encounter in daily life. Since being launched by Andreas Heinecke in Germany in 1988, the exhibit has been to twenty countries and one hundred fifty cities worldwide, delighting millions of visitors.

Visit http://www.dialogue-in-the-dark.com to learn more and enhance your empathy.

Cradle to Grave

Developmentally, it is important to understand what each child is capable of at each age in terms of empathy and other social-emotional skills. Subsequent chapters drill down into each age group, from babies to high schoolers, to help you focus on your children or, if you're a teacher, those in your classroom.

Importantly, if you want to get the emotional work done, it helps to know what's hindering empathy from the biological perspective as well.

Barriers to Empathy Development

If your child is stressed or constantly distracted, that will be a barrier to empathizing. Not surprisingly, if your child is under stress, being bullied, or excluded, not only will he or she be unable to focus on studies, but he or she will also be unable to have caring concern for others.

A lack of physical and social-emotional nurturing is another biological barrier. Nurturing relationships are essential for intellectual as well as social development. Children require nurturing care to build capacity for empathy and other social-emotional skills. Starting in infancy, supportive, warm, and nurturing interactions foster not only language but also the beginning of emotional cues and social-emotional skills. Renowned pediatrician T. Berry Brazelton insists that "the ability to understand another person's feelings and to care about how he or she feels can arise only from the experience of nurturing interaction. We can feel empathy only if someone has been empathetic and caring with us. Children can learn altruistic behaviors to do 'the right thing,' but truly caring for another human being comes only through experiencing that feeling of compassion oneself in an ongoing relationship."[18]

In fact, in Susan Pinker's *The Village Effect*, in which she discusses the benefits of caring for each other collectively, she points to the latest studies in psychology neuroscience to illustrate that early learning is driven by the motivation to connect face to face.[19] Social cues highlight what and when to learn. Even young infants are predisposed to look at people and copy the actions that they see. They can more readily learn and reenact events and feelings when they see them in person as opposed to on a screen (repeated for emphasis: screens are not substitutes for people's faces). That speaks to the importance of modeling, discussed in chapter 7, which discusses teaching empathy to infants and toddlers.

Not surprisingly, a lack of face-to-face time is a big challenge for today's children. I raised two children in the 1990s and early 2000s. I'm ashamed to admit how technology really sneaked up on us in our house. If I could do it again, I would have managed time in front of the TV and computer screens much differently—and they were *waaay* less intrusive than smartphones.

It's actually easy to visualize the terrible biological brew that screens cause in a young brain. Have you ever been to the primate house at the zoo and seen the gorillas sitting with a nice banana watching *Dr. Doolittle* on Netflix? Screens just don't do much of anything for animals. It stands to reason, then, that they don't do much for our youngest children, either. Despite the American Academy of Pediatrics's recommendation to not provide screen time to kids younger than two, it happens aplenty. About 40 percent of kids are watching by age three months, and 90 percent are by their second birthday.[20] The prime driver for language learning is *face-to-face* connection with another human being; media compromises babies' future language skills and vocabulary. In fact, research shows that early television exposure (at ages one through three) is associated with attentional problems at age seven.[21] As Pinker says, we have changed from group-living primates skilled at reading one another's every gesture and intention to a solitary species—each of us preoccupied with our own screens—and not surprisingly, we are witnessing our empathy decrease overall.

Empathy: The Slow Emotion

As anyone who's tried to lose weight can tell you, there's no get-slim-quick solution out there that really works. It's the same for empathy, experts tell us. There's no get-empathetic-quick trick out there. In *The Shallows: What the Internet Is Doing to Our Brains*, Nicholas Carr, a finalist for the 2011 Pulitzer Prize in general nonfiction, tells us that more sophisticated deep thinking requires us to be calm and attentive. Empathy and compassion are *slow* mental processes. It takes time for the brain to transcend the body and comprehend the moral elements of a situation. The more distracted a person is, the more emotions and comprehension will be compromised. Moral decision-making takes time and reflection.[22]

"I was inspired to write the book after I realized that I was losing my own capacity for concentration and contemplation," Carr wrote in an article in the London-based *Telegraph*. "Even when I was away from my computer, my mind seemed hungry for constant stimulation, for quick hits of information. I felt perpetually distracted."[23] He pointed to one study in which half a class of American university students was allowed to use internet-connected laptops during a lecture, while the other half wasn't. Those who were on the web scored much worse on a subsequent test. In short, Carr says, we need to prize this historically ingrained, bioevolutionary behavior known as empathy.

I'd have to agree. It's gotten human beings this far.

How Did HAL Know?

Only an empathy specialist like author Nicholas Carr would realize that in the ground-breaking film *2001: A Space Odyssey*, the computer HAL is the only one who shows much in the way of human emotion. You have to marvel at how far ahead  of his time author Arthur C. Clarke was when in 1968 he wrote the science fiction novel on which the movie was based.

Activity option: Watch the movie with your family. What was the emotion that HAL demonstrated?

In conclusion, we know that the roots of empathy derive not only from our genetics and physiology but also from our evolutionary beginnings. Starting with the single act of parents anticipating their offspring's needs, evolutionary success creates and sustains a bond. From there, the building blocks continue. A family unit's cohesion can build to that of a small band of humans or tribe. Indeed, we observe this in many animals, in whom empathy becomes the foundation for a survival tool. In short, if our ancestors weren't really good at this, we wouldn't be here. Empathy is the glue that holds families and larger groups together.

Charles Darwin's "survival of the fittest" never mentioned empathy per se, but he did mention "sympathy" emphatically and often, and he seems to have ventured into empathy turf intentionally. Darwin's phrase is largely thought of in cutthroat terms: strong species driving the weak to extinction. But I think that's a misrepresentation of his full intent. After all, "survival of the fittest" meant the survival of species that were best adapted to their surroundings. To me, he seems to have been a believer in "survival of the kindest." Early in 1871, Darwin seized on the importance of empathy, writing the following in *The Descent of Man*:

[T]he basis of sympathy lies in our strong retentiveness of former states of pain or pleasure. Hence [in the words of Alexander Bain], "the sight of another person enduring hunger, cold, fatigue, revives in us some recollection of these states, which are painful even in idea." We are thus impelled to relieve the sufferings of another, in order that our own painful feelings may be at the same time relieved.[24]

In short, Darwin was one of the first to understand that "survival of the fittest" included empathy. Where empathy is present, humans have a better chance of passing on their genes. Where empathy is not present, one could argue, those humans are not as well positioned to produce future generations.

Today, researchers emphasize that empathy is a critical twenty-first-century skill and needed by children now more than ever to succeed. I hope this chapter has solidified your understanding of empathy and has you motivated to give this gift of caring to the children in your family or, in the case of teachers, the students in your classroom and beyond. Nothing could be more important than doing so as early and as consistently as possible.

empathy 101
defining how empathy fits in with other social-emotional skills

I do not ask the wounded person how he feels,
I myself become the wounded person.
——Walt Whitman, *Leaves of Grass*

The best way to learn is to teach.
——American physicist Frank Oppenheimer

When I first embarked on my journey of teaching empathy and other social-emotional skills at the Kidsbridge Tolerance Center, I had a general sense of the importance of character education. But if I was going to walk into a classroom and ask educators to entrust me with their students, I couldn't just wing it. I had to read—a *lot*. I had to do research, and then test and retest Kidsbridge lessons to make sure we had evidence that kids were really learning and blossoming with new prosocial attitudes. I've spent twenty years doing just that: observing and interacting with thousands of children, parents, and educators so I would truly understand the Empathy Advantage.

In short, teaching is really the best way to learn, because if you're passionate about a subject, you'll go digging in every corner: reading academic journals, interviewing experts, and exploring websites throughout the ever-expanding cyber world to discover best practices and obtain the latest research. Then, knowing you have good facts in hand, you decide which morsels are the sweetest and most nutritious and serve them up to the kids.

Relax, I'm not asking you to do *that* level of work on empathy. That's why I wrote this book; I did the hard work *for* you. But to teach children these concepts, I think it's helpful to take a few minutes to build a solid foundation and understand what empathy is, what it is not, and how it fits into the grand scheme of the family of social-emotional skills.

You've done this kind of nurturing before, and you can do it again. After all, hasn't every parent taught his or her child the concept of "love"? Every parent has a unique perspective on love and teaches it in his or her own unique way. Although it's a difficult task, parents by and large pull it off. There's the love that mommies, daddies, and caregivers have for their children. There's the love that mommies and daddies have for each other. There's the love that exists between friends. Then there's the love of birthday cake, ice cream, Double Stuf Oreos, vanilla cream donuts with chocolate frosting and rainbow sprinkles drizzled perfectly on top, and ... oops, sorry, kind of got off track there. But you get the point. Although teaching about love is complex, it's not work at all. Teaching love is beyond doable. It's pure joy! So is teaching empathy.

Intuitively, I think we all know what empathy means: kindness, respect, compassion, concern, and consideration for others. At the Kidsbridge Tolerance Center, we define empathy as *walking in another person's shoes* because this is a very easy concept to understand, especially for kids. The second part of empathy is labeled "empathic concern" in most circles, but at Kidsbridge we reengineer it into language that children can understand: action or empowerment.

Another way we describe action or empowerment is by using the word *UPstander*. An UPstander, one who is empowered by empathy and chooses to get involved, is the opposite of a *bystander*. UPstander was coined in 2002 by Samantha Power, who later served as US ambassador to the United Nations. In *A Problem from Hell: America and the Age of Genocide* (a very difficult book for a hypersensitive empath like me to read, but I forced myself to complete it), I recognized the brilliance of this new term immediately, and, to my knowledge, I was the first in the country to start employing it regularly. I introduced the term *UPstander* into the Kidsbridge vernacular more than fifteen years ago. Now we see the word appreciated and integrated into the American vocabulary nationwide. Thank you, Samantha, for getting us started.

In chapter 6, defining empathy together during a family meeting is one of the first things I recommend you do. It should be a team exercise that involves everyone. The words *kindness*, *respect*, and *compassion* are good for starters. For older children, perspective-taking is a great concept, too. Of course, I highly recommend saying "walk in another's shoes," but feel free to create a definition that works for the entire family. There are no hard and fast rules. It should be a concept that everybody understands and embraces, to promote buy-in and engagement.

My all-time favorite definition is strangely from Adam Smith, known to the world for his breakthroughs in economics. Smith was ahead of his time in more ways than most people realize. In 1759, Smith defined empathy as *fellow-feeling*. He explains in *The Theory of Moral Sentiments*, "When we see a [blow] aimed and just ready to fall upon the leg or arm of another person, we naturally shrink and draw back our own leg or our own arm; and when it does fall, we feel it in some measure, and are hurt by it as well as the sufferer."[1]

A Few Other Favorite Empathy Definitions

- *The ability to get inside another person's feelings and worldview*—Grant Wiggins and Jay McTighe. This really gets to the core of empathy.[1]

- *Seeking to understand rather than be understood*—Stephen Covey. This one is heartwarming. I love how the focus is first on listening and then on being listened to.[2]

- *[T]he intellectual or imaginative apprehension of another's condition or state of mind*—Dr. Robert Hogan. Hogan pairs "apprehension" with empathy to make the point that it is not always easy to be empathetic.[3]

- *[O]ur ability to identify what someone else is thinking and feeling, and to respond to their thoughts and feelings with the appropriate emotion*—Simon Baron-Cohen. A great definition by the famous British researcher.[4]

- *Our tendency to care about and share other people's emotional experiences*—Jamil Zaki. He based this idea on the research of Sara Konrath, a professor from the University of Michigan, who conducted a meta-analysis combining the results of multiple studies on empathy. She found precipitous declines in empathy among today's college students.[5]

Notes

1. Quoted in Jessica A. Hockett and Kristina J. Doubet, "Empathy through Academic Inquiry: A 'Controversial' Approach," *Learning with Empathy* 13, no. 1 (2017).

2. Ibid.

3. Robert Hogan, "Development of an Empathy Scale," *Journal of Consulting and Clinical Psychology* 33, no. 3 (1969): 307–16.

4. Quoted in Julian Powe, "The Practice of Empathy," *Forbes*, September 11, 2012, https://www.forbes.com/sites/trustedadvisor/2012/09/11/the-practice-of-empathy/#4ca289be58d6.

5. Jamil Zaki, "What, Me Care? Young Are Less Empathetic," *Scientific American Mind*, January 1, 2011, https://www.scientificamerican.com/article/what-me-care/.

Where does the word *empathy* itself come from? It's all Greek to me, and it's definitely worth knowing. The word derives from the Greek root "pathos," which means emotion, suffering, or feeling. The Greek root "em" means "enter into." When we join the two parts, we have "entering into emotion and feeling." Many emotion researchers define empathy as the ability to sense other people's emotions, coupled with the ability to imagine what someone else might be thinking or feeling.

The Germans created a great word for empathy in the nineteenth century, *Einfühlung* (pronounced EIN-foo-loong), which means "feeling into" or "in feeling."[2] I love the interpretation of this word by one of my favorite primate researchers, Frans de Waal (originally from the Netherlands), whom I heard lecture at a conference years ago in Atlanta. He defined this German word as "one individual projecting him or herself onto another."

The Difference between Empathy, Sympathy, Social-Emotional Skills, and Emotional Intelligence

We have a good idea at this point what empathy is. Now it's time to define what empathy is not: sympathy. For some people, empathy and sympathy are synonymous and are used interchangeably. Adam Smith did an excellent job of distinguishing between the two. He noted that when we feel sympathy toward someone, we may feel pity or compassion without having a corresponding feeling within ourselves.

In our society, with its twenty-four-hour news cycle, I think we actually go on sympathy and empathy overload. Very occasionally, we'll see something on the news and feel compelled to act with empathy by, say, giving a donation to the Red Cross if it's a story about hurricane or flood victims. More often, we'll feel sorry for the victims but not feel compelled to act. The most common reaction is to feel nothing at all. We become desensitized. We go into our shells and, sadly, live our lives on autopilot. It is unrealistic to try to help the entire world, but with empathy, we can make a conscious decision to determine where we can help and give it our best effort. Mother Teresa famously said, "If you can't feed a hundred people, then just feed one."

In our personal, daily interactions, however, empathy should play a much bigger role. In particular, our children should want to help if a schoolmate is bullied. If your child sees another being pushed around, it's not enough for him or her to feel sorry for that other child and just watch. Remember, we want both the feeling of "walking in the shoes of another" *and* helping that person.

Social-emotional skills is another key term. Empathy is just one of a larger set of skills that also involves managing emotions, establishing positive relationships, and making responsible decisions. I'd argue that empathy is the most important of all those skills and is, in fact, their foundation. You cannot really care for others until you care for yourself, in other words, learn self-empathy. That is why self-empathy (also called self-compassion) is job one at the Kidsbridge Tolerance Center. It is followed by job two, empathy and compassion for others, and job three, empathetic action to help.

> *[Y]our kids will need emotional intelligence*
> *to be on a team or lead the team.*
> —Doris Kearns Goodwin

Emotional intelligence is another key term. I credit Maurice J. Elias, professor of psychology at Rutgers University and director of the Rutgers Social-Emotional and Character Development Lab (and one of the cofounders of the Social Emotional Learning Alliance for the United States, SEL4US), for helping me understand it. I am lucky enough to know him and be able to ask him questions at social-emotional learning (SEL) meetings and bullying prevention conferences in New Jersey.

He deems emotional intelligence to be the set of abilities that help us get along in life with other people in all kinds of situations. "It's our ability to express emotions, to detect emotions in others, to regulate our strong feelings when we have them," he says. "It's our ability to focus our energies on goal setting and problem solving—to be able to take the perspective of other people that are in our social world. And finally, it's our ability to have the basic social skills that we need to manage everyday relationships."[3]

This definition sounds like empathy-plus. I think Elias would agree that empathy is one of the critical foundation skills to build emotional intelligence. Since emotional intelligence improves people skills, we can conclude that empathy is a building block for emotional intelligence.

Elias has made another contribution through his pioneering work at the Collaborative for Academic, Social, and Emotional Learning (CASEL), a national collaborative that provides insight and programs to schools nationwide. Elias was one of the founders. Over the years, CASEL has provided many resources for teachers and parents across the country, including a wheel diagram that does an excellent job of mapping out core social-emotional learning competencies (see figure 4.1).

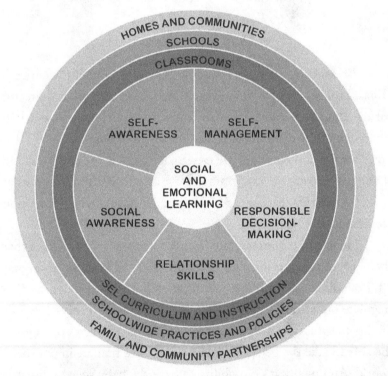

Figure 4.1 Social-emotional learning competencies

When I examine this chart, I feel we could insert empathy in every portion of the wheel. Furthermore, I would place empathy at the hub of the hub. It is the core of social and emotional learning.

Q: What is the difference between empathy and sympathy?

A: Sympathy means pitying others or feeling badly for them. The word *sympathy* does not include an impetus for action. Empathetic children might take action and try to help.

Q: What is the relationship of empathy to social-emotional skills?

A: Empathy is one component of social-emotional skills. Others include managing emotions, setting goals, establishing relationships, and making responsible decisions.

Q: How do empathy and emotional intelligence relate?

A: Emotional intelligence is the set of skills that helps us through life in all kinds of situations. We aspire to be in control of our feelings and have the ability to regulate them, meaning that when we express them, we do it with empathy, kindness, and respect.

Putting It All Together

Different psychologists and researchers create different stages and definitions for empathy. They all agree on one thing, however. The process starts with caring and concern for another. The final phase involves being an active ally: feeling empowered, taking action, being an UPstander, or otherwise helping another. In upcoming chapters I discuss how reading and literature can be an important tool for teaching kids about empathy, then get into more detail about teaching it to children and teens in different developmental age groups.

five
empathy, media, and social media

If you're not part of the solution, there will be no solution.
—Jaron Lanier, *Ten Arguments for Deleting Your Social Media Accounts Right Now*

raise your hand if you've ever deleted a social media account, or at least taken a *looooong* vacation from it. Facebook, and especially Twitter, have often gone from being places to share fun pictures of vacations or pets to places where false information and haters are to be found. Jaron Lanier, an internet guru whom I've heard speak at some gaming conferences in New York City, gets that.

In *Ten Arguments for Deleting Your Social Media Accounts Right Now*, Lanier says Facebook and Twitter have made us less empathetic, and certainly a lot meaner. "Negative emotions such as fear and anger well up more easily and dwell in us longer than positive ones. It takes longer to build trust than to lose trust. Fight-or-flight responses occur in seconds, while it can take hours to relax. This is true in real life, but it is even more true in the flattened light of algorithms."[1]

In fact, Lanier says, although it wasn't some evil plan, the designers of these algorithms knew what they were doing by tapping into these negative emotions. Chamath Palihapitiya, former Facebook vice president of user growth, who is mentioned in Lanier's book, provides supporting evidence that his company realized what could happen when it came to breaking down societal norms: "The short-term, dopamine-driven feedback loops we've created are destroying how society works. . . . I think we all knew in the back of our minds . . . we kind of knew something bad could happen." In fact, his only solution is to stop using these tools. He himself has given them up.[2] (Algorithms are designed to manipulate us, but that's another book.)

Recognizing empathy's importance, Lanier's argument number six is phrased this way: "Social media is destroying your capacity for empathy." He affirms, "Empathy is the fuel that runs a decent society. Without it, only dry rules and competitions for power are left."[3] He concludes, "What's really going on is that we see less than ever before of what others are seeing, so we have less opportunity to understand each other."[4]

Children and Media in the United States: Stats and Facts

There's little argument that media rules our children's land. The only thing that varies is which type of media is used by which age groups. For our younger kids, it's television. Kids aged five to eight spend more than an hour in front of the TV (more time for kids aged two to four). Teenagers, however, do their viewing online, using services such as Netflix and YouTube. In fall 2018, 38 percent of teenagers' daily video content was consumed via Netflix, with an additional 33 percent through YouTube. Overall, North American teens and young adults spend an average of 170 minutes—nearly three hours—per day on social media.[5]

All of us are bombarded in the news by stories about people whose lives have been destroyed by violence, disease, natural disaster, or poverty. It's natural to feel helpless and overwhelmed and to create walls to protect ourselves. Curling up on a couch to watch TV or immersing ourselves in a smartphone is an understandable escape from it all.

But is it really such an escape? Children frequently have their first experience with violence when watching television or a movie, or playing a video game. This exposure introduces them early to pain and suffering. So it's no wonder that they are desensitized to emotion early. I'm not saying that these shows or video games turn our kids to violence. But they do desensitize our kids, and we want to reverse that trend because it crowds out the sensitivity and empathy they need.

"The research is getting clearer over the long term, people with more exposure to violent video games have demonstrated things like lower empathy to violence," says Jean Brockmyer, a clinical child psychologist and professor emeritus of the University of Toledo. "Initially, people are horrified by things they see, but we can't maintain that level of arousal. Everyone gets desensitized to things."[6]

In fact, Brockmyer's recent research shows physiological changes to teenagers' brains, revealing that the areas of the brain where empathy sits become compromised by long-term exposure to violent images. Her paper followed another study by Canada's Brock University that indicated constantly playing violent video games makes children less morally mature than their peers.[7] I can't think that parents' views on video games would be unchanged if they understood the facts about the impact to their children's physiological and emotional health. If I had a magic wand and a time machine, my son would have spent fewer hours playing video games.

Addiction and Media

A chapter on media would not be complete without mentioning harmful addictions, whether to social media or video games. An article on addiction to the game Fortnite explained that tweens and teens love this postapocalyptic world, but teachers and parents complain that kids are falling asleep in class and that their grades are plummeting, in large part because they're too busy playing to get enough sleep. You need to set limits for everyone in the family, but for kids in particular.

"This game is like heroin," says Lorraine Marer, a British behavioral specialist who works with kids battling game addiction. "Once you are hooked, it's hard to get unhooked."[1]

In Japan, kids are sent away from home to withdraw from gaming addictions. Set your rules when your kids are little so these addictions don't sneak up on you in the form of disrespectful behavior or a bad school report card.

Note

1. Quoted in Jef Feeley and Christopher Palmeri, "Fortnite Addiction Is Forcing Kids into Video-Game Rehab," Bloomberg, November 27, 2018, https://www.bloomberg.com/news/articles/2018-11-27/fortnite-addiction-prompts-parents-to-turn-to-video-game-rehab.

However, even though the ever-powerful pull of smartphones seems insurmountable, it's not. Parents can manage and control media in their homes while encouraging empathy and other social-emotional skills. Paraphrasing the Little Engine That Could, "Yes, you can!"

Remember Nick Carr from chapter 3, author of *The Shallows*? Carr reminds us that the brain is plastic, and we can change its nature. Just as too much time spent online rewards our brain in a bad way, quiet reflection and boredom can stimulate it in a good way. Hey, who knew boredom had its good points?

Media Literacy

Now for more good news. Media literacy is a relatively new discipline that is evolving to prepare more effective tools and strategies for parents, teachers, and youth. When we talk about media, we are talking about a wide variety of things: popular culture, music, film, video, internet, and advertising, not to mention print. The National Association for Media Literacy Education (NAMLE) defines media literacy as the ability to access, analyze, evaluate, and communicate. In short, it involves teaching kids to think critically about what they're watching and not simply accept things at face value. Having those media literacy skills in hand will make your kids smarter media consumers.

When I first heard about the discipline of media literacy, I was fascinated. Upset by what was on television and the internet and knowing that parents, including myself, and even many educators had no clue how to battle this onslaught, I was thrilled to know there were others out there who were ahead of the curve trying to help.

One of the first books I bought on the topic was *Media Literacy Is Elementary: Teaching Youth to Critically Read and Create Media* by Jeff Share. To me, it is the bible of media literacy, teaching us to critically analyze media with our families. I relied heavily on his groundbreaking work when I started working as director at the Tolerance Center, and I later met him at a NAMLE conference. He and I are in the same camp: "moderation in all things" and "the earlier, the better" to teach children to develop independent critical-thinking skills with respect to media's indirect and long-term effects.

In his book, Share recalls how a fourth-grade teacher explained the consequences of poor media literacy for students: "They're going to have to have a better way of, at a younger age, to be able to evaluate what they're able to get into and a lot of the negative things that are coming in their way." If children aren't taught critical inquiry skills properly in this age of rapidly changing technology, they will be at risk of struggling to be active participants in a democratic society as adults, especially a multicultural society like the United States, where the same message can be interpreted very differently.[8] We want a society in which we really understand each other. We don't want to just tolerate one another; we want to embrace different perspectives. How prescient my colleague Jeff was in 2009.

Share expounds on the importance of teaching media literacy in the classroom in a book with UCLA colleague Douglas Kellner called *The Critical Media Literacy Guide: Engaging Media and Transforming Education*. Kellner and Share found that 80 percent of teachers using critical media literacy skills in their K–12 classes think these methods improve those students' skills. In an interview discussing the book, Share tells a story about their work with a third-grade teacher in central Los Angeles. "She had the students choose a topic they felt was most important to them, analyze it, and create a piece of media about it," Share says. "The kids chose school gun violence, the [2019] terrorist attack in New Zealand, Islamophobia. . . . They did this in a proactive way and invited guest speakers to the class. Now, a group of these third graders are actually pushing the administration to bring a restorative justice program into their school."[9]

NAMLE has wonderful content on its website at https://namle.net. For parents to get started on media, I especially recommend the "Parent's Guide to Media Literacy: Building Healthy Relationships with Media." It won't overwhelm you, I promise. Also, check out the wide-ranging resources on Media Literacy Now (https://medialiteracynow.org).

Another media literacy guru focused on multiculturalism, Carlos Cortés, is a nationally known and award-winning author, teacher, and consultant on a wide variety of issues related to diversity, the impact of media, and cross-cultural understanding. In *The Children Are Watching: How the Media Teach about Diversity*, Cortes discusses in detail how the media frames diversity-related themes such as race, ethnicity, gender, religion, and sexual orientation—often in ways we would not like. He suggests how schools and parents can take more control of how children learn about these complicated issues.

Because media literacy is so important, I come back to it in upcoming chapters on the elementary, middle, and high school years, providing tips tailored to these different age groups.

Memes

While listening to the radio in my car, I happened upon a story about a high schooler who was accepted into Harvard and would have gone on to attend if he hadn't fallen into the trap of posting harmful memes.

Memes are humorous images or videos with word captions that are shared rapidly by internet users.

Before the internet, memes didn't exist, and now they regularly go viral. Kids as young as elementary school age share memes of cute animals and silly photos with captions. Teens and adults, however, often share images with snarky sayings and putdowns.

At Kidsbridge, when we learned about memes, we were

horrified to hear from parents and teachers that so many kids made fun of others' religion, skin color, or ethnicity. We knew we had to educate ourselves, then teachers and kids, immediately.

Back to this young man's tale on the radio. This young man became enraptured with a cool incoming freshman chat group. Others were posting vicious, insensitive memes devoid of empathy, and he felt the need to fit in. Before he knew it, he was trying to "one up" fellow incoming students and posting cruel memes about persons with disabilities, immigrants, and so on.

That was the end of his Harvard career before it began. A bright young man with everything going for him received an email that his acceptance to Harvard University had been revoked. Imagine what it felt like to be him or his parents.

If you can do just one thing about media, tell your kids that it is all permanent, and they should assume it is not private. They won't understand you, really. This is why it's a good idea to tell this story (or a similar one) and have them walk in the shoes of the "almost" Harvard University student.

Virtual Reality

Virtual reality (VR) is a simulated experience that requires just a computer and a headset placed over the eyes. What you see resembles the real world, historical events, or a fantasy land in a 3-D immersive environment. VR technology can be used for gaming, entertainment, and/or educational purposes.

When you try VR, you quickly understand how it can transport you into a whole other empathy realm. At a recent American Alliance of Museums conference, I saw a long line for one of the VR exhibits. I figured everybody must be onto something if the wait was that long, so I got in line, too. When I had the chance to put on the headset, I was instantly transported back into the past. I was civil rights pioneer Rosa Parks on the bus. I walked up the steps in the bus and took a seat in the front row. The bus driver said that I had to move to the back, but I decided to stay where I was. Other passengers started to stare at me, and I felt very uncomfortable. The pressure to move to the back shook my nerves. Wow, I was really walking in Rosa Parks's shoes and understood how courageous she was in a whole different way!

Jamil Zaki, a professor of psychology at Stanford University and director of the Stanford Social Neuroscience Laboratory, is optimistic about VR's ability to inculcate empathy. His Stanford research team found it likely that virtual reality could decrease stereotyping and discrimination as well as build empathy.[10]

In *The War for Kindness*, he talks about the artist Chris Milk, who celebrates VR as the "the ultimate empathy machine." In 2014, Milk created a new VR film called *Clouds Over Sidra*, which tells the story of a twelve-year-old girl in a Syrian refugee camp in Jordan. Viewers can experience what a young girl in the camp does, spending time with her and her family. Milk says, "You're not watching it through a television screen. . . . You're sitting there with her. When you look down, you're sitting on the same ground that she's sitting on. And because of that, you feel her humanity in a deeper way. You empathize with her in a deeper way."[11]

I don't know that VR has enough research behind it to justify claims of empathy gains in a statistically significant way. But although the jury is out, I'm excited about its prospects.

Reality TV

Do you ever watch reality shows with your children in which contestants are humiliated? Remember how Simon Cowell became a household name with his nasty putdowns of *American Idol* contestants that drove them to tears? Ask yourself (and your family) why it's funny to watch others' pain and embarrassment. It's one thing when others perform silly antics and want you to laugh. It's another when they're singing their hearts out and then having their hearts broken.

I think there's a lot to learn from reality TV. Sit with your family and discuss whether a person's privacy is being invaded. Discuss why there is so much humiliation and exclusion shown, often with a "laugh track." Would you emulate what you see on TV and repeat it in your home or classroom? Would you try to embarrass a spouse or a child? Of course not.

10 Simple Rules for Empathy and Media

1. Limit each family member to one hour a day of media and stick to it (you may want to increase the media time for tweens and teens).

2. Reduce exposure to shows with violence and negative emotions; in research studies, these shows have been seen to increase aggression.

3. Set a goal of no media one to two hours *before* bed. Media disrupts sleeping patterns.

4. Use technology to install a software program on tablets and phones that powers them off. Not because you're the boss, but because it is good for your children.

5. Watch over all devices, including phones, tablets, desktops, TVs, and any other media. In other words, kids should check them "in" and "out."

6. Talk to your family about social media—especially kindness, respect, and permission. Rule No. 1: Don't embarrass others.

7. No media during mealtimes. Period.

8. Be aware of your own behavior. If you are restricting your kids, you must set limits for yourself and your spouse. You are a role model.

9. Discuss media with your kids. Watch their favorite shows with them and analyze together what you're viewing. Discuss violence, competition, exclusion, and meanness and tell stories of how kids got in trouble relating to privacy issues.

10. Make sure that media content is developmentally appropriate. Make sure an elementary schooler is not watching what a teenager would.

Fewer than one in three parents limit screen time and videos. Do your part to up that percentage.

six

parent tips
strengthening moral compasses

You teach me, I forget.
You show me, I remember.
You involve me, I understand.
—E. O. Wilson

[W]e must take care of our garden.
—Voltaire, *Candide*

as a parent, your heart is stolen the moment your child is born. This cuddly, soft person shares your DNA and even *looks* kind of like you! Your smile broadens when you discover your baby's developing personality includes some of your very own traits. Maybe you both are picky eaters with a stubborn streak: "There's just no way you're getting me to eat those disgusting-looking peas!" (When I was ten, I once sat at the table for an hour after dinner because I refused to eat them. My parents won that battle.)

Part of you wants to fast-forward to meet the people your children will be when they grow up. Will they share your hopes and dreams? Will they be kind? Will they become doctors, artists, athletes? Will they support you in your old age? (OK, that's probably rolling the dice *too* much!)

Nature is a strong influence in molding your infant. However, nurture is every bit as impactful (as demonstrated in chapter 2). Here's your chance to teach your most precious human all of your most important values about love, respect, morals, and more. Here's your chance to see whether you can develop even better offspring with empathy.

In short, now's your chance to teach empathy. And you *can* do it. I know that with every fiber of my being. By nurturing, modeling, and enhancing your child's "people skills," you can create a caring and compassionate person full of empathy. You can offer your child a positive life's journey in which treating others with kindness earns reciprocal kindness and trust. It's very beneficial for your whole family and rewarding for you. Watch your child develop as he or she grows into not only a good person but also one whose traits and skills offer the promise of success and living with joy.

Of course when you have a new baby in your hands, it can be difficult to see years down the road to the challenges that lie ahead. But for those whose children are edging toward their teens or have already arrived, you totally get it (along with my deepest sympathies and a little advice—don't worry, they'll turn into real people again by their mid-twenties; mine did). You're dealing with "clear and present danger" issues like bullying, grades, dating, drugs, and smoking.

In these challenging times, empathy is more than ever a much-needed companion and critically important as schools continue to push character education out of the classroom to spend more time on academics. The problems are serious. Consider these gloomy results of a recent survey:[1]

- Forty-nine percent of students reported being bullied or harassed in a manner that seriously upset them.

- Thirty-one percent believed physical violence is a big problem in their school.

- Twenty-four percent believed it is OK to hit or threaten someone who makes them very angry.

- Fifty-seven percent of teens stated that successful people do whatever they have to do to win, even if others consider it cheating.

- Fifty-one percent reported cheating at least once on an exam.

Clearly, parents and educators need to step up to better infuse morality and ethics into our children, because many schools are leaving a void.

Before I get into the nuts and bolts of what you can do as parents/educators to instill empathy, here's one more kernel of alarming news, something that you probably already know: it is much harder to be a parent or teacher today than it was ten or twenty years ago. At the Kidsbridge Tolerance Center, I have had the opportunity to talk with hundreds of teachers, counselors, and other educators over the years. I often ask them, "Is it harder to teach students today than it used to be?"

You should see their faces. They look at me like I'm crazy for even asking. In the words of one educator, which are representative of what the vast majority tell me, "It's so much harder to teach kids today than it used to be. Kids are less respectful, more distracted, and kids do not even know how to hold a conversation today."

Such responses to my query are supported by experts in the

field. D. Stanley Eitzen notes that a breakdown in social connections is making children less civil in school. He has written in detail about the isolation we see within the home itself, pointing to the numerous hours that they spend alone. Writing in 2004 (when the iPhone was just a gleam in Steve Jobs's eye and the idea of pausing live TV was just bonkers), Eitzen noted that some children had a landline, computer, TV, VCR, microwave, refrigerator, and other devices in their rooms, isolating them from the rest of the family. "Family members are often too busy and too involved with their own individual schedules to spend quality time together as a family," he observed. "These homes may be full of people but they are really empty."[2]

Sadly, I am sharing my personal five top concerns for youth:

1. Narcissism is up.
2. Empathy is decreasing along with other social-emotional skills.
3. Immediate gratification is up.
4. Face-to-face time is diminishing.
5. Media and the internet are compromising kids' social-emotional skills.

Should we give up as parents and educators? Absolutely not! But with our eyes wide open, we need to work harder. We need to work smarter and educate more strategically. This is why, as parents, we need to arm ourselves with the best tools and tips to create empathetic children. In our children's weekly activities and schedules—many parents are guilty of overscheduling their kids with soccer games, recitals, coding classes, and other activities—how much time is devoted to empathy and other social-emotional skills?

Top Ten Reasons to Spend More Time Working on People Skills

1. People who can "read" feelings and other non-verbal cues are more emotionally adjusted, better liked, and more successful.

2. Empathy is a critical relationship-building skill that will enhance your child's ability to have better people skills.

3. Individuals with better people skills interview better, a key factor in their having both higher employment rates and higher wages.

4. People with better social-emotional skills have lower rates of substance abuse, obesity, and criminal activity.

5. People with higher measured rates of empathy usually have lower rates of ethnic prejudice and aggression. Those with higher empathy are more willing to use nonaggressive means to solve problems. Those with higher empathy are less prejudiced.

6. Those with higher empathy have better problem-solving skills and are usually kinder and more compassionate.

7. Those rated higher in social-emotional skills have improved behavior and enjoy superior academic achievement.

8. Empathetic children grow up to be empathetic parents and relatives.

9. Empathetic children care for others and will make our communities and world a better place to live for all.

10. Those ranked higher in empathy make better leaders.

Let's get started on understanding the concepts and components that will help us enhance empathy to benefit our children. I begin with face-to-face skills.

Step One: Get Face to Face

The most important rule at the Tolerance Center is no technology: none, zero, zip. It's at the very core of everything we do. All of our discussions are in small groups and face to face. In the center, we practice having all eyes on the speaker as a demonstration of respect. We emphasize "only one person talking at a time" and ensure that every child gets to be heard in a group, including the shy children.

When we announce this to classes at the beginning of Kidsbridge programs, a look of shock comes over the kids' faces, but they all hang in there and buckle down to do the activity. Why the no-technology policy? The main reason is that children have way too much media in their lives. As parents, our best weapon—and the only way we can compete and counteract media—is to regularly spend quality face-to-face time with our children and students.

Face-to-face time is a critical skill that is best taught early. As you know, our children are constantly observing us—far more than we realize, and *earlier* than we realize. Knowing that, we can role model and inspire empathy quickly and consistently in small, bite-sized chunks of teaching time.

What does face-to-face time consist of? It involves the following four elements, all of which we need to teach our children to recognize and understand:

1. nonverbal cues

2. tone of voice

3. body language and gestures

4. facial expressions

Your children's people skills will be improved if they can observe and decipher the critical components of interpersonal communications with you and their peers. For example, a person who's being sarcastic might be doing so with a smiling face: How does a child navigate what a peer is really trying to communicate? A classmate who is being bullied might be angry and asking for help. Will your child be able to discern this?

Strengthening children's social-emotional skills will improve their ability to "read" people. Over time, such an increase will enhance quality face-to-face time, a critical component for fostering empathy and strong people skills.

What Do the Experts Say?

Author Susan Pinker says the case for face-to-face contact is a clear winner. "Programs that promote face-to-face conversations and interactive reading between parent and child have had *more than twice* [author's emphasis] the impact on the language and literacy skills of kids from impoverished backgrounds than laptop programs have had," she says, noting that spending a year with a skilled teacher face to face is far more effective than a laptop.[1]

Pinker also encourages families to eat together, highlighting that the outcomes will be young kids who read and write better as well as teens who are happier and healthier and have higher SAT scores and lower rates of drug and alcohol use. "If the kitchen is not just a place to scarf down calories but an arena for sharing stories, confidences, lessons learned and gossip, then families who talk and eat together might have children who are psychologically healthier and who do better in school," she writes. Sadly, she has even seen the opposite, with predictably negative results: parents so uncomfortable in their own homes that they circle the block when arriving home until certain the nanny has tucked the kids into bed.[2]

Likewise, Sherry Turkle's research supports face-to-face communication. An MIT psychologist, Turkle has written a lot of insightful books about the value of face-to-face investment, including *Alone Together: Why We Expect More from Technology and Less from Each Other*. In another book, *Reclaiming Conversation*, her research indicates that social media leaves us feeling more isolated and alone. Turkle admonishes us to realize that our children's constant obsession with being connected digitally actually results in loneliness and reduces empathy.[3]

Notes

1. Susan Pinker, The Village Effect: How Face-to-Face Contact Can Make Us Healthier, Happier, and Smarter (New York: Spiegel & Grau, 2014), 207.

2. Ibid, 106–7.

3. Sherry Turkle, Reclaiming Conversation: The Power of Talk in a Digital Age (New York: Penguin Books, 2015).

Don't ask your children, "How was your day today?" That lets them get off the hook using the famous one-word answer: *OK*.

action tips

Instead, try these questions: "What was the most important thing that happened to you today?" "What was the best thing?" "What was the worst thing?" And, of course, stop and listen. Be face to face. Be in the mindset to sit down with them for five minutes. Otherwise, your nonverbal communication gives an unintended message: that you really don't care.

Once you're on the face-to-face bandwagon, you'll notice a difference in the quality of your communication fairly quickly. Then you'll want to kick it up a notch! Now that you're paying attention to your children closely, take a moment to pay attention to what this is translating to on the clock and on the calendar. Ask yourself, "How much time am I spending face to face with my children on average per week?"

Well, this book is all about steps you can take as a parent that won't require much sacrifice of time or energy. I have figured out a way to make this easy on you. I have designed a simple, complete, face-to-face time log chart so you can track your interactions (see figure 6.1). The results might surprise you! You might have earned a well-deserved pat on the back, or you might realize you need to ratchet up your face-to-face time. Regardless, it's important to get started.

At the bottom of the chart is an empathy meter. If you're consistently spending at least three hours face to face with each child each week, go treat yourself to something (whether that's a spa treatment, ballgame tickets, a bag of peanut butter cups, or some other reward; I'll leave that up to you!). If you are putting in less than three hours, think about what you can do to increase the time you spend.

Some of you will say that three hours is impossible. Don't throw up your hands and walk away. Can you do at least two hours a week? Anything you can do will benefit your child and your whole family.

Figure 6.1

Warm-Up for Step Two:
Realizing Empathy Can Grow

In this section I am part teacher, part motivational coach. If you think that you can bring out some empathy in your child, but that its seeds can only grow a fixed amount, you're thinking too small. You can grow more than a small flower. You can shoot for a towering oak. You can shed what experts call the "fixed mindset" and try on a "growth mindset."

Carol Dweck is a growth-mindset guru. She's a world-renowned psychology researcher and teacher at Stanford University who has been studying what makes children successful since the 1970s. Her teachings have motivated me, and they energize both parents and educators everywhere. She frees us from the handcuffs of the fixed mindset—the idea that children's basic qualities such as intelligence and talent are fixed traits—and shifts us into the growth mindset—the idea that hard work and new strategies allow your children to take their abilities and strengthen them.

Dweck's personal story has much to say to us. When Dweck was in the sixth grade in Brooklyn, New York, her teacher, Mrs. Wilson, seated students around the room according to IQ. Those without the highest IQ were not allowed to carry the flag during assembly or even to wash the blackboard. "She let it be known that IQ for her was the ultimate measure of your intelligence and your character," she said. That demoralizing experience would later motivate Dweck to illustrate that traits like intelligence and empathy are not fixed from birth. A research study that she coauthored really got my attention. The study found that junior high students with a fixed mindset fell back academically, while those with a growth mindset moved ahead, and when an intervention program that provided students with study skills was introduced, some of the struggling "fixed mindset" kids began to discover they, too, could grow. "You mean, I don't have to be dumb?" one boy asked with tears in his eyes.[3]

Dweck has integrated that research into numerous empathy studies. In one, she and fellow researchers gave materials to one group of participants that were designed to prompt them to have a fixed mindset about empathy. The second group of participants received materials designed to persuade them that empathy could grow. Then all participants were asked to volunteer in various ways to help cancer patients. Those who had read the "growth mindset" materials were more likely to volunteer for a support group in which they'd have to come face to face with cancer patients, as well as to volunteer in other ways.[4]

In short, Dweck counsels us to praise hard work and effort, what many in the educational field now attribute to the widely accepted term *grit*. Not only can we teach empathy, but with our efforts and our children being willing to cooperate alongside us, our kids can also change and expand their ability to walk in the shoes of others.

If we and our children have a "fixed mindset" about empathy, empathy is halted in its tracks. If instead we believe in a "growth mindset," we might be able to comprehend that we can behave more empathetically toward others whose characteristics differ from ours.

When we are challenged to "feel" for those *outside* our tribe, a growth mindset for empathy can be bigger than a small step. It may even be a leap. But knowing and caring for others makes the world a better place.

Although the US Supreme Court didn't rule on empathy in *Brown v. Board of Education* in 1954, when it issued the landmark ruling banning segregation in schools, it clearly had some of that concept in mind. White children in an all-White school had less chance of understanding the experiences of Black children when they were in two different schools than when they saw children of color every day in the same halls and classes. If we integrate different types of children, in classrooms, lunchrooms, and buses, their empathy grows.

The inclusion principle for empathy works similarly when we integrate children with special needs into the classroom. Including children with mental and physical challenges in the classroom produces fantastic results, as those without disabilities become more empathetic. Diversity comes in many shapes and sizes, and its overwhelming benefits for youth in the empathy studies by Dweck are plain to see.

Step Two: Family Meetings

Nurturing empathy can be broken into three important family-inspired processes, as suggested by researchers Kevin J. Swick and Nancy K. Freeman, professors of early childhood education. Their suggestions are so spot on that I quote them here verbatim:

- Providing children experiences with caring relationships based on mutual trust, empathy, and responsiveness to others

- Modeling kindness, peacefulness, and caring and bringing children's attention to examples of these kinds of pro-social skills

- Validating children's efforts to care for and about other members of their ... communities[5]

Next I explore one of my favorite rituals to foster empathy, self-esteem, and self-compassion: the family meeting. (Feel free to watch a few old episodes of the *Brady Bunch* or *The Partridge Family* to get yourself into the right mindset; my apologies in advance for any theme-song music or cries of "Marcia, Marcia, Marcia!" playing in your head for the next few hours.) It's important to lead, but to be successful you'll also need buy-in. As E. O. Wilson said in the quotation at the beginning of this chapter, don't fall into the trap of just teaching or showing your children. You need to involve them. Then they'll learn.

Your family meeting could be at dinner time or on the weekend—whatever's convenient for all of you. Don't overwhelm your kids; just start with fifteen minutes. Following is a sample agenda to start (obviously, don't feel you have to adhere to this exactly):

The Family Meeting Agenda

1. Start with a silly icebreaker, such as asking about a favorite color, food, or game. In my educational career I have learned from the best, and my former boss, Dr. William Gutsch, director of the Hayden Planetarium of the American Museum of Natural History in New York City, was all that. He taught me that education is more powerful when it is fun and entertaining. At first I disagreed with him, but I have learned in subsequent years how right he is. Have some fun while you learn.

2. Share how amazed you are that empathy can be taught successfully and explain the "growth mindset."

3. Share that empathy can be fun.

4. Define empathy for your family (see chapter 4 for "family-friendly" definitions) and provide examples. Then ask them to express the concept in their own words.

5. Explain the benefits of empathy, particularly how it improves people and communication skills.

6. Have everyone complete the face-to-face time chart together, assessing how much time each family member spends face to face with the others. Discuss the results in a nonjudgmental way.

7. Ask everyone if they think it's a good idea to increase face-to-face time. Brainstorm the possible benefits, including people skills; together, set very small goals for increasing face-to-face time together.

8. Brainstorm some fun family activities, like reading together, games, outdoor walks, museums, and community service projects. Make sure they involve interaction, cooperation, and *fun*. Every family member should make a suggestion.

9. Agree to meet together in a week and discuss what you have learned.

10. Perhaps think of a fun name for your empathy quest. I sometimes use the term *empathy portal*, which has the feel of jumping into a mysterious hole full of surprises as in *Alice in Wonderland*.

11. Suggest engaging in an empathy or kindness contest, as well as perhaps a prize.

Feel free to go rogue if you have other ideas that will increase face-to-face time and make it more enjoyable. If your kids want to create a rhyme, a jingle, or a song to celebrate or announce empathy moments or meetings, go for it. Maybe T-shirts? Creativity raises the fun factor!

Fun Fact That Isn't Fun

For all you lovers of having your child sign a pledge or a contract to stick with a certain behavior (like empathy), *fuhgeddaboutit*. I am sorry to say the research  does not relect kindly on pledges. Child pledgers are not prepared to understand why they should change their ways, are not able to practice the skills necessary to make it work, and do not have the stick-to-itiveness. Don't waste your time!

Here's a fun activity you can do in the car, where your kids are trapped. Take away their cell phones for twenty minutes. When you see a person walking on the street or driving a car, challenge your kids to tell a story about that person. *Did that man have a good day? . . . Where does he work? . . . Does he have a family? . . . What is that woman looking forward to? . . . What if you gave her a hundred dollars? . . . Would that change her life? . . . What makes that child happy or sad? . . . Does that child have two parents? . . . Has that child ever been hungry? . . .* Make up your own questions, or, even better, ask your kids to create questions.

Step Three, Nurturing: Meeting Your Child's Emotional Needs

If you have a small child, have you ever yelled at him or her for crying over something silly like not getting to watch a certain TV show or not being able to stay up late? Did the yelling (1) stop the child from crying or (2) make the crying get worse? I suspect the answer is number 2.

Children can best develop empathy when their emotional needs are met. When they feel secure and loved, children evolve to care about themselves and others. Studies tracking children from early ages conclude that kids with secure attachments "show greater empathy, stronger emotional coping skills and more developed moral sensibilities."[6]

Nobody's perfect, but parents or caregivers who tend to nurture their kids to cope with negative situations by discussing them in a kind, problem-solving way have children who are more empathetic and show positive emotional expression. By contrast, parents who minimize or ignore their children's emotions with a "man-up" attitude have kids who are less socially competent. An angry, tense parent will more likely have young children who have more difficulties with their peers.[7]

Why "Manning Up" Doesn't Work

Everything that you have read in this chapter is the opposite of "manning up." Several years ago, I was delivering a presentation on empathy and its importance to school parents. When I was packing up to go, a man sauntered up to me and proudly proclaimed, "I'm glad that my father was tough with me. It made me the man that I am today. Life is tough and my father taught me to tough it out, so I don't believe in this empathy thing."

I listened respectfully and answered, "I hear you that it worked for you and you're happy that your father was tough on you, but our children are growing up in a different world that is even more challenging than yours. Some of them don't have the capacity to 'man up'; instead, they do drugs, cut themselves, and some of them even kill themselves. I don't think we're willing to take a chance with even one child, are you?" He didn't have much to say after that. He turned to walk away, and as he did, I hoped he might be starting the journey of walking in the shoes of kids today.

Nurturing your children and meeting their needs plants the seeds of empathy and kindness. Here I circle back to the second quote at the beginning of this chapter, in which Voltaire suggests that we nurture our gardens.

David A. Levine, author of *Teaching Empathy*, underscores the importance of using "trust, modeling, support, and intentional emotional imprinting" as a way of accomplishing that nurturing.[8] We know our children are watching us, so we need to model what we want them to copy. I love the term Levine has coined: *emotional imprinting*, or *emo-imprinting* for short. Emo-imprinting is easy to visualize and understand; just as ducklings know to follow their mother swimming in a pond or lake, kids will copy or emulate what their parents are doing.

John Gottman, an award-winning research psychologist, has done a lot of research on raising children. He is alarmed that one-on-one time is decreasing and advises parents that for the best shot at raising an empathetic child, parents should be in their kids' lives while being emotionally available: "Stay engaged in the details of your children's everyday lives . . . stay emotionally available to them."[9]

Being emotionally available requires that you embrace or recognize the child's distress rather than dismissing it. Helen Riess, in *The Empathy Effect*, encourages parents to acknowledge children's feelings and their need for security. She provides many examples of what to say to validate children's fears rather than negating them.[10] For example, when a child is frightened of an animal, you might say, "Are you scared of that animal? What scares you about the animal?" Riess certainly would not be in the "man-up" camp of teaching children.

In exploring the neuroscience behind empathy and nurturing, Riess recommends that parents start early and be realistic. She says that parents should not overreact by being intolerant of "a single second of unhappiness in their child's life." It's healthy for children to run up against obstacles. Challenges will teach them to develop the grit, perseverance, and resilience that are key to success in life. Her best advice for parents when faced with a child's difficult emotions? "Explore what's behind the feelings—the back story."[11]

Riess also suggests that parents talk to their children about other people's feelings, which brings me to the next topic: walking in another person's shoes.

Step Four, Cultural Empathy: Walking in Another Person's Shoes

One of the unique attributes of empathy is that it requires us to be "present" and still. I have already mentioned that empathy can be a slow emotion. Sometimes it requires more processing time than the other social-emotional skills, because it can ask a child to "walk in another's shoes." In a very busy world, it can be challenging to slow down, but it is worth it.

Creating empathy by walking in others' shoes can be accomplished in a variety of ways. "Walking in others' shoes" can be categorized as (1) historical empathy, (2) cultural empathy, and (3) peer/family empathy.

Historical Empathy

This type of empathy is a tried-and-true educational process used in museums around the United States. It is evidence-based, meaning that it is measured to have a statistically significant effect on improving empathy attitudes. Here is an easy visual example. In New York City's Lower East Side Tenement Museum, guides travel up and down the stairs through old tenements and neighborhoods from the late 1800s. They take visitors on a journey through time, inviting them to walk in the shoes of an immigrant who has no skills, is poor, and may not know English. What was it like to come to this country with less than five dollars in your pocket? What was it like to be responsible for a family? What was the daily routine for a poor child? Youth who take these journeys back in time understand how challenging it was to come to this country as an immigrant and to be a hungry child or adult.

When is the last time your family visited a museum? Museums are shifting away from being collections of stuffy cases of artifacts (which I personally love) to reengineered institutions that welcome families with interactive activities and dialogue about current issues that society is facing.

As always, children's museums specialize in and offer real "play" in their exhibits, which strengthens both creativity and imagination muscles for children. Other museums around the country are beginning to refocus on social justice, civic engagement, and actively engaging members of the communities they represent. This is an exciting paradigm shift toward empathy and diversity appreciation, and a trend to watch. Research the museums in your area!

Cultural Empathy

We teach this type of empathy at the Tolerance Center. For middle schoolers, we visit the topic of Native American sports mascots, which are called names such as Braves, Warriors, and Redskins. (For those of you who don't know, *redskins* historically means bloody scalps and is considered a slur by Native Americans.)

Because most of the students are comfortable with Native American characters as sports mascots, we challenge them to walk in the shoes of a Native American. We ask them: What does it feel like to be reminded of scalps and the violent death of your people when you are a Native American at a sports event? How does an indigenous person feel about his or people being referred to as savage or primitive?

Most Native Americans are uncomfortable about being the only living humans used as a sports mascot. After showing kids some Native American sports mascots in the center, some of the students seem to get it and change their minds about how acceptable that is. They have entered the empathy portal, walking in the shoes of Native Americans, and upon leaving the portal, they understand that it is not right for sports teams to benefit from a false representation of Native Americans. This is a good place for me to give credit where credit is due: "Don't judge a man until you have walked a mile in his shoes" is an old Cherokee proverb.

Native American sports mascots usually represent all indigenous peoples as brave warriors; sounds great, doesn't it? Not when you learn that most Native Americans today do not want to be represented this way. Today, Native Americans are doctors, lawyers, ballet dancers, scientists, and so on; in other words, they are human beings. Would you want to be characterized repeatedly as an angry warrior? Would you want to be represented this way to your children?

Peer/Family Empathy

This type of empathy is represented by walking in the shoes of a parent, a sister, a brother, a cousin, a friend, or a neighbor. At the Tolerance Center, one of our main focuses is bullying prevention, and you can imagine that teaching children how to stop bullying, how to stop being a target, and how to intervene is not as simple as saying "do the right thing." At the center, we teach children various strategies so that the next time they are called a name, are bullied, or see someone being bullied, they have a variety of strategies from which to pick. Getting involved requires such strategies. Following is a sample activity about Native Americans that is rarely done in schools. You don't have to follow all of these steps, but when teaching empathy it is good to consider doing much of this and to go slow.

Activity: Walk in the Shoes of a Native American

1. Ask your children if they know any living Native Americans.

2. Ask what they have learned in school about them.

3. Ask if they would like to learn more, because you know Native Americans are living in your state but you don't know any personally.

4. Do some research on the internet to explore

   - how many Native Americans live in your state.
   - how many Native Americans live on reservations and how many do not.
   - what kind of jobs Native Americans have today.
   - the history of Native Americans in your state.
   - what words or place names that you use today come from Native Americans.
   - what foods are Native American (hint: squash, beans, corn).
   - what you can do to be an ally today to Native Americans.
   - whether naming sports mascots for Native American is respectful.

"Walking in another's shoes" is a process in which we have to go slow. It takes time to work through these emotions and thoughts. Consider the following steps, recommended by writer Steve Mueller in his blog:[12]

1. Walk a mile in someone's shoes. Ask yourself how a situation looks from someone else's perspective.

2. Ask yourself what the person's motive is. Is he or she being selfish? Helpful?

3. *Let it go.* Take some time to process what's happening, replacing anger with compassion.

4. Discover the similarities, not the differences.

5. *Don't judge too hastily.* Empathy is a slow emotion; sleep on it. Take more time to process what's going on.

6. Become aware of your own emotions. We all have good days and bad days. Accept that as you evaluate the situation.

7. Ask others about their perspective. You can be more objective if you ask your relatives or friends what they think.

I use step 7 frequently at home. When I present an unpopular decision or conclusion to my husband or children, I ask them to ask other people about it. What do other people say about my opinion or stand? What do others think?

Bonus Step: Is Empathy Being Taught or Modeled in Your Child's School?

It is vital for parents and caregivers to know that they can't rely on schools anymore to teach social-emotional skills. School administrators usually want to teach character education but are increasingly pressured to prioritize testing, academics, grades, and sports. Social-emotional skills have been reclassified in many schools as a low priority. It's up to you to get children to step back and recalibrate what their school is all about. There are things you can consider to improve your child's school.

Ask yourself these questions:

- What social-emotional programs are being taught in your child's school?

- Are they effective programs; that is, is someone measuring or assessing them?

- Do they address empathy? Do they include other important social-emotional skills?

This is difficult for many people. I get it. But if you have it in you to be a change maker, you can make all the difference. I've done it, and so can you. It's better if you don't go it alone. It is not only easier but also more effective to gather a couple of other concerned parents to schedule a meeting with the principal or the school counselor. Start by asking your friends whether they are passionate about this issue and, if so, to join you for a premeeting. Have coffee before the meeting at the school and listen to one another.

At your first meeting with the school staff person, be friendly and ask a lot of questions. Job one is to learn about the school's inventory of social-emotional learning (SEL). What programs are they doing, what are they measuring, and what are they planning for the future? Don't be surprised if an SEL inventory doesn't exist; push for one.

Regroup with your team and discuss what you've learned. Then perhaps as a team or just as a committee, ask for a second meeting. Subsequent meetings could follow wherein you and your group encourage the school administrators to improve on social-emotional skill programs for all students. It takes a village to teach empathy, and we are anointing you—or one of your friends—"Mother Empathy," "Father Empathy," or "Person Empathy." (A sample agenda for your meeting might be the three questions just listed; I created the agenda to discuss these issues with my child's elementary school counselor.) When organized and steadfast, parents can be empathy drivers outside of the home, and teachers can inspire caring class-rooms and schools.

I have similar advice for teachers. In some schools, the principal and counselors might not be interested or feel they have time to focus on social-emotional skills. Find some allies to leverage power in numbers and see whether that helps.

So there you have it, a series of ideas and steps to turn yourself into the parent or teacher you want to be and help you bring more empathy into your home or classroom. All families are different and learn and process at different rates. As you begin your quest, don't expect immediate results. In my own family, change was often slow and incremental. If you don't see immediate change, don't despair; you have the growth mindset in your corner.

I noticed in my own family over the years that sometimes it would take my kids a few hours to process what I'd tried to teach them. Sometimes it would take a few days, or even a few weeks. (It usually takes my husband at least twenty-four hours to process anything that I have to say, but that's a whole other story.) So give your kids some time to step up.

Know that you are growing a variety of seeds, watering them, and fertilizing them. One day, you and others will notice the beautiful flowers and plants that you have been nurturing in your garden.

As parents, when we get tired or exasperated, we resort to bribes ("rewards" if that takes the sting  off) like food, internet, or TV time. A word to the wise from college professor Peter M. Vishton in *Scientific Secrets for Raising Kids Who Thrive*. He counsels, in so many words, "Don't do it." We want our children to engage in positive behavior without expecting a reward. Bribing creates an undesirable link that we want to avoid. We want our children to learn to be naturally cooperative and be good people. Sharing, cooperating, and helping others should be rewards on their own.[1] Being lazy, my husband and I occasionally bribed our kids; without hesitation, I can tell you that this strategy was shortsighted and ultimately didn't work.

Note
1. Peter M. Vishton, Scientific Secrets for Raising Kids Who Thrive: Course Guidebook (Chantilly, VA: Teaching Company, 2014).

seven
teaching empathy
infant to three years

We learn to listen by being listened to. We see our work as a "baby step"
toward giving every person a voice from the moment of birth. Perhaps it
will also be a first step toward restoring empathy in our society.
—Dr. Claudia M. Gold[1]

I can't stand to hear babies cry. As a young mother, it was difficult
for me, especially if I couldn't figure out what was wrong, which
happened more than I care to admit. I felt as if I, too, were in pain
and trapped, with no way out of this awful feeling that pierced my
heart. But it always passed eventually. And those first few smiles sent
me soaring to wonderful heights.

Come to think of it, I can't stand to hear toddlers cry, either.
What's more, as they start to learn words and phrases, they develop
sometimes adorable, sometimes cunningly brilliant ways of pushing

your buttons. No matter how many years pass, I still hear echoes in my mind of little sentences starting with "I need . . . I want . . ." And who among us is unfamiliar with the one-word medieval torture that toddlers wield like a weapon: the word "why?" "Please put your toys away. . . . *Why?* . . . So your room will look nice and neat. . . . *Why?* . . . Because I don't want to trip and break my leg. . . . *Why?* . . . Just do it!!!"

In case you haven't figured it out yet, that's my way of saying that the earlier you can start your kids on the Empathy Advantage, the better off you and your entire family will be. In this chapter I explain that the seeds of empathy exist even in infants. I also explore some tactics for nurturing that empathy and then discuss how to apply some serious strategy before toddlerhood arrives.

Infants

Infants are remarkable in ways that we would never expect. At the ripe old age of one or two days old, infants cry in response to other infants crying in the hospital.[2] With as much as I know about empathy, even this fact surprised me—and reassured me. How amazing it is to know that infants are hardwired for empathy. Nature gives most of us the gift of some empathy, although we receive different amounts. It's just waiting there for loving parents to nurture it and help it grow.

Active empathy, rather than just an innate response, begins to develop in late infancy. During the first year, the infant has feelings and begins to develop cognitive skills.

The importance of the parent's role in encouraging empathy as early as possible can't be overemphasized. Researchers point out the importance of babies developing a strong and secure bond with their parent figures. Security fosters empathy. When parents and other caregivers express concern and provide comfort, empathy is exactly what they are modeling. Children are just beginning to regulate their emotions, and that sensitive response to their needs helps them do that. In contrast, if caregivers and parents ignore their children's needs or stress the child consistently, they may compromise the child's ability to develop empathy. So it is important that parents maintain a positive and safe home environment from early on.[3]

As we learned in previous chapters, the more face-to-face time you can provide your children, the better your family's quality of life will be. Infants are smarter than we think and are watching us closely. If you model anger, they will pick up on that. If you model caring and concern, they will remember that, too. Yes, this is the time to plant the seeds of emotional stability.

If you get yourself into the habit of modeling the behavior you want early, it will be more natural for you to teach empathy to your kids as they grow older. Am I asking you to react perfectly every time your infant spits up on your favorite shirt and every time he or she cries when you're already ten minutes late for work? Of course not! But if you do your best, if you take a breath and remain aware of your actions and emotions, the calmer and less tense your baby and household will be.

It follows, of course, that if a focus on the quality of your interactions with your infant is beneficial, a focus on increasing the amount of time you spend interacting will also help. The American Academy of Pediatrics (AAP) estimates that for each hour that a child younger than age two spends in front of a screen, he or she spends about fifteen minutes less interacting with the parent. Creative play also drops, by about 10 percent. The AAP's overall recommendation for children younger than eighteen months is straight and to the point: zero screen time except perhaps for video chatting.[4] Infants are just not ready for it. Remember those *Baby Einstein* videos? Subsequent research says they accomplish nothing.[5]

Just in case you need a bonus sales pitch, I'm happy to oblige. While mothers who work outside of the home spend an average of eleven minutes daily with their children, fathers spend only about eight minutes of quality interaction time on weekdays.[6] Not hours. *Minutes!* Full-time at-home mothers spend a little bit more face-to-face time with their children, averaging thirteen minutes of quality interaction a day, but wouldn't you think it would be much more? Emotional unavailability and a lack of face-to-face time rob our future generation of empathy and other social-emotional skills.

How do you increase that face-to-face time? There are plenty of options besides using media as a babysitter. When you have chores to do around the house, you could

- carry your baby on your body in a carrier;
- ask a sibling to be the entertainer (more about "little helpers" elsewhere in the chapter); or
- if you are in the kitchen, move the child in a car seat or stroller so he or she is always observing you.

There are lots of other ways to do it. The ideas are limited only by your creativity!

action tips

Toddlers

I will always preach the gospel of restricting screen time. So let me start this section with the AAP's recommendations for toddlers.

- Eighteen to twenty-four months: If you feel the need to introduce screen time, it should involve both parent and child watching high-quality programming, such as content offered by Sesame Workshop and PBS.

- Two to five years: just one hour per day of high-quality programming—with a parent if possible.[7]

All right, I saw some of you shaking your heads. Well, not literally, but I had a mental image of you doing it because I know how busy we all are and the statistics as far as what's really happening with screen time. The American public doesn't know, or in many cases just doesn't care about, the AAP's recommendations. One study in 2002 found that nearly half of those between twelve and twenty-three months of age, and more than 40 percent of those between twenty-four and thirty-five months, were in front of screens beyond what the AAP recommended at the time.[8] And that was many years ago.

But I hope by now I've coached you to move past that initial reaction. You're already starting to be empathy pros. You know you can do this! Even if you can't meet those goals consistently, you can UP your game a little bit to start on the path to a more attentive, caring child or student.

Of course, it's not all about screens. Let's discuss some of the other aspects of the young child. Around eighteen months, the child is more aware of how other people feel. As infants mature into toddlers, they begin to understand the connection between emotions and desires, and, of course, separation or independence. Do the "terrible twos" sound familiar?

In surveys, parents *say* they place more value on caring than achievement. Well, it's time to put your money where your mouth is! This is when you get your empathy muscles to work. Reinforce caring by complimenting acts of compassion and kindness. But don't throw your compliments around willy-nilly; use a little nuance. Researcher Mark Davis specifically recommends that parents compliment the child's *behavior*, not the child. Here's why. Studies show that when actions become a reflection of who a child is, when the child is judged by what he or she does, that child is more likely to make better moral choices.[9]

In other words, complimenting specific behaviors is better than complimenting the child as a whole person. It's the difference between saying, "You're such a good girl!" and "You did such a great job putting your toys back in your cubby!" This way, children are not always under the microscope of being classified as *good or bad kids*. They are critiqued for their behaviors, which can be changed to meet expectations.

The flip side for misbehavior should be fairly obvious: it's better to criticize children's behaviors than to criticize the child as a person. For example, you would say, "I didn't like that you hit your baby brother. That was not a good thing to do," rather than saying, "You are a bad boy." We hope that children will conclude there are better options to consider in the future. We know and they know that they are capable of better choices.

Adam Grant, a professor at the University of Pennsylvania's Wharton School, amplifies this strategy by suggesting a way to strengthen our parenting skills that is a cousin to "criticize the behavior, not the child." Grant says that using a little guilt is better than using shame. He argues that shame is an ineffective technique with poor consequences, but guilt, when used carefully, can be a powerful motivator. *Whaaat?* Guilt can be good? (Many may find this strange, but having grown up around old-fashioned Jewish guilt, it seems perfectly natural to me—what a motivator!) As Grant reminds us, in the famous words of humorist Erma Bombeck, "Guilt is the gift that keeps on giving."[10]

For example, if a child does something wrong, shaming communicates to the child that he or she is not a good person, while guilt is a better motivator for more positive behavior in the future. "Shame is the feeling that I am a bad person, whereas guilt is the feeling that I have done a bad thing," Grant writes. He points to a study by psychologist Karen Caplovitz Barrett in which toddlers were given a rag doll and the leg fell off during play. "The shame-prone toddlers avoided the researcher and did not volunteer that they broke the doll. The guilt-prone toddlers were more likely to fix the doll, approach the experimenter, and explain what happened. The ashamed toddlers were avoiders; the guilty toddlers were amenders."[11]

You may ask what guilt and shame have to do with empathy. Guilt prods youngsters to understand that their behavior hurt someone else: the core of empathy. The child wants to do better so a playmate will feel better. Shame is toxic. Guilt builds a desire to do right. Some parents can't tell the difference and don't discipline at all, leaving children without boundaries or a sense of right and wrong.[12]

Building self-worth is key. Grant recommends that before toddlers evolve into preschoolers, we should ask our children to be helpers. Involving your children provides them with self-esteem and makes them feel like they have something meaningful to offer. You can enhance your child's new identity by asking other questions, such as "Will you be a sharer? A carer? A caring person? Can you play with your baby brother for ten minutes to help mommy?"[13]

As mentioned previously, part of building a strong parent-child relationship rich with interaction is engaging in face-to-face activities and minimizing exposure to technology and media. Little children are natural lovers of the outdoors, losing themselves in wonders ranging from the colors of leaves in the fall to blowing dandelion seeds to make a wish. Don't forget the fun of reading, puzzles, and playing board games. (My favorites were Candyland and Chutes and Ladders. Chutes is still a great starter kit for the young game player and, boy, did I hate that *looooong* chute down to the bottom.)

And don't feel that you have to overschedule. I know when I was growing up I had a lot of alone time. Alone time is invaluable because it allows the young brain to take off in creative play and flights of imagination. The AAP wisely recommends that parents establish screen-free times, such as dinner and other mealtimes, and screen-free zones, such as children's bedrooms.

A great toddler tip comes from Dr. Markus Paulus, a professor of developmental psychology at Ludwig Maximilian University in Munich, Germany. He recommends taking toddlers on an exploration of empathy-related behaviors like sharing, helping, and comforting others. He recommends that we guide children into the colorful world of feelings. He cites one intriguing study in which researchers observed parents reading picture books to their toddlers and discovered that the children who were asked to discuss emotions in the books tended to share more quickly and more often. How wonderful! His research shows that when parents and caregivers motivated toddlers to assist at home with empathy, they were more likely to be helpful around the house as they grew older.[14] Who doesn't like that?

I wish I had done this with my children when they were toddlers. By the time I started asking my children to help around the house at the age of eight or nine, it was too late. There were battles because they were not accustomed to helping at all. It needs to be part of the household's routine. Learn from my mistakes: start asking for assistance with simple tasks at an early stage.

Interestingly, several studies say that parents should avoid bribing their children for good behavior. OK, they don't usually use the word *bribe*; they generally use the word *reward*. But I'm willing to say, "Don't bribe! Don't offer action figures and dolls! Don't offer lollipops and other sweets!" Bribing is a strategy that only works in the short term.

Good behavior isn't something that should be bought with toys and food. We should be tapping into children's natural reservoir of wanting to do good. Praise is the only reward they should need. (Note: I'm not going to be unrealistic and say you should be perfect; we all give in once in a while. Parenting is tough work!)

Toddlers Can Help Around the House, and They Want To!

Why bother trying to get your toddler to help around the house? Because he or she will build confidence, learn that cleaning and straightening up is a lot of work, and—most important—subconsciously appreciate and empathize with the parent's/caregiver's ongoing responsibilities. Following are some great activities. Feel free to come up with your own.

1. **Dusting using old, mismatched socks**. Let the toddler slip each hand into an old sock. Then let him or her go to work wiping dust from books, tables, shelves, and anything else that is dusty and safe to touch.

2. **Putting away folded laundry**. Your toddler can help by carrying folded laundry to the room where it belongs and assist you in putting the laundry away.

3. **Picking up dirty clothes**. This has two parts. (A) Pick up the item from the floor and put it wherever your family places dirty clothes: in the clothes hamper, in the wash basket, and so on. Next time, have the toddler pick up and deposit the dirty item with you accompanying him or her. By the third time, he or she will be able to do this task alone. (B) In the laundry room, make a game by having the toddler help you sort the clothes by color.

4. **Picking up toys and books**. You, the parent, make a home for different types of items—in other words, "a keeping place." In the beginning, together with your toddler, pick up the toy or book and walk it to its keeping place. Open-top baskets and bins work well for toys, low bookshelves for books. Gradually, the toddler can pick up independently. If he or she forgets, make a game of pickup:

"Do you see the ball? Show me where it goes." Hint: Do not talk in generalities. Instead of saying, "Pick up the playroom," say, "Please put your blocks in the bag."

5. **Cleaning up their own messes**. If your toddler spills a cup of milk or juice, give him or her a paper towel or damp rag to

   help you clean it up. Of course, you may want to reclean the spill area with a disinfecting wipe later when your child isn't around (you don't want to give the idea that he or she didn't do a good enough job), but the toddler gets the message of what's expected. Often singing a catchy song helps the cleanup go better. (To the tune of "Here We Go 'Round the Mulberry Bush," try singing, "This is the way I clean up the spill, clean up the spill, clean up the spill. This is the way I clean up the spill, and make everything so clean.")

6. **Sweeping the floor**. Most toddler boys and girls find sweeping enjoyable. (And it uses up lots and lots of toddler energy, thankfully.) Purchase a child-sized broom and dustpan and let him or her help you sweep the kitchen floor or the outside walk as you sweep along with your adult-sized equipment.

7. **Unloading the dishwasher**. Younger toddlers will be able to start with handing you items one at a time, starting with spoons, for you to put away. As you add different items, model how to carefully hold the item safely and then observe the toddler following through. Older toddlers can graduate to taking out the item and putting it in its proper place safely.

8. **Carrying and putting away groceries**. Start younger toddlers with carrying a lightweight, nonperishable item that will not be damaged if dropped, such as a roll of paper towels. Older toddlers can help put the items where they belong.

9. **Setting the table**. Young toddlers can bring paper napkins and place one at each setting. Older toddlers can transport spoons, plastic cups, and plates and put one at each setting.

10. **Taking care of the family pet**. Let your toddler fill a just-the-right-size plastic scoop with the amount of dry food needed and pour the food into the animal's food dish. Your toddler can also use a small plastic pitcher to pour water into the pet's water bowl.

11. **Washing the car**. Here, you and your toddler work together with a bucket, sponge, soapy water, a hose for rinsing, and a soft cloth for drying. Too ambitious? Your toddler can wash his or her tricycle while you wash your bike!

No parent can do it all. But every parent can do a little bit more. That includes you! Start with "baby steps," adding a little more empathy in your daily routines each week. Before you know it, your little ones will start to reap the rewards.

- Acknowledge your children's emotions and help them describe the feelings they are feeling.
- Reduce the time your children spend with technology and media.

- Create cooperative face-to-face activities every week that are fun and include exercise.
- Role model caring and various feelings like sadness, fatigue, hope, exhaustion, caring for others, concern, happiness, and joy. You are role modeling that it is OK to be angry, but it is also OK to be sad. There is nothing wrong with being angry or frustrated and nothing wrong with being afraid.
- Maximize face-to-face time with your little ones. They are watching.

eight
teaching empathy
three to six years

For in every adult there dwells the child that was,
and in every child there lies the adult that will be.
—John Connolly, *The Book of Lost Things*

as we get older, the thought of flying to, say, California or Florida leaves many of us stressed for weeks ahead of time about the hassle of remembering everything to pack, long security lines, traffic, and so on. And heaven forbid if we are flying in winter. Then we have to worry about the possibility of snow, delays, missing connecting flights, and other issues.

Now look at flying through the eyes of a threeto six-year-old child. *We're going on an airplane! How high will we go? Does that puffy cloud look like a rhino or a hippo to you?* One of the big surprises of parenthood for me was seeing the world through the eyes of a child again. My children were teaching *me* to remember what a wondrous and beautiful place this world can be. Being a parent and spending time with your child often knocks that jaded, cynical, timeworn perspective on life right out of you.

There are many things going on in the psychology of the preschool child, but ranking high among them is that sense of wonder. Part of our job as parents is to nurture that and to use it as rocket fuel to lay their foundations for joy, curiosity, and play. Defined as "early childhood," this stage of life is when children are watching you very closely, so make sure you are leveraging that sense of wonder. Remember, when you're little, you think your parents can do no wrong, so roll with it! (Note: I have yet to see a single case in which the "perfect parent" notion persisted into the tween years. In middle school, if my kids saw me in the school hallway, they were too embarrassed by my existence to even acknowledge me; they walked right past me, even though I was volunteering *my* time at *their* school!)

Mystery Walks Outside

It was now or never, I said to myself. It was raining and I was reminiscing about my childhood days, of being out in the rain and not minding a bit. The more I got soaked and smelled the rain, the more those soggy childhood memories warmed my heart. I already knew that life as a parent was passing by too quickly, and I said to myself, "It's time for my kids to put on the raincoats and boots and get soaking wet!" Yes, that's right. It was not a cold day, so out we went—my six-year-old daughter Rachel, my three-year-old son Jake, and me.

I grabbed my camera before we left the house, and we walked, heading in whatever random direction we felt like. We looked around at how everything was getting wet. We jumped in puddles. We giggled. We found ourselves in our neighborhood park, where I snapped photos of my kids splashing in even more puddles and waving at people who were smiling back at their exuberance. People looked at us like we were nuts. Perhaps we were.

My children, Rachel and Jake

Soaking wet, we sloshed back home. The first thing I did when I got home was take more photos of them, sodden and dripping in the hall, before giving them a hot bath.

What an experience. We survived outside soaking wet, and the best part of all is that we had fun. Among the thousands of pictures I've taken of my children, these photos might be my very favorites. I framed them and treasure them. They remain to this day proudly displayed on the living-room wall, taking me back to that fantastic, unusual rainy-day shared adventure.

And you can do this, too, with your kids. If rain's not your thing, take your kids on a sunny-day "Mystery Walk." When they ask where you are going, tell them, "I don't know." The uncertainty will mystify them. Let them decide whether to turn left or right. Let them enjoy the power of control. Their curiosity and creativity will soar, and you just might learn something new as well. Coach them to use their five senses. In addition to sight, stop to smell, feel, touch, hear, and—if you come across a tree with ripe fruit—taste. Warning: This just might become addictive.

Reading and Discussing

I'm not sure who appreciated reading time more, my kids or I, during what we called "Reading Hour" (feel free to come up with a more inventive name). Admittedly, reading Dr. Seuss's *Go, Dog, Go!* dozens of nights in a row started to fray my nerves, but having them cuddle on my lap and (spoiler alert) their joyful reaction each time we got to the end—"A dog party! A big dog party! Big dogs, little dogs, red dogs, blue dogs"—gave all of us a giggling payoff.

With books, we can sneak in empathy lessons without children even realizing it. Simply initiate the practice of reading books aloud to your children at bedtime and on the weekends. Then observe what they can learn through their openness to wonder. And though I have a thing about kids and screens, I have news for you: while I love the touch, smell, and feel of the printed page, if you want to read from a tablet, I'll let you slide.

In the following sections, I provide some question prompts for you to ask your children that will get them to think about the mental states and emotional situations that the book characters are feeling. Even preschoolers can begin to understand others' perspectives and "walk in their shoes." The more stories you read, and the more stories you discuss, the more you will maximize your preschoolers' empathy and communication skills. So, do as we do with preschoolers who visit the Tolerance Center: "Teach it and teach it often." Discuss sharing, caring, and cooperation so they become second nature to the children.

By the way, there's no rule that you have to empty your wallet and buy the books I introduce here and in other chapters. Go to the library! One of my favorite memories of being a young person was my trips there. I loved the way the library and books smelled as well as the quiet and the solitude. And I treasured my library's summer reading club. One year, the club's theme was a "rocket to the stars"; as we read more books over the summer, the librarian would move our rockets higher and higher until we got to the moon. I felt such a sense of achievement and aspired to read more books until I did, before the summer was out, reach the moon. Let your child reach for the stars and the moon, too!

Following are some of my favorite empathy-inducing books, which I still have in my home even though my children are now grown (I am saving them for my grandchildren).

The Little Engine That Could

Most people focus on the engine and the gumption it needs to go over the mountain, but who worries about the poor children waiting who might not get their toys? I did when I was a child! Discuss this with your kids: How are the children feeling? Sometimes it's fun to switch it up and not focus on the main, obvious character.

Books Featuring Baby Animals

You can't go wrong with photos of baby animals. They are naturally empathy inducing and will inspire a love of nature and wildlife in your family. In my home, we had lots of nature books and magazines. I want to give a shout out here to the National Wildlife Federation's magazine *Ranger Rick* and, for younger kids, *Ranger Rick Junior* and *Ranger Rick Cub*.[1]

The Giving Tree

If you haven't read this book by Shel Silverstein, take a deep breath and get out the tissues. I won't ruin the ending, but there was one character with a lot of empathy and there was another character without it. After you read the book with your child, have a discussion.

A Tale from the Care Bears: The Trouble with Timothy

This was a classic in my house. It was read over and over again by both my children. In it, young Timothy is having trouble getting along with his peers in kindergarten. From out of nowhere, magical Friend Bear comes to the rescue. Friend Bear empathizes with Timothy and coaches him to be nice in school the next day. Timothy "walks in the shoes" of his classmates. The next day Timothy goes back to school and guess what happens? Friend Bear's job is done, and she disappears.

Chicka Chicka Boom Boom

This is a rollicking tale of mischievous "toddler-esque" lowercase letters that climb a coconut tree in alphabetical order, oblivious to the consequence that the weight will cause the tree to bend and send them tumbling out. Kids will feel empathy for the lowercase letters that wind up with minor cuts and scratches, later to be comforted by the parenting/caregiving uppercase letters.

The True Story of the Three Little Pigs

The classic tale of the "Three Little Pigs" is one that we all remember. But have you had the opportunity to read this version by Jon Scieszka? I love this book, in which the author flips the story. The pigs are mean, and the wolf is misunderstood. It's a howl (pardon my pun) to walk in the paws of a lonely, misunderstood wolf! See if this works for you and see if you can find other books that present a different point of view from a familiar book or character. Or imagine one together.

This is a great place for a reminder of the importance of a nighttime routine for preschoolers. You probably know that they need an unsurprising series of consistent, predictable steps. That will make them feel safe and cozy in their beds when they are winding down from a busy and stimulating day. With the screens away, now's the time to read books to inculcate empathy.

Some children's books come with a discussion guide at the end, but you can make up your own prompts for any story. Put on your new thinking cap and ask questions like these:

action tips

- How do you think the little girl was feeling?
- Did the boy feel bad about grabbing the toy?
- What would you do in this situation?
- Do you think that was a kind thing to do?
- What is the nice thing to do?
- Do you like Character A? Character B? Why or why not?
- What questions do *you* have?

Simply put, discuss feelings and maybe motivations as well.

It might be helpful to make your own customized questions for reading prompts. This way you don't have to invent new questions every night. As your kids get older, you will have to work on them and improve them. I have provided you with a start in the above textbox.

Storytelling

It's never too early to start storytelling—just going off in your own direction to wherever your imagination takes you. After a little practice, putting on your creative thinking cap should come fairly easily. According to Elizabeth Erickson from St. Catherine University, "As the child absorbs language, [he or] she also comes to better articulate her thoughts and experiences. One can effectively guide children to the language they need to be successful in communicating their emotions and understanding the emotions of others through storytelling."[2]

Free Play

Free play has real value, including for empathy. When your child plays with other kids, it enables him or her to listen and pick up social cues, even at this age. In order to get along with peers, your son or daughter has to discover and consider how the other person feels. "Social play also requires children to share ideas and express feelings while negotiating and reaching compromises," writes Leah Shafer in a blog published by the Harvard Graduate School of Education.[3]

Of course, playtime with parents is great empathy time as well. Sadly, researchers have discovered that free play declined by at least a third between 1981 and 2003, meaning a resulting decline in face-to-face time.[4] Recent research confirms this is a trend. When parents can't be around, they often put their kids in other supervised activities. Those have value, but there's a loss of the initiative, creativity, and confidence that free play allows. Too much structured time can lead to a decline in social-emotional skills. That can also lead to behaviors—among them bullying and attention seeking—that we don't want our kids to internalize.

Did you know that, in China, parents ship their children away to schools as young as age five? And that at these schools, the rich parents pay the teachers to hug their children? As a result, poor children may not receive hugs at all. How distressing!

DID YOU KNOW

Fun Activities, Including Puppet Shows

Talk about sense of wonder. This is *the* age for a puppet show. (I'm channeling Mister Rogers, in relation to King Friday, the proud ruler of the Neighborhood of Make-Believe. By the way, I vote to bring Mister Rogers back to the internet and TV.) One of my favorite activities at Kidsbridge is making puppets and performing puppet shows. Why puppet shows, you ask? When kids pretend to be characters other than themselves in the Tolerance Center and bring them to life, it's amazing to watch them take on different perspectives.

One good idea, say researchers Carla Poole, Susan A. Miller, and Ellen Booth Church, is to suggest acting out various situations with puppets using voices that accurately invoke the intended feelings (such as caring, happy, or sad voices).[5] During kindergarten, children can learn how to create caring friendships and develop a vocabulary related to feelings, enabling them to convey their emotions.

If puppets are your thing, you can make fancy ones or just keep it simple. It's a fun activity just to make stick puppets; a piece of paper folded in half and glued to a Popsicle stick will suffice.

Next, it's time to act out scenarios or skits that will teach your child more about feelings. Following are some examples:

- Mean-spirited scenarios
- Exclusion scenarios: someone is not included or invited
- Helping others, getting along, and kindness scenarios
- Sad scenarios

action tips

You should let your child pick and vary the character

that he or she wants to play: the mean puppet, the target puppet (we don't use the word "victim" anymore), a "helper puppet," or whatever else you invent!

But that's far from the only play activity that can exercise that empathy muscle. Any type of face-to-face interaction is helpful, such as walks, playing games, helping prepare meals, baking cookies, and arts and crafts.

Other Ways to Support Your Young Child Socially and Emotionally

I hope I have stimulated your thinking and now you are aware of enjoyable ways to use your child's sense of wonder to strengthen his or her empathy. Understanding how the mind of the threeto six-year-old operates will open the door to other ways you can assist in your child's social-emotional development. I'm willing to bet that these activities will be as fun for you as for your child.

But even though I suspect you don't need a reminder, this is a good place to mention that parenting is the toughest job you'll ever love. It involves a lot of commitment, thinking on your feet to turn difficult situations into teachable moments, establishing structure to allow the space for quality time and empathy to flow, and more. It's time to talk about strategic parenting.

But before I do that, keep in mind the way the brain of the threeto six-year-old functions. Experts in psychology tell us that at these ages, children are developing a "theory of mind," defined as children recognizing that others are separate and apart from themselves. The terrible twos are just the beginning, when children are realizing they are distinct creatures. This emerging self-awareness spurs new emotions, needs, and desires as they hit the preschool years.

Strengths and Weaknesses

One key lesson we like to teach at the Tolerance Center is that every person has strengths and weaknesses. This is an invaluable lesson to teach a child, because it means every child is special. Or as Mister Rogers used to sing:

> You are my friend.
> You are special.
> You are my friend.
> You're special to me.
> You are the only one like you.
> Like you, my friend, I like you.

Here's a good activity for the whole family to do to tickle your child's interest about strengths and weaknesses.

action tips

1. Pass around pieces of paper and pencils or pens.
2. Each person should write down his or her own strengths and weaknesses (you can write it down for your kids).
3. Share the pieces of paper and discuss what you wrote with each other.
4. Choose a person and guess what his or her strengths and weaknesses are.
5. Then share what those strengths and weaknesses are.

Don't be surprised if this activity ends with a few giggles. And don't be astonished if you learn some surprising things about each other! (In the classroom, I would just share and discuss strengths.)

Praising Kindness

One way to reduce the frequency of difficult behavior is to catch your kids in the act of being good and make them want to be so again and again. It just takes a little extra energy to praise your children for any signs of empathy or kindness that you observe. You can also praise other children and adults in your child's presence so they understand early that you value empathy and all of your relationships. Everyone can be a role model.

I loved one parenting expert's idea of going into "growth mindset mode" to put deposits in the "Positive Recognition Bank," in which the deposits are praise instead of money. While you should try to be consistent in praising your child for, say, sharing that favorite stuffed animal with a sibling or a friend, it's no biggie if you accidentally miss a day. That's because you had the foresight to operate in stealth mode rather than having committed to praising the child's every good action. You have covered yourself by banking a day off with all your other praise.[6]

Teaching Moments

Once you're aware of your child's array of good deeds, you will observe teaching moments everywhere. For example, let's say your child grabs a toy from a sibling or another child. You could say, "When you grabbed your sister's toy, you made your sister upset. What can you do to make her feel better?" You could also say, "How would *you* feel if your sister grabbed your favorite toy from you?" Then listen to your child's response closely. Don't rush.

The time to find those teaching moments is now. The earlier you start, the easier it will be to create a culture of empathy as your kids grow older. Following is a great list of recommendations adapted from those on the Babycenter website:[7]

1. Label the feeling.

2. Praise empathetic behavior.

3. Encourage your preschooler to talk about his or her feelings and yours.

4. Point out other people's behavior.

5. Teach verbal and nonverbal cues.

6. Teach and role model politeness.

7. Don't use anger to control your child.

8. Give your preschooler small jobs.

9. Role-model acts of empathy.

10. Be sensitive to gender and be careful that your children are doing likewise.

Did you know that the United States is participating  in a study that will measure empathy? The International Early Learning and Child Well-Being Study is assessing three thousand five-year-old preschoolers in each of the United States, England, and Estonia on literacy, mathematics, self-regulation, and social-emotional skills, specifically including empathy. I'm thrilled to see that the Organisation for Economic Co-operation and Development is on the empathy team and eagerly await the results, due to come out in 2020.[1]

Note

1. For more information, see Linda Jacobson, "Pre-to-3: New 'Baby PISA' Study to Include US 5-Year-Olds," Education Dive, March 8, 2019, https://www.educationdive.com/news/pre-to-3 -new-baby-pisa-study-to-include-us-5 -year-olds/549810/, or go to the study's site at https://www.oecd.org/education/school/ Early-Learning-Matters-Project-Brochure.pdf.

Self-Esteem versus Self-Compassion

One of the best things that we can do is teach our kids about self-compassion. When I was raising my kids in the 1990s, the self-esteem movement was hot. Apparently, if our kids had more self-esteem, they would be more successful in the world. There were a lot of books and videos instructing us how to compliment our children for anything they did. Self-esteem was the goal, so if they competed on a soccer or baseball team, all the kids got a trophy regardless of the effort they put forth. (That's still common today.) My kids were not competitive, and from the sidelines, I was horrified to watch them spend more time *socializing* on the field than defending the goal. Embarrassing, and not really trophy-worthy!

With more research and observations of the unintended consequences of praising too much, we now know it's not about self-esteem. Falsely praising children for just existing is not the answer. Instead, scientists and psychologists are recommending that we promote self-compassion for our children. Self-compassion means that we encourage our kids to value themselves and to not be too critical of themselves. We don't want our kids to beat themselves up for making a mistake. It's up to us to remind them that everyone makes mistakes and that it's OK. As an empathy fanatic, I define self-compassion as "empathy for oneself." Springing from that, your child can better feel empathy for others, building on a foundation of self-empathy. It might be analogous to the maxim "You can't really love someone else until you love yourself."

Here's one idea to teach your children self-compassion: Ask them to remember how it feels when someone hugs them. Then tell them to give themselves a hug when they feel bad, because it's important to love ourselves and make ourselves feel better, too.[8]

Sharing

I hated sharing my toys. My younger sister destroyed all my board games and dolls. Lucky for me, my parents had some empathy and allowed me to *not* share just a few toys, which I still have to this day. Yes, folks, I still have Ken and Barbie in their original carrying cases. They're worth a lot of money, and they were wonderful things to share with my daughter when she was young, a treasure I hold dear. I am saving them for my grandchildren one day (hint! hint!).

This leads me to recommend creating a "sharing area" in your house. Not every toy should live there, but some toys should. Your child(ren) can cycle stuff in and out, but teach sharing early and the benefits will last a lifetime. Sharing is a core concept of empathy, because it teaches children to think about how another child will feel when he or she gets to play with others' special game or toy.

Summing Up

Letting your kids use their sense of wonder, catching your kids in the act of doing good, and setting up some useful structure to leave time for closeness and quality time are all vital components in teaching your children empathy in those preschool years. Keep in mind that these are just guidelines and suggestions. Good ideas become great ideas when you tailor them to your children or students. And the best ideas are often those you come up with on your own. The one thing to keep in mind is that teaching empathy is a two-way street. Don't do all the talking. Your child has a lot to say, too.

A quotation from Erika Christakis, a preschool teacher, will tie this all up in a bow:

> The real focus in the preschool years should be not just on vocabulary and reading, but on talking and listening. We forget how vital spontaneous, unstructured conversation is to young children's understanding. By talking with adults, and one another, they pick up information. They learn how things work.[9]

nine

teaching empathy
elementary years

If we can let them connect with people they would never meet otherwise,
they're going to learn about people who look, live, and learn differently.
—Kathi Kersznowski, school district technology specialist[1]

kathi Kersznowski is an educator after my own heart. This lover of global education was frustrated when she learned about Empatico, a web platform for linking classrooms across the United States and around the world, because her school district didn't have the webcams necessary to implement it. But she didn't give up. She contacted the organization for help, and it offered $2,000 worth of webcams in return for her school district becoming the first to set up the video chat capability in every class-room and training teachers how to use it.[2]

She took the deal. Now there's a hallway in southern New Jersey's Wedgwood Elementary School with a pushpin for all the places where students have connected by video chat, including towns in Minnesota, Kansas, Hawaii, and Canada. Second graders at nearby Bells Elementary got to talk to second graders at Ibime School in Mexico City. They discovered that the Mexican kids love taquitos and they learned about the Day of the Dead, when Mexicans make *ofrendas*, offerings of food left with pictures of dead ancestors in the hope their spirits will come by for nourishment during the night. But they didn't just learn about their differences. They learned how much they are the same. Bells Elementary students sang the song called "Baby Shark," complete with gestures to mimic the chomping of jaws, and the Mexican kids were soon following right along.[3] "Baby Shark" has gone viral; check it out online and get ready to dance.

In elementary school, kids are wide open to new experiences. They also have the ability to understand empathy in a way that they could not when they were preschoolers. By age six or seven, children are cognitively capable of "walking in somebody else's shoes." They are ready to feel empathy and act on it in the form of sharing, supporting, and helping. With that in mind, this chapter presents strategies to turn your elementary schoolers into superpowered persons with strong empathy muscles.

Let's begin by discussing *mindfulness*, a strategy that will help get your child in the empathy mindset. From there I go on to cover giving your child the kind of structure, wrapped in high expectations for empathy, that will let him or her thrive. I include coaching from some social-emotional skills pros. Then I discuss some more strategies appropriate for this age level, including everything from great books that will tickle your kids' imagination to community service projects that, rather than striking them as the equivalent of eating their veggies, will be enjoyable and rewarding.

Mindfulness

At the Tolerance Center (or in our mobile outreach programs in schools), before we teach empathy, we start with mindfulness. This is the relaxing, calming warm-up that every young mind can use (every stressed-out adult mind needs it even more), as it sets the foundation for enhancing empathy. Mindfulness refers to being in the present moment and includes focused breathing and accepting thoughts and feelings for what they are without being judgmental. This technique is increasing in popularity, and rightly so, because at Kidsbridge we find this activity truly effective for both increased focus and decreased distraction.

The scientific benefits of mindfulness have been demonstrated in many studies. Children who practice mindfulness reduce their stress and become more aware of feelings, tension, and actions. It also is a foundation for social-emotional development, creating increased capacity for kindness, respect, and compassion. Some schools incorporate mindfulness into circle time, and some faith-based organizations do it, too. One mindfulness method is S.T.O.P. As described in the *New York Times* by reporter David Gelles, author of *Mindful Work: How Meditation Is Changing Business from the Inside Out*, the process goes like this.[4]

- Stop. Just take a momentary pause, no matter what you're doing.

- Take a breath. Feel the sensation of your own breathing, which brings you back to the present moment.

- **O**bserve. Acknowledge what is happening, for good or bad, inside you or out. Just note it.

- **P**roceed. Having briefly checked in with the present moment, continue with whatever you were doing.

How well does this work? Here's what one elementary school child told me after having taken part in a Kidsbridge mindfulness activity: "My brother hit me, then I went to my mom and she screamed at me, so I decided to go upstairs to my room. I closed the room, did my deep breathing with a little pillow buddy on my belly. I calmed myself down and when I was done, I went downstairs with a smile on my face." I was so proud to hear that. What a rewarding revelation from that youngster!

In my household, both my husband and I worked full time, were stretched too thin, and struggled to focus on all the things that deserved attention. If only we had known about mindfulness! I recommend the following three books for introducing mindfulness to your family:

Breathe Like a Bear: 30 Mindful Moments for Kids to Feel Calm and Focused Anytime, Anywhere: This book by Kira Willey (illustrated by Anni Betts) provides thirty easy breathing techniques that kids can learn from bears and other wonderfully illustrated animals.

Mindful Games Activity Cards: 55 Fun Ways to Share Mindfulness with Kids and Teens Cards: This is a "deck" of fifty-five mindfulness games by Susan Kaiser Greenland. The book focuses on what the authors call the "new A, B, C's" for learning and a happy life: attention, balance, and compassion.

Mindfulness for Kids: 30 Fun Activities to Stay Calm, Happy, and in Control: Carole P. Roman and J. Robin

Albertson-Wren wrote this kid-friendly guide to help children navigate scenarios that they encounter at home, at school, and with friends.

Family Culture and Structure

Have you ever been in a classroom or at a youth group meeting where kids just don't know how to react to discipline? I've seen and heard about plenty of kids who do their own thing in the classroom, speaking out of turn or getting out of their seats, even bullying schoolmates at recess or in the halls. If they don't understand discipline from and don't respect a teacher, it's not necessarily the teacher's fault. Often students are not learning discipline and kindness from their parents. Such kids tend to lack structure at home, meaning there is no consistent set of expectations.

Structure is a tricky discussion, though. You want to be in the Goldilocks zone: "not too much, not too little, but *juuuust* right." You want to have rules, but the right kinds, and only enough to create structure without stifling your child. As organizational psychologist Adam Grant writes in *Originals*, kids with too many rules tend to make "excellent sheep." They crave their parents' and teachers' approval and have a hard time learning to function in the world because they always look to someone else for answers. Grant writes, "Creativity may be hard to nurture, but it's easy to thwart."[5] I argue that the same thing pertains to social-emotional skills. Successful parents emphasize moral rules instead of specific rules, Grant says.

Don't worry about what everyone else is doing when establishing your own personal caring family culture. When my kids were little, they were always comparing our rules to those in other kids' houses. My husband and I had to explain that the rules in our house were unique and special; other parents were entitled to set their own. Not the answer they wanted to hear (*harrumph*), but neither threatened to run away to the "better" house. (Well, actually one day my daughter did threaten to move to the better house.)

In the culture that you create for your home, you can try to direct your children to be attentive to other children being called a name, bullied, or excluded, thus generating an opportunity for empathy. Compliment them, for example, for including a new kid in their game of tag.

Grant coaches us to explain the impact of a child's behavior and keep it developmentally appropriate. However, when your child lashes out meanly, such as making fun of a kid's clothes or difficulties with math, this is the time to use guilt in a positive way. It's a chance to tell your child that it's never too late to right the wrongs of the past by behaving better in the future (remember the growth mindset). Hopefully the lesson will lead to action.

Telling Them to Say "Sorry" Doesn't Work

Since we are talking about guilt, this is an appropriate time to discuss apologies. Although we were taught apologies were good when we were kids, experts recommend against insisting on an apology as a strategy. Please don't instruct your kids to apologize, because the apology is usually rote and not heartfelt. Is there a parent out there who hasn't seen his or her child perfect the maneuver of saying *sorrrrrry* with either an eye roll or a smirk? What you want, as in the example about guilt in the previous section, is for them to decide on their own to give an apology when the situation calls for it. It is *especially* harmful to ask a child who bullies to apologize to a victim or a target. This is a no-no, causing unrealistic expectations, and it's frightening for the child who is being bullied or ostracized.

Instead, experts recommend helping your child with strategy, such as ways to redirect the conversation or how to get away from the confrontation. It also helps if your child tries to understand why bullies act as they do. Ask your child questions such as "How do you think they're feeling? What can you do different the next time you're being bullied?"[6]

If children insist on apologizing and it's heartfelt, I would let them do it—in person or by writing a sincere note.

Family Meetings

I talked about family meetings in the last chapter, and of course as your kids get older you should continue with these meetings, making them more developmentally sophisticated and changing up the fun factor. As your fun instigator, I recommend that you start this meeting with an icebreaker to get your family smiling and laughing.

Here are a few that work at the Tolerance Center:

- Take turns saying your favorite color, hobby, or food.

- Identify something each person has in common with each family member, as well as something different about one another.

- Have everyone say what his or her favorite family activity is. You might be surprised what you learn! In a similar discussion on a vacation, a friend of mine found out, to his shock, that while at summer camp his daughter had developed a love of fishing, something they'd never done together.

Clearly the object of family meetings will be to see what kind of empathetic culture everyone would like to see in the family. It is easy to discuss the value and benefits of more peaceful cooperation in your home. Following are some questions that can help you dive into your family culture discussions:

- Do you think our home can be more peaceful?
- Do you think there are ways that we can help each other?

- Do you think that we can help each other reduce stress and anxiety?
- Do you feel that you are listened to?
- Do you feel that we use media respectfully or that it is dominating our family culture?

Tip: You might consider scheduling a family meeting once a month, or maybe even once a week. Don't make them too long; we want the family to look forward to them, not be eyeing the clock the whole time. Encourage family members to bring their own agenda items.

Chores, Contracts, and Kindness

While we want to limit the rules, it's valuable to have buy-in for the ones you have. Then they don't feel like rules! Elementary school age is an excellent time to introduce the concept of family behavior contracts. In my family, contracts were initiated with a sit-down, face-to-face, one-on-one discussion of current behaviors and attitudes and what we wanted going forward.

If you start when your kids are in middle or high school . . . well, c'mon, do I even need to finish that sentence? Your chances of success might be just as good as hitting the lottery! I've seen plenty of family contracts or chore charts hanging on the fridge in other people's houses with a bunch of checkmarks on the first week, a couple on the second, and then vast wastelands of untouched real estate thereafter. If you start when your kids are younger, you get more buy-in, and family behavior contracts become a habit. As my kids grew up, I would contract with both to do their chores and be kind to one another. (Wish I had done contracts with my husband!) The whole family would sit down for a meeting. We'd sign the agreement and even date it, revisiting it in a month and then every three months.

Not sure what you want out of a family contract? Here's a sample of expectations you might want to consider:

Do your weekly chores around the house.

- Do your homework every night.
- Get up in the morning in plenty of time to catch the bus.
- Use media in moderation.
- Be kind to your sister or brother.
- Be respectful to your parents/caregivers.
- Make your mother breakfast in bed every week. (You never know, it might sneak through!)

We didn't bat a thousand with our contracts, but just as in baseball, if you get at least a few hits out of every ten times up, you might just be a star! Our kids knew the expectations and grew accustomed to them. Contracts are also handy for the kid who's got the denial routine down cold, as in "I never said I'd do that" or "You never told me to do that." (Yes, we had one of those, and no, it wasn't my husband.) Now you have documented proof in writing, with their names and the dates attached to it. You don't even have to say a word; just point to that piece of paper hanging on the fridge and watch them shuffle away and comply.

Coaching Time

This is a good place to introduce advice from one of the real pros about what else we can talk about—not just in our contracts and family meetings but also in our parenting and teaching in general. To me, one of our national treasures in social-emotional learning is Maurice Elias, director of Rutgers University's Social and Emotional Laboratory. He is a champion of all social-emotional skills and the philosophy of holistic social-emotional learning for all.[7] He and others have launched a national movement known as SEL4US, a volunteer collaboration of many agencies across the country working to ramp up holistic social-emotional learning for kids, parents, and educators in schools.[8] This program is in eighteen states and growing—an indicator of the growing recognition of these skills' importance. I am a proud participant in New Jersey's SEL4NJ group, whose formation Elias spearheaded, and am privileged to have Elias as a resource in my home state of New Jersey (great resources for educators are available at sel4us.org).

For elementary-age kids, he specifically advises these strategies:[9]

- **Understanding your child's emotions can help you both build empathy.** Elias recommends that you truly listen to your children and be fully present. When you genuinely care about your child's thoughts, emotions, and actions, you are strengthening your relationship and modeling what it means to be a good, active listener.

- **Bedtime is a good time to review conversations.** Tucking your kids in is a good peaceful time to digest the day and to share feelings, especially when there have been disagreements during the day. You could say things like "When I put myself in your shoes, I can see why you feel this way," or "I understand where you're coming from."

- **Consider attending a play or getting your child involved in acting.** What better way to get kids to gain perspectives on others than through theater shows or practicing skits at home?

While I'm on the topic of quality time, I have another recommendation. Before your children catch a case of middle school sass and start wanting as little to do with you as possible, take the opportunity to maximize your face-to-face time with puzzles, sports, puppets, arts and crafts, and board games. Ask them what they would like to do. Don't fade completely into the background just because they're mature enough to play independently. Katie Hurley, a psychotherapist and the author of *The Happy Kid Handbook*, recommends, "Teach them to play your favorite card game, bake with them or find another activity you can share. They may say no at first, but keep trying."[10]

More Coaching: What Doesn't Work and What Does

Some experts say that parent training is the most critical piece of the social-emotional skill puzzle. Barbara Gueldner, a school psychologist who worked on a University of Oregon study evaluating anti-bullying criteria, cautions that you need to work on yourself before you can work well with your kids. "A lot of kids don't have their basic needs met and that's inherently stressful. When you don't feel that great, you're not that nice to other people," she says.[11]

Sadly, many parents and guardians and educators hold onto the archaic "man-up" short-term strategy. Parents or guardians with a "man-up" philosophy believe that life is a zero-sum game and that their children just need to suck it up and deal with life's challenges. They also think there's only room for winners in this world, and they don't worry about losers or consider their feelings. This book's philosophy disputes that idea; empathy has benefits for everyone. Children need to treat their classmates as cooperators and colleagues, not as competitors. Cooperation is a long-term, successful strategy for both friendships and careers.

Gueldner believes that teaching kindness is critical to social and emotional learning and espouses a two-pronged approach. The first is teaching emotional literacy to adults. She advises adults, "First, you have to be aware of your own behavior and what you're modeling to your kids. This requires a certain amount of self-reflection—you have to care about what your behavior says about you." Second, parents need to be aware of social situations and talk about them with their kids. She suggests you ask, "What did you see? What would you want someone to do if you were in that situation?"[12] This two-pronged approach can reduce both aggression and bullying and produce happier and more academically successful kids.

Increasing Playtime

When I was a kid, I was allowed to run around outside and play with my friends until the sun went down, even if it was eight o'clock at night. That would *never* happen today with our culture of heightened concern about safety. (I'm not saying that's wrong, although perhaps we've drifted too far to the other extreme.) Everything wasn't structured around kids' dance recitals, travel to soccer games, and specialized summer camps. We were free to come up with our own games, make mud pies, ride bikes, put on a puppet show, participate in arts and crafts—do anything we felt like.

So many parents fall into the trap of thinking they have to keep their children busy all the time, scheduling them in dance classes, sports, or whatever. Moderation is the key. There's a time and place for everything. There's a time for the quality parent-child interaction I've espoused in this chapter in addition to structured activities. Recess and independent play time provide opportunities for children to learn social-emotional skills, including empathy. When children play together without an enforced structure, they learn how to take turns, resolve conflicts, and walk, hop, skip, or run in "the shoes of another child." They also learn how to manage their own emotions and behavior, a fundamental life skill at this age.

Many schools, under the pressures of academics, have cut out recess. But the American Academy of Pediatrics says "recess is a crucial and necessary component of a child's development," and I agree. Sacrificing it for academics and boosting test scores is shortsighted.

Making an Impact on Your Child's Classroom

It's important to be an advocate for your child in school in many ways, not just in regard to academics. You can advocate for recess. And of course, you can advocate for social-emotional skills.

As my kids were growing up, I would visit their classrooms from time to time to volunteer or to present an activity. I learned so much by studying the teacher. Being there was a great opportunity to engage in a friendly chat with my child's teacher and ask about the social-emotional program inventory for the year. Be curious about the programs. How many are there? Are they assembly or small-group discussions? Are they evidence-based (meaning have they been measured to be effective)? With limited resources, social-emotional programs generally need to come with proof they are effective. By the way, assembly programs aren't effective, except as a chance for kids to learn how to pass notes from row to row; that's what I did with my friends.

A research study reveals that not only does improving the emotional quality of classroom interactions positively affect life skills, but it also predicts growth in reading and math achievement.[1] Way to go, empathy!

Note

1. Robert C. Planta et al., "Classroom Effects on Children's Achievement Trajectories in Elementary School," American Educational Research Journal 45, no. 2 (2008), https://doi.org/10.3102/0002831207308230.

The Ups and Downs of Media for the Elementary Schooler

Let's face it. Much of your child's time is going to be consumed with media. Some kids get smartphones in elementary school and some don't. Undoubtedly they'll be in front of the television or on the computer. So, since screens are going to be a major component of their time, let's deal with them head on.

As mentioned in chapter 5 on empathy and media, your children watching violence on TV doesn't mean they are doomed to a life of crime or will become incurable bullies. But research shows that viewing violence can have a significant effect on their developing brains and how they think and act. Young minds can't necessarily differentiate between what is real and what isn't, so they may copy some of the behaviors they see. It can even have a similar effect to what is seen in post-traumatic stress disorder, leaving the child feeling as if he or she has been emotionally abused if the content is sadistic enough. One well-known expert and author, Gail Gross, says the result can be children who have less empathy, use aggressive strategies to solve problems instead of dealing with conflict peaceably, and deal with frustration through kneejerk reactions instead of thoughtful ones. These are characteristics seen in bullies.[13]

It is comforting to know, however, that experts can coach us as parents and teachers how to use that very same type of violent imaging in a positive way. In one study, the researchers divided a group of boys into two groups. The first group was asked to consider the feelings of a victim *before* viewing a violent cartoon, while the second was not. The study found that the children in the first group liked the perpetrator in the cartoon less and thought he was mean, in contrast to the second group. The second group's empathy measurement was significantly lower than the first group's.[14] Therefore, it makes sense to monitor what your child is watching and, if you spot a violent show on the TV, to either change the channel or talk about it in a way that strengthens the empathy muscle. Pause the program at an opportune moment and ask questions like the following:

- What did you think about this?
- Did anything scare or upset you?
- Would you like to change the ending?
- Were you upset that one character was being mean to another?
- In this show, are these people actors? Are they paid to act mean? Why?

This book discusses developing empathy in your home and school, but as adults worried about the name-calling, division, and general lack of empathy today, it is imperative that we teach our children to care for others whom they might not know.

Here's a quick, fun activity to do with the whole family in twenty minutes. Draw concentric circles as shown below, only copying the capitalized words (the words in italics are to get your thinking caps going). Discuss who they care about THE MOST, A LOT, SOMEWHAT, and NOT SO MUCH, and then write the names in the appropriate circle. Have each family member share and discuss.

Who Do YOU Care About?

NOT TOO MUCH

SOMEWHAT

A LOT

my soccer team

close friends

school nurse

my family

THE MOST

best friends   my dog

strangers

my teacher

bus driver

endangered animals

snakes

I did this activity with my young son and daughter, and it generated some good discussions. Following are some additional discussion prompts for this activity:

- What about the girl who's new in school and sits alone in the classroom? Do you care?

action

tips

- What about poor children in other countries?

- What about cats and dogs that have no home?

Awesome Books

Now that I've covered developing a culture of empathy in the home and the classroom, as well as how to deal with topics such as screens, I want to explore some awesome books that are effective in giving you the Empathy Advantage.

I was walking in the children's section of a well-known bookstore, strolling and scanning for children's books with faces that were of color, not just White. Sadly, there was only one. I told the manager what I was looking for, and she struggled to find another. How sad it was to realize that the bookstore didn't have enough empathy for parents of color to think that perhaps Black or brown kids would feel left out with books only having White kids' faces on them.

It can be exciting to explore diversity with your child at this age by reading books about different types of children. Seek books about skin colors and ethnicities unlike your own. Let your children walk in the shoes of a refugee, an African American, an Asian child, or a child from Appalachia. You will learn together to appreciate the tapestry of diverse backgrounds, heritages, and ethnic cultures. How rich our multicultural variations are! Let's strive to appreciate others' worth.

By taking this Diversity Challenge, you will teach your children not to be afraid of "the other." In that vein, I want to share with you one of my favorite stories. Hidden at the back of Dr. Seuss's *The Sneetches and Other Stories* is a short story called "What Was I Scared Of?" The main protagonist is walking along and is frightened by a pair of "pale green pants." Everywhere the character goes, the pants appear and scare the "pants off of him"! The character regularly runs away, but near the end of the story he finds the pants crying:

> I never heard such whimpering
> and I began to see
> that I was just as strange to them
> as they were strange to me!

Can you guess the ending?

As kids get busier and academic pressure ramps up, reading for fun is diminished for many children. In 2019, Scholastic's *Kids and Family Reading Report* found an alarming decline of nearly 40 percent in children who read frequently between ages eight and nine, even though a majority of kids in general agreed they ought to read more books for fun.[15] That suggests there's a lot of room for improvement. "The high-stakes tests and academic pressure aren't likely to disappear any time soon, so it's up to parents and teachers to convey to kids that reading isn't a chore," writes the *Washington Post's* Mari-Jane Williams. "We need to teach them that it can be a fun way to explore different places and life experiences, or that it's a simple escape from everyday life."[16] With that said, the following sections discuss some of my favorite books that children should find fun to read, while learning a little empathy along the way.

The Zach Rules Series

One of my favorite book series for empathy and emotional skills is by William Mulcahy, a licensed professional counselor and psychotherapist. The titles are *Zach Apologizes*, *Zach Gets Frustrated*, *Zach Hangs in There*, *Zach Makes Mistakes*, and *Zach Stands Up*. In *Zach Apologizes*, Zach does something mean, and his mother asks him to write or draw what happened. The exercise helps Zach to process self-respect and negative feelings, engendering empathy. I strongly recommend this series and especially the author's notes in the back of the books, including his inventive concept of the "four-square apology." It includes (1) what I did to hurt somebody, (2) how the person felt, (3) what I can do next time, and (4) how I'll make it up to the person. Very clever, and no apologizing! Life is so much more complicated than saying, without meaning it, "I'm sorry."

Sam and the Firefly

This book, by P. D. Easton, is one of my childhood favorites. Sam is an owl being bugged by an obnoxious, show-off firefly named Gus, and that firefly is a real troublemaker. I won't give away the ending, but Sam, feeling empathy for Gus, knows that Gus will rue all his antics.

Eggbert—The Slightly Cracked Egg

This book by Tom Ross is another empathy favorite. I was fortunate enough to meet Tom in New York City when we were both attending Columbia University. I had no idea that he had children's stories on his mind as we both negotiated graduate school.

Eggbert is an egg who loves to paint pictures, not realizing that he is slightly cracked. He is ostracized by the other eggs for this disability and excluded by the vegetables in the refrigerator. He leaves the refrigerator, unwillingly, to discover and travel the world outside. Again, I will not reveal the ending, but Ross tackles diversity, disability, and empathy in this beautifully illustrated children's book.

Ruby Bridges (for Fifth and Sixth Grades)

I must mention the real story about the first African American child to desegregate an all-White school in 1960. Talk about an empathy opportunity! There are many good books about this topic. What was it like, day after day, with adults yelling and throwing tomatoes, trying to scare Ruby as she walked to and from school? She was about seven years old, with the National Guard by her side to protect her.

Share with your kids the fact that the White parents would not send their children to school, so the teacher taught Ruby alone, one on one. And talk about how that teacher might be feeling. The teacher, Barbara Henry, was White and very loyal to Ruby; what daring! She tried to make Ruby's school experience as normal as possible even though Ruby was the only student in the classroom for the entire year. What courage she had to stay the course! Show your children a photo of the real Ruby Bridges and ask the following questions:

- How must she be feeling?

- How does this make you feel?

- Why are the adults so angry?

- Would she be anxious or scared about the ride home?

- Why was it important for her to do this day after day?

- What is segregation? Are schools segregated now? Why not?

My Name Is Yoon (for First and Second Grades)

Yoon is encouraged to Americanize her name and chooses a new one from the Name Jar, but in the end she realizes she likes her own name best.

Who's in a Family?

This book by Robert Skutch presents no preconceptions about what makes a family a family, which makes it a great gateway for kids to understand families different than their own. It even has animal families!

The Family Book

This book by Todd Parr also celebrates all kinds of families, including adopted families, stepfamilies, one-parent families, and families with two parents of the same sex, as well as the traditional nuclear family. It has bright, catchy illustrations.

It's Okay to Be Different

This is another book from Parr that reassures kids that it's OK to be different and that diversity is something to celebrate. It addresses kids of every shape, size, color, family makeup, and background. The author uses wit and beautifully drawn, brightly colored, childlike figures.

Oliver Button Is a Sissy

In this book by Tomie dePaola, a boy is teased and ostracized because he'd rather read books, paint pictures, and tap dance than participate in sports. This gives your child a sense of why teasing someone for being different really makes no sense when you think about it. In fact, being different is what makes us special!

Toys and Strategy

Whenever I travel out of town, I check out the local museums. My daughter calls me a museum nerd. One of the museums I checked out recently was the Baltimore Museum of Art. As I walked from room to room enjoying paintings, sculpture, furniture, and random videos, I came across work by an artist I had never heard of before, Ebony G. Patterson. What caught my eye in a corner of the gallery was about seventy-five guns all bejeweled with faux crystals and gemstones. Puzzled, I read the artist's statement on the label: "Toys condition children for adult rules, uneven power relationships, and violent futures." That blew me away: I had never thought about this before.

Of course, as parents, we know that toy rifles send a message to our children, although that message varies depending on your views on guns, as some might consider them helpful in teaching responsible gun ownership, while to others they connote violence. As we become more thoughtful and strategic about what affects children, it helps to be cognizant and sensitive about our purchase of toys and the messages they send to our children. As an empathetic parent, think carefully of what you are implicitly communicating and choose toys carefully. If your child receives as a gift a toy that you deem inappropriate, explain why you do not think that the toy communicates the right morals and values. Discard it discreetly or donate it to a charity.

Intergenerational Interaction

If you are lucky enough to live near your parents, by all means arrange for your children to visit their grandparents regularly. Think of what it will mean for your grandparents and your kids if they're not doing this already! Depending on your parents, it might be awkward for you to give them a short and sweet verbal instruction manual. But if you drop off the kids, try to prevent the grandparents from falling into the trap of letting the kids play with their smartphones or watch TV. Explain the importance of empathy and face-to-face time, suggesting walks, museums, trips to the zoo, walks in the park, arts and crafts, baking, board games, or anything else that gets your parents to look into the eyes of your beautiful child(ren).

If the grandparents aren't nearby, think of all the lonely seniors in your area who would love to see a young child. Consider ways to explore taking your children to a senior home (one that you have inspected beforehand to make sure it's suitable for a child to see). People volunteer to take dogs into senior homes. Perhaps you will be clever enough to have your son or daughter visit with an elderly and lonely person, with or without pet in hand. Can your youth group or school class visit with seniors? They light up—it's such a gift.

I recently overheard a gray-haired senior at a local community service event say, "I love volunteering next to a seven-year-old—together we can make the world a better place." Boy, did that warm my heart! There are millions of grandparents lonely and isolated around the country. Their love is a huge asset that is squandered.

Other Fun Empathy Activities

At Kidsbridge, practice . . . practice . . . practice has resulted in time-tested activities for generating empathy among elementary-age children (and others). Following are a couple of favorites that we use at the Tolerance Center.

Telling Our Stories

This activity asks children to talk about a time when they wish someone had shown empathy toward them. The script goes something like this:

1. Close your eyes.

2. Try to remember if there has ever been a time that you may have been called a name, bullied, or excluded.

3. If you can't think of a time when it happened to you, try to remember a time when you saw this happen to a friend.

4. Write or draw about what happened or how it made you feel.

5. Would you like to share your stories? (This is optional, of course.)

Of course, kids being kids, you can't count on them to have something to say all the time. If you feel like you're in the Grand Canyon and your request for a story is just echoing into a never-ending void, I recommend sharing *your* story. For example, you could say, "When I was your age, I was not invited to my friend's birthday party. I felt awful and cried. I went to my father and he said . . ."

The main goal of this activity is to let kids know they are not alone. Millions of kids are bullied or left out of activities every day. It's not so much that misery loves company, but it's great for your child to learn that there is nothing wrong with him or her. The power of realizing you're not alone is indeed strong. A note from one of our ten-year-old students, Jennifer, tells it best. "I didn't realize that I wasn't the only one being bullied," she wrote. "When I learned at Kidsbridge that thousands of kids were called names every day, I thought it was awful, but after that, I didn't feel so alone."

Another major goal is to learn about prejudice, bias, discrimination, and the emotions associated with them. When learning about others' experiences, kids discover how other children have felt, struggled, and dealt with incidents involving name calling and exclusion. And it's actually a good thing when parents have to share their stories. I can still remember my kids' sense of shock when they found out that I had actually been called names and teased as a child, too.

Some kids just don't like to talk about their feelings. But don't consider that a stop sign, just a detour. Parent like a pro by having children draw and write down their experiences. This type of activity reflects a form of emotional intelligence that can serve as art therapy. It's a powerful means of communicating feelings and experiences. Research has shown that art therapy is an opportunity to learn and, for example, can be a sophisticated way to draw out experiences of being bullied.[17]

Persons First

Persons First is our "special needs and disabilities" activity at Kidsbridge. It teaches us to think of other people as individuals, not labels. Juan is a little boy with an intellectual disability. Satjeet is a little girl with a physical disability. They are not "disabled children." Juan and Satjeet are Persons First.

This activity is best conducted in small groups. The fun is kicked off with a huge basket full of puppets, all of whom have disabilities. Some puppets have a mental challenge, some cannot see, and some have other physical hindrances.

The puppet with leg braces is our featured teacher. She is a beautiful puppet named Esther who is wearing a cute outfit, but kids' eyes always gravitate to her leg braces.

When we ask the kids what Esther wants them to recognize, most need to be encouraged to look at her other attributes. Esther wants them to notice her assets—her hair in two braids, her beautiful eyes, her being a member of the glee club—and she especially wants them to adore her really cool, colorful outfit. (You will recognize that we are asking our visitors to "walk in the shoes" of Esther.)

Next, we introduce other puppets with mental or physical disabilities. The kids are assigned a photo and a description for the new puppet with a disability. They might learn about Juan and what his strengths and weaknesses are. Or they might get to know Satjeet and her challenges. Again, they walk in the shoes of these diverse puppets. Led by the facilitator, the group members rejoin the circle to discuss which puppet they were assigned to and what they learned about their assigned puppet child.

The bottom line is to inspire empathy. Through collecting data, we've learned that it works. We've also got some cool quotes from the kids to prove it:

Thank you so much for teaching us about kids with challenges. You taught us that people who are blind or have a disability aren't scary, just different. You showed us that we shouldn't be afraid of people who are different than us and that it's ok to ask questions or to be curious about someone.
—Jaquan

Thank you so much for the cool puppet theater! It was fun to solve problems using crazy puppets and humor. I also learned how saying little things that are mean could still hurt the same as the big things that are mean. Just by having fun we could still learn about how not including or being prejudice can hurt a lot. Thank you for teaching us about diversity.
—Sophie

Thank you for the puppet activity. It was my favorite one because I love art. My puppet was being bullied by a smiling clown. Bullying is wrong, so a fashion model puppet came to my rescue. Once again, thank you for the amazing lesson and for teaching my class about bullying.
—Michael

The late Paul Winkler, who was the longtime director of the New Jersey Commission on Holocaust Education, introduced me to one of my favorite activities to generate empathy. He called it Shoebox. It puts students in the shoes of a child suffering in the Holocaust or any other genocide, including present-day Syria or Yemen. You give your child a shoebox and ask him or her to pretend you are leaving home tomorrow and can only pack a small shoebox full of belongings. What would they select? Toys? Photos? Candy? Food?

Don't force it. Wait until they get older if it makes them too upset. But when it works, they learn empathy and another key social-emotional skill, gratitude, as they learn to appreciate and prize family, shelter, security, and love.

Have you ever felt a rush of emotion and joy singing in a choir? Dancing in a troupe? Acting in a play?

Have you ever seen the wave of happiness in your kids or students and how proud they feel of themselves when they participate in such activities?

When we do things together in coordination, whether it's synchronized swimming, rowing, playing music, singing, or dancing, it can be a synchronized activity, or "synchrony." Tal-Chen Rabinowitz, a researcher from the Institute for Learning &

Brain Sciences at the University of Washington, says, "Synchrony is like a glue that brings people together—it's a magical connector for people." In studying synchrony, she says, "The findings might be applied to formulate new strategies for education in our effort to build a more collaborative and empathic future society."[1]

Note

1. Quoted in Molly McElroy, "Game Played in Sync Increases Children's Perceived Similarity, Closeness," University of Washington news release, April 8, 2015, https://www.washington.edu/news/2015/04/08/game-played-in-sync-increases-childrens-perceived-similarity-closeness/.

Strengths and Weaknesses Activity

At the center we have discussions in small groups about strengths and weaknesses. Because even the smallest gift can make the largest impression on a child, we make sure *after* our Kidsbridge program that every child leaves with a Kidsbridge strengths bracelet, on which each child has recognized and printed his or her strength. Sometimes staff share their weaknesses with students in small groups, and I encourage educators to consider this as well.

We can't all be good at everything; it is important to communicate this to your children. Although the fact that Mommy and Daddy aren't perfect might not sink in at this age, I highly recommend that you share your personal strengths and weaknesses, and that your spouse or significant other do so as well. Parents being on a pedestal is unhealthy for any parent-child relationship.

Community Service Doesn't Work Unless . . .

Some families go to a soup kitchen and serve food to the needy on Thanksgiving every year. That's great, but it's not for everyone. Some children have different ideas on how they can make a difference that connect for them. This is a great time to listen to them, because community service without emotion is empty and pointless.

In fifth grade, my daughter became involved with a group of kids who organized a coat drive for a nearby urban town with disadvantaged families. I was so delighted that she wanted to participate. Her skill set was art, so she created a poster illustrated with sweaters and coats being donated, topped with a drawing of a rocket, filled with coats, zooming to the poor. Yes, that's right, it zoomed. She drew a rocket, not a car. At the bottom of the poster she printed, "Help the poor for the winter." I was so proud of her using her artistic talent to get more kids and parents to donate coats and winter clothing.

Discuss the needy in your community, and not only at holiday time. Give your kids an amount of money you're comfortable donating, and have them research some charities online with you. Then discuss which charities to choose and how to divide the money among their choices. Learning how to select, prioritize, and make decisions to help others is a lifelong asset. And the empathy muscle they'll develop, whether it be toward those who get only one meal a day, are homeless, or cope with disabilities, is priceless. A thoughtful, real discussion makes community service come alive and is effective in developing empathy. (Continue or initiate this in middle or high school.)

In the end, when it comes to empathy, it's all about meaningful communication. It's all about talking, listening, and just being there. Whether you're teaching mindfulness, sharing a book, holding family meetings, or figuring out where to make donations, the better your communication is, the more empathetic your child will be. And the bond of love, caring, and respect that you and your child share will be stronger, hopefully for a lifetime.

ten

teaching empathy
middle school years

The Golden Rule is not an option—it's the key to our common survival.
—Karen Armstrong, author

maybe all we need to bring more empathy and caring to our world is a little *hygge*.

A little *whaaat*?

Before I give you the answer to that cliffhanger, let me tell you about one of the world's greatest social-emotional success stories.

Denmark is the undisputed heavyweight champion of the happiness world, at least in the eyes of the Organisation for Economic Co-operation and Development (OECD). Since the 1970s, this tiny little European nation has been at the top, or close to it, in the organization's "Better Life Index," more commonly known as the happiness index.[1]

How did this happen? Jessica Joelle Alexander and Iben Dissing Sandahl, an American writer and her Danish psychotherapist husband, claim to know the secret sauce. In their best-selling book *The Danish Way of Parenting*, they say it all comes down to one word: upbringing. Danes are happy because of how they were brought up by their parents. America may have "pursuit of happiness" built into the Declaration of Independence, but with our country's focus on grades, testing, Ivy League schools, and competition, we barely crack the OECD's top twenty in the index. It's all about how children are brought up, including their *hygge*. I'll let the authors explain the concept, which I think is awesomely helpful and age-appropriate for middle schoolers:

> *Hygge* is the uniquely Danish word for a special kind of togetherness. Image that hygge is a space that your family can enter into. This special space will be *hyggeligere* (cozy) if everyone understands and makes an effort to follow the hygge rules. The hygge oath is something to discuss and think about in advance so that all participants who enter into the hygge space for a family dinner, a weekend barbecue, or a simple everyday family gathering will understand the "ground rules." When everyone knows that it's hygge, they can each make an effort to foster closeness for the sake of the whole family.[2]

Alexander and Sandahl describe spending Sunday dinner in *hygge*. Phones and iPads are turned off. Drama is left at the door. Family members focus on making sure they actually taste their food and drink instead of scarfing it down to get on with their evening. Controversial topics like politics are avoided. And they tell funny and uplifting stories about one another, play games, and emphasize gratitude.[3]

What an amazing concept. Just being together and fostering closeness is infused into their lives. Playing is emphasized. Telling kids that getting their homework done is the be-all and end-all is forbidden. That's just part of the Danish recipe, of course. But what a beautiful approach to life. And I'm pretty sure there's no law that says you have to be Danish to have some *hygge* in your own family.

Imagine that *hygge* is an empathy portal that your family can enter. If everyone participates and makes an effort, this new special space truly can be *hyggeligere*.

I'm not naïve enough to think America is going to import this custom and that we'll suddenly rocket up the OECD's charts. But we live in difficult times, and I wanted to send a message at the start of my discussion of this challenging age of transition for children that face-to-face time, *hygge* or not, is critical at this point. Middle school is rough enough without adding in society's external challenges. Kids have those hormones flying. They're drifting into more adult situations. They think they always have to prove they're cool, because they're not mature enough to know that trying super hard to be cool *is not cool!*

In the case of my family, while it wasn't *hygge*, face-to-face time did something special for us in a specific situation. It was uplifting during a difficult period for our country, and I couldn't have been prouder of how it led to my then middle school-age son rising to the occasion.

Our time was in 2005 when Hurricane Katrina devastated New Orleans. As it turned out, we had a wedding to attend in nearby Lafayette, Louisiana, about six months later. Out of the blue, my son came up with an idea during a family discussion: Could we take a tour of the poor areas impacted by the hurricane, specifically the Ninth Ward, which was ground zero for the flooding? Jake, who was in a video production course, wanted to borrow a camera from his school and film the damage and destruction. Astonished, we said yes, and a month later we were touring the Ninth Ward with my son's camera and his nose pressed against the van window. A month after that, his film premiered on the middle school's video channel. We were so proud that he wanted to share this poignant and sad story with his schoolmates and teachers.

Parents need to seize the middle school years and grow their children's empathy. New research from the University of Kansas shows that students transitioning to middle school show declines in empathy, as evidenced by being on the giving or receiving end of bullying behavior. Prevention is critical, because as bullying rises, learning outcomes fall.[4]

What actually is going on these days? I quote here from an *Education Week* article citing recent statistics from school principals, reported by University of California at Los Angeles researchers:

- Nine in ten said incivility and contentiousness in the broader political environment had affected their school communities. The overwhelming majority reported contentious classroom environments, hostile exchanges outside class, and demeaning remarks about people's political viewpoints.

- Eight in ten report[ed] students had made derogatory remarks about people's race or ethnic group.

- Six in ten said students had made derogatory remarks about immigrants.

- Eight in ten said they had disciplined students for "uncivil behavior" toward other students in the past year.[5]

In the face of such disheartening statistics, can empathy make the future better? Yes, it can.

Teaching via Books, Videos, and Internet Sites

To help our middle schoolers during these years, let's first learn a little more in depth about empathy. I want to give some brief detail about different types. Reading can be an indispensable tool for tackling social empathy at the middle school level. I discuss three categories here. Category one is what this book has largely focused on up to this point: social empathy, getting children to understand how others are feeling during school, play, and other situations. I introduced historical empathy in chapter 6 and will revisit it. But I'm going to introduce you to two others: multicultural empathy, plus a mystery "bonus" category.

Category One: Social Empathy

To me, the best book for teaching social empathy to middle school children is *Wonder* by R. J. Palacio. I made my whole family read it, even my husband. Not one of us could get through the book without the tear ducts turning on.

Wonder is about a young boy with a facial disfigurement that makes other kids cringe. The boy, Auggie, endures constant name-calling and bullying and is constantly excluded from activities by the other kids because of his deformity. Palacio deftly advances the story by "walking in the shoes" of not only Auggie but also other characters in the book. Hers is powerful storytelling. I recommend that you follow my family's lead and have all members of your family read and discuss it. If you want to take the shortcut and watch the movie, I won't tell. But the movie runs a distant second. Don't cheat yourself. Go for the book.

Category Two: Historical Empathy

Historical empathy is another great part of the mix. Just let your imagination do the talking; relying on a historical figure such as Abraham Lincoln, Jackie Robinson, or Susan B. Anthony allows us to teach with a twist. It involves asking your child to go back in time to revisit a real person or even a fictional character who encountered challenges (I touched on this subject without delving into the mechanics of it in the elementary school section). Travel back in time with your middle schooler to dig into lessons on empathy.

Speaking of Abe Lincoln, I read in Doris Kearns Goodwin's book *Leadership: In Turbulent Times* that as a boy, Lincoln admonished his friends for torturing turtles. Wow, that is impressive. Goodwin dwells on empathy throughout the book as a foundation for future leadership skills for presidents.

Thomas Hoerr, author of *The Formative Five: Fostering Grit, Empathy, and Success Skills Every Student Needs*, has some of the best suggestions for middle schoolers to develop historical empathy. Hoerr recommends, "Consciously teach about stereotypes and discrimination, the history and evolution of attitudes, and the reasons why people's degree of empathy vary. From the Crusades and Westward Expansion to the subjugation of blacks, Jews, and women, there is no lack of fodder. Ask 'What caused some groups or individuals to be so insensitive to the needs of others?'"[6]

Hoerr also recommends that students examine historical examples of innocent people who were wrongly accused. He suggests, "Study the trial of Galileo, the Salem Witch Trials, or the Dreyfus Affair [which involved injustice and antisemitism in turn-of-the-twentieth-century France]. The goal is to help students see the perspectives not only of the wrongly accused but also of the other characters involved. It may be easy to feel empathy for the protagonist, so it is important for students to see the interplay of perspectives so they can speculate on which other character(s) might warrant their sympathy or empathy."[7] Finally, he recommends that students reflect on a time when they were wrongly accused. Have them examine how they felt, and how it connects to those historical incidents.[8] It's a brilliant strategy. (I highly recommend his book for both parents and educators.)

One of my favorite books for teaching historical empathy is *Refugee* by Alan Gratz, which made it to the *New York Times* bestseller list. It talks about three youths with a common mission—to escape—but for entirely different reasons, in challenging historical situations. One is a Jewish boy in 1930s Germany with the threat of concentration camps looming. Isabel is a Cuban girl in 1994 hoping to escape the riots and unrest of her country and find a new life in America. Mahmoud is a Syrian boy whose country has been torn apart by civil war and seeks to make his way with his family to Europe.[9]

It's up to you to decide whether your middle schooler is ready for some heavier material and can be taught through accounts that he or she reads in the news. But you don't have to dwell on big political clashes, violence, or the like. You can keep it lighter if you want.

Now I add two new categories of educational empathy to your toolkit.

Category Three: Multicultural Empathy

This is a big one in today's society. We're taught growing up that America is a "melting pot," but kids today don't always see a lot of melting going on. Immigrants are viewed with suspicion because they look different or speak a different language. American Muslims think of themselves as just, well, American, but others view them with suspicion. Muslim youths at the Tolerance Center often share that they have been called terrorists.

I saw someone rip a hijab off my friend's head and run away.
She started crying and I didn't know what to do.
—Yolanda, age twelve

Use contemporary cultures to help your child understand that cultural beliefs vary. Challenge stereotypes and bias. Remember your diversity challenge from chapter 9, and step up your game to represent heritages, traditions, and cultures that are different from your own.

There are innumerable ways to help children learn about multicultural empathy. One of the best ways to literally "get the flavor" is to use something as simple as food to explore differences. "Food taboos and delicacies often arise from cultural and religious beliefs; one person's meat is another's poison," says an article in *National Geographic*. "The humble hamburger, a mainstay of U.S. cuisine, is a forbidden food for Hindus. Pork is off the menu for many Jews and Muslims. More than 1,400 species of protein-packed insects are part of African, Asian, Australian and Latin American cuisine, but one would be hard pressed to find these creepy crawlies at a U.S. restaurant (at least intentionally)."[10] My husband and I once bought a box of freeze-dried insects; there were no takers, but it led to some interesting family discussions about alternative protein sources in other countries.

Many kids are ruthlessly teased about the lunches they bring to school. So teachers, you could bring foods into your classrooms that are indicative of the various cultures represented among your kids. Parents, you could have a diversity appreciation party along the same lines at which each guest brings in food from his or her cultural background. It's easy and fun to immerse youth in other cultures, and there is a host of books out there if you're looking for some exotic, savory ideas.

I've seen multicultural empathy have a terrific impact at Kidsbridge. Students who visit say it best: "I knew things happened in the world, but this woke me up," said Sam, a seventh grader. "Hearing real kids talk about this and not just reading about it really opened my eyes to a whole new world. I was extremely moved by every activity. Decisions will be much easier for me now."

There is a plethora of wonderful middle school books in this category; search online using the keywords "multicultural middle school books."

Bonus Category: Creating Empathy for Our Planet

With my own special brand of youth empathy, I have added a new category for something that needs all of our help and respect urgently: our planet. We need to understand and have feeling for the miracle that provides us with the air we breathe, the food we eat, and the gorgeous flowers and fauna that the next generation will inherit.

With a booster shot of empathy, surely our children can do a better job of providing cleaner water and purer air to help both

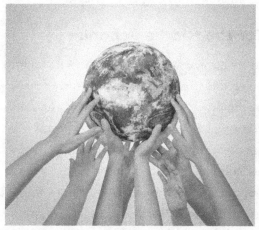

themselves and Earth's creatures on land and sea. The ocean is rising along our coasts and throughout the world, slowly destroying island cultures in parts of the South Pacific. As I write this, fires are raging in Australia, and

Photo 176591496 © Rangizzz | Dreamstime.com

Venice is suffering floods that are supposed to occur once every hundred years but are happening for the second time in a month. Our eyes can glaze over about the tragedy for cultures that exist outside our community, but it's not so easy when we read headlines like this about our own nation: "Alaskan village threatened by rising sea levels votes for costly relocation."[11]

In this article, the *Guardian* reported that the residents of an Alaskan island just north of the Bering Strait called Shishmaref, in a real-life case of "voting themselves off the island," decided to move their village to the mainland after decades of rising sea levels tied to climate change. But they weren't sure they had the funds to do it, meaning they might be trapped. Federal government officials state that there are thirty-one Alaskan islands faced with imminent threats from flooding and coastal erosion.[12]

One book I highly recommend for reading and discussion is *Rising: Dispatches from the New American Shore* (2018). Elizabeth Rush's book will get you and your middle schooler feeling empathy for Americans and wildlife all across our country as she describes in a nonshaming way the effects of climate change in places from the Gulf Coast to Miami, from New York City to the Bay Area.

Media Literacy for the Middle Schooler

In a world of divisiveness and with the term *fake news* making its way into everyday language, understanding the power and principles of media literacy is more important than ever in its own right. But as discussed in chapter 5 on empathy and media, there are many ways that media literacy is important in the realm of empathy.

As a reminder, media literacy is the ability to access, analyze, evaluate, and create *media* in a variety of forms. You know the old adage from the real estate business, "location, location, location"? My adage for parents of middle schoolers regarding media would be "literacy, literacy, literacy." By the time kids hit grades six to eight, they are ready to stop accepting what they see at face value. They are ready to analyze what's in the mind of someone who writes an article or creates an advertisement, as well as how different people might react who are polar opposites.

For example, in 2017 the company that makes Dove soap posted an ad (a three-second GIF) showing a Black woman taking off her brown shirt to become a White woman wearing a white shirt. A great classroom or at-home activity would be to be ask why an African American might find this soap ad offensive. Unilever (the maker of Dove) put out an apology, admitting the company "missed the mark."[13] See if your child or student can figure out why many took the advertisement to suggest that the color black signifies dirty and white represents clean. Analyzing media content is a great avenue for both perspective taking and building a moral identity.[14]

I also have a personal example when it comes to media literacy. You can just imagine what kind of teachable moments the TV show *South Park* could provide. In middle school, my son liked to watch the show. I found it distressing. It was not developmentally appropriate for middle schoolers, and I wasn't sure how to address the problem. It seemed to me that the show was teaching my eighth grader how to make fun of everyone and everything. I turned it off; he turned it back on. Sometimes I sat down with him to try to explain that the show was not good for him, but all in all, I felt I was losing the battle.

It wasn't until he was older and more mature that he again found empathy for others. Here's what I didn't do, but should have:

1. Disconnect the TVs in the house. (OK, this really wasn't an option for us. Actually, there aren't too many families for whom it is.)

2. Put the children in the car and drive them to a park or to an activity. As a working parent, I wasn't there as much as I would have liked. I wish I had a found a way to do this more.

3. Watch the show with your child and discuss what he or she observed from the program and learned. Discuss how unkind it is to make fun of others. Remind your child how it feels when others make fun of him or her.

4. Limit the amount of *South Park*–type shows your kids can watch and balance them with other, healthier programs. In other words, create a media calendar with a better menu of programs.

To pull off item 4, it's best to use a family media assessment log (see figure 10.1). The log I've developed lists on what device the kids watched a show; with whom they watched it; how long they watched; whether it involved violence, meanness, sex, or profanity; and what the parental rating was.

FAMILY MEDIA ASSESSMENT LOG

CHILD:	TV/PHONE/ DVD/INTERNET:	PROGRAM NAME:	ALONE = A FRIENDS = F SIBLINGS = S PARENTS = P	DAY WEEK:	LENGTH IN HOURS:	VIOLENCE = V MEANNESS = M SEX = S PROFANITY = P	PARENTAL RATING:
Jake	DVD	Planet Earth	P	M	1 hr		G
Tanisha	phone	Mean Girls	S	S	1.5 hrs	S + P	NI

PARENT RATING KEY: Great = G / Okay = OK / Needs Improvement = NI

Visit healthychildren.org to create a healthy family media plan.
Visite healthychildren.org para crear un plan familiar de medios saludable.

Figure 10.1

While having the TV or smartphones taken away for an indefinite period could lead a person to spontaneously combust in today's world (kids today can't even imagine a world without internet, or even, heavens to Betsy, a world with only dial-up access!), that doesn't mean we should abandon the idea entirely. How about putting them away for one evening? For one weekend? Or even longer? During family meals, for sure.

In one study, preteens went to a sleepaway camp, where the counselors took away their phones for five days. The kids were measured to be better at reading nonverbal emotional cues than the control group of kids.[15] Wow, and that's after only five days!

"Children on average spend more than 7.5 hours a day watching television, using computers, downloading music, and instant messaging," writes Dr. Kenneth R. Ginsburg in *Building Resilience in Children and Teens*. "For most of the time, each child is unconnected to other people."[16]

That last sentence is a gut punch. Your child can be in a crowded room but making no connection with anyone. That's not a picture any parents want for their children. That's why we need to be even more strategic about media than ever.

I would be remiss if I didn't suggest that you can inculcate more empathy by delaying cell phone and social media privileges until after middle school. What is the rush, especially when the payoff is a child who is more present and empathetic? (OK, I can virtually hear you saying, "But all of their friends have them!")

Maybe this will inspire you: Bill and Melinda Gates, who are among the most tech-savvy couples in the world, did not give their kids cell phones until they were high school age. You might want to discuss this topic in a family meeting. Explain the benefits of waiting. You never know; perhaps there's room for a negotiated settlement.

Media Detectives Activity in the Tolerance Center

I have talked about policing what our kids watch. But here's a fun way to use TV to inject empathy into their systems. Turn the kids into media detectives!

When my kids were middle schoolers, something that got me really angry was watching *America's Funniest Home Videos*. I watched kids get injured and pets get hurt, but what really upset me was the program's showing senior citizens falling down, with a laugh track and vibrant, silly music in the background. It's one thing to have an inconsequential slip and fall after which the person ends up laughing at himself or herself. Then you're laughing *with* the person. It's entirely different when there is actual injury, and humor is only in the eye of the viewer, not the viewed. Then you're laughing *at* the person. I resolved to create an activity to teach children awareness and empathy, also known as media literacy, and piloted it at the Kidsbridge Tolerance Center.

To start the activity, we showed a video clip of senior citizens falling down and getting hurt. First we watched it with the sound on, and then we watched it with the sound off. We asked the middle schoolers these questions:

- What did you observe?
- What did you hear?
- What was the difference between the first and the second clip?
- Did the music and laughter make you feel differently about the video?
- Is it funny when senior citizens fall down?

Then we asked them:

- Are the elderly people in the video really hurt?
- How can we tell?
- Do they need to go to the hospital afterward?
- If this happened to your grandparents, would this be funny?
- What would you do if your grandparent got hurt?

To create empathy and teach kids to more critically analyze media—or, in other words, to have them graduate to the media detective level—we do the following with this activity:

- Coach them to be aware of canned laughter.
- Analyze why media producers use laughter and music.
- Raise awareness of the meanness in media.
- Discuss how media can influence them in middle school.

The activity discussion culminates with asking why this program was on TV. Some very bright students get it right away. Raising their hands, they offer answers like "to make people laugh" and "to get good ratings." And then we hone in on the issue of why shows manipulate TV viewers with laugh tracks and music. You would be surprised how many middle schoolers demonstrate significant gains in sophistication by figuring this out right away: money! TV shows and many videos on the internet are there to make money.

When the thirty-minute activity is finished, we do a short survey to assess its effectiveness as part of our ongoing efforts to ensure we are producing activities that achieve statistically significant improvement. As we have fine-tuned the activity, I have been pleased to measure more and more of the kind of results for which we were hoping. At the center, kids do develop empathy for the people and pets being hurt on television and other media.

Wow. I never thought about this before. And thanks for teaching us about memes. I never thought of them as cruel and causing harm.
—Zain, grade eight

Sadly, when teaching media detectives at the Tolerance Center, I have observed teachers laughing at the very things on TV that we are working to coach the kids not to find funny. When this happens,

I need to take a breath. Does it surprise you that we also find our-selves educating adults at the Tolerance Center?

When watching TV or YouTube at home with your kids, are you laughing when characters are mean or people are getting hurt? Please appraise what you are modeling. Your kids are watching.

Plays and Role Plays

My father used to take me into New York to see Broadway shows. Besides introducing me to classical music, it was one of the best gifts he ever gave me. One of the most memorable times of my life was when as a teenager I saw *Death of a Salesman*, in which the lead role of Willy Loman was played by a famous actor. (You'd think with such a memorable performance that I would be able to recall if it was George C. Scott or Jason Robards. But I can't. Maybe I still have the Broadway Playbill? *Sigh.*) As my father was a working salesman, working six days a week and rarely home for dinner, he was dumb-struck by the play, and I remember comparing notes, so to speak, on the way home and discussing where we agreed and disagreed.

It's what he told me afterward that was most significant. Empa-thetically, he walked in the shoes of Willy Loman, a character created by playwright Arthur Miller, and decided after leaving the theater that he would not travel the same path. The play was fictional, but it revealed an essential truth, and it transformed his life—and the lives of our entire family. After that, I noticed my father had more "spring in his step." While he didn't change careers, he did change his entire outlook. He found new passion and motivation, visible through his newly scribbled sales scripts and the presence of more sales books on our kitchen table.

The power of seeing a play at the theater, whether a Broadway show or a school play, can be far greater than seeing the same thing on TV. I encourage you to take your middle schooler to the theater, but I also encourage you to put on your own plays or skits at home.

Drama can be scripted, or you can incorporate "improv" to create scenes in which your children can take on the roles of characters, real people, or heroes from history. Or you can act out a dilemma in the school halls.

"Cultural art forms allow us to share these experiences and perspectives with one another, leading to the development of cooperation, compassion, sympathy, and empathy," writes Sarah Lynne Bowman in her book on role-playing games.[17]

Before you jump into skits and role playing in your home, have your family agree on some ground rules (a perfect time for a family meeting). Here are some suggestions:

- Everyone should be respectful to one another.
- No teasing or name calling.
- No pushing or shoving, even in fun.
- Following are some great discussion questions from Bowman for after you engage in role-playing with your children:[18]
- Does this character relate to your personality? Why or why not?
- Do you feel this character represents a part of you?
- Why do you find this character interesting?
- How does your character change over time?
- What did you learn from playing this character?

Following are three fun and thought-provoking ideas for role-playing from another author, Amanda Morin:[19]

Giving someone a compliment: It's not easy to give a genuine compliment. It needs to be about something your friend would take pride in or would want noticed. As Morin says, "Demonstrate by asking your child which is more meaningful to him [or her]: 'It's great that you like to eat eggs,' or 'You're a really good soccer player.'"

Dealing with clique behavior: Tweens often have trouble fitting in. Help your child understand that kids in cliques are looking for a reaction when they exclude or tease someone. "Practice some simple ways he can defuse situations humorously ('You're right, this shirt really *is* ugly—maybe I should just take it off right here') or calmly ('That's OK, I can sit somewhere else')." Make sure your child always knows that he or she can come to you to talk about these incidents.

Starting a conversation with a friend: This is often a hard one for kids who struggle with social skills. Let your child practice on you by having him or her give you a compliment, comment on what you're doing, or talk about something you have in common.

Role-playing is one of our most popular and most effective activities at Kidsbridge. Following are additional scenarios that we use at the center:

- a new girl in school eating alone
- a student who is being bullied
- a Muslim girl who gets teased for her religion
- a child being teased because his or her family can't afford cool sneakers
- a girl being teased for being a tomboy
- a boy being teased for taking dance lessons
- a child being bullied for having two same-sex parents

I'm going to try to stop saying "You're so gay."
—Ethan, grade six

Teaching Strengths in the Tolerance Center

In chapter 8, I discussed what a treasure Mister Rogers was, teaching our preschool kids that everyone is special and has his or her own strengths. Well, even though your middle schoolers have outgrown Mister Rogers, that doesn't mean the lesson is any less important. How painful it is to watch a middle schooler's face in a Kidsbridge Tolerance Center program and realize that personal strength is a concept that child has never considered. When I share this with other adults and educators, they are either aghast or nodding in agreement.

In American society, we are so busy striving for grades and higher test scores that we forget to remind children that they all have qualities that have real *worth*. This is why at Kidsbridge we create something wearable, a wristband on which children write their core strengths. Typically, when we ask students what they're good at, they will cite a sport or a school subject. "No," we respond, "what quality as a human being makes you good at what you do?" Most kids are confused by that question, but we persevere to accomplish our goal. Every child leaves a Kidsbridge program knowing he or she intrinsically has a strong point—whether it's creativity, humor, perseverance, or some other awesome character trait—and wearing it proudly. How much better our kids will feel if we take the opportunity on a regular basis to make sure they remember how special and unique they truly are.

*Kidsbridge taught me to believe in myself; I learned that
I am good at some things and I have perseverance.*
—Kayla, twelve years old

> *Kidsbridge helpers touched my heart by them showing me how*
> *to use what I am good at—being a problem solver. That helped*
> *me understand that this is something I can be proud of.*
> —Jose, thirteen years old

Labeling a Child

In the early 1980s, designer jeans were all the craze. It drove me absolutely nuts trying to figure out why teenagers thought it was so important to spend large chunks of their parents' money on Jordache or Gloria Vanderbilt jeans (or why their parents went along) and looked down on other kids who were content with wearing no-name brands made of the same exact material. But there will always be people for whom labels are integral to their identities. As busy adults bombarded by media and rushing at work and at home, we use labels to communicate as a status shortcut.

Some labels are OK, but they can get nasty really quickly. In the Tolerance Center, one of our main focuses is teaching kids not to stereotype, such as believing that all Italians like spaghetti, all African Americans love rap, and so on (you can picture the more vicious stereotypes that I won't repeat here). As a parent, alert yourself to any stereotypes used in your home and then bring everyone's attention to them, creating teaching moments. Don't be shy about exploring the ones the adults use in the house, either.

Then there's the truly dark side of labeling people, in which parents label their children as bad, stupid, ugly, worthless, and more (adults do it to each other, too, of course, and sometimes much more maliciously). It's bad enough that kids do this to each other in school and online. It's terrible when it happens at home, too.

Labels are not good for anyone. For a child to be defined by one characteristic is unhealthy mentally and emotionally. And even if the label has some basis in reality—some children really do cause a lot of trouble in class—calling them a troublemaker is hurtful and short-sighted. As I just pointed out, kids have their own unique strengths, but a label may cause them to dwell only on their negative traits. Remember Carol Dweck's "growth mindset." Our children are not fixed; they are constantly evolving. You don't want to do anything to hinder them from outgrowing their negative traits.

The Center for Parenting Education (https://centerforparenting education.org/) is one of the best sources for information on why labeling your children is wrong and a shortsighted strategy. I summarize here some of the center's key points on the subject:[20]

- **Labels stick to children**: Children aren't born with a positive self-image. Parents act as "psychological mirrors," meaning that what we teach them is what will reflect back. So make your words count and avoid the negative labeling before the glue hardens and those labels are stuck in their psyches.

- **Labels speak to children**: Calling your child "bad" or a "troublemaker" can lead to a vicious cycle wherein he or she begins to live down to these labels. And don't go crazy on positive labels, either. Calling your daughter "Princess" once in a while may give her warm fuzzies. But do it too much and, as the Center for Parenting Education says, "When 'Princess' is asked to clean her room, she may refuse, stating that it's too much work and someone else should do it for her."

- **Labels cost children**: Just as that Michael Kors purse might cost you a week's salary, labeling your child may come with a cost, in terms of damage to the parent-child relationship. You, too, can fall into the trap and think of your child as "mean" or "lazy." That limits your own ability to see your child's full potential.

- **Labels "live on"**: Labels are difficult to remove. Your child may carry that label into playtime or classroom activities and end up being treated however he or she has been described—as nasty, sneaky, and so on. Children tend to cling to their self-defeating ways.

In short, if your child misbehaves or has a negative characteristic that needs correcting, focus on the behavior, not the child, in your choice of words. If your middle schooler refuses to get homework done all the time, don't call him or her lazy. Instead, point out that refusing to do homework is unacceptable and consequences will follow, such as losing cell phone privileges or the chance to go out with friends to a movie.

You may have noticed one label that I haven't addressed yet. Yes, I've saved the worst for last: *bully*.

As Kidsbridge is in the business of preventing bullying, I want to share with you specifically why labeling someone a bully is a short-term strategy that will blow up. For one thing, the child may bully a younger child one day and then be bullied the next. Furthermore, you don't know all the factors involved.[21] In a teacher's shoes, perhaps that child is abused at home and is modeling the only behavior he or she knows. With bullying being such a hot button (rightly so) in today's society, we can't throw such language around loosely. In particular, that's a label we don't want to see "stick," extract a "cost," or "live on." When we address that behavior at the center, we are careful how we do so. We may talk about "kids who bully," or "kids who cause harm," but we never label the child a bully.

A diary or journal is a great place to process obstacles and feelings. I kept a diary in elementary and middle school. I still have it, and it is beyond fun to read as an adult. Buy your child a cool diary or have him or her pick one out in a store. And remember *not* to peek or pry.

Keeping a diary helps children to "develop empathy as they express personal feelings about things they may be experiencing," say authors Pamela Tiedt and Iris Tiedt in *Multicultural Teaching—A Handbook of Activities, Information and Resources.*[1]

Note

1. Pamela Tiedt and Iris Tiedt, Multicultural Teaching—A Handbook of Activities, Information and Resources (London: Pearson, 2009), 116.

Listening . . . Really Listening

Throughout this chapter and this book, I talk about face-to-face time. The central part of this is listening: truly listening. In a Woody Allen movie called *Zelig*, whenever the character Zelig would listen to somebody, he would put his entire self into it, and beyond. He would become so engaged that his body would morph into an exact replica of the person to whom he was talking. I'm not asking you go to that extreme, but actively listening to someone is important when it comes to empathy. It demonstrates to the talker that you care about what he or she has to say. So don't focus only on your listening, but also consider what the rest of your body is doing.

Is there a better way to position yourself to demonstrate you are really listening? Author Adam Bryant provides the following tips, which work for kids as well as adults: Do lean in and nod encouragingly. Don't cross your arms or seem like you don't care. "Listening, done well, is an act of empathy," Bryant writes. "You are trying to see the world through another person's eyes, and to understand their emotions. That's not going to happen if you are judging the other person as they're talking. It will dampen the conversation, because you will be sending all sorts of subtle nonverbal cues that you have an opinion about what they're saying. If you go into the discussion with the main goal of understanding their perspective, free of any judgment, people will open up to you, because they will feel they can trust you to respect what they are saying."[22]

When you only have five to fifteen minutes, play a fun quick listening game with your middle schoolers.[1]

Telephone (aka Whispering Down the Lane): See what happens when students form a line and a message is whispered from one end to the other. See whether the message gets mangled.

Blindfold obstacle course: This is another classic that really depends on trust. One student is blindfolded. One partner gives verbal directions on how to navigate the course, and the other must follow the directions to move through an obstacle course. Safety first!

Stand up/sit down: Have students stand up or sit down any time a specific word or phrase is mentioned during a prepared lesson or speech.

If you think middle school is challenging, hold on for the high school ride. High school kids are still working on identity and searching to define themselves, but their desire to interact with you is—well, if you have a high schooler, feel free to find out for yourself if you can ever get him or her to come out of the bedroom. So every moment counts more.

Note

1. Michele Meleen, Listening Activities for School, https://teens.lovetoknow.com/listening-activities-middle-school.

teaching empathy
high school years

If you don't like the way the world is, you change it.
You have an obligation to change it.
You just have to do it one step at a time.
—Marian Wright Edelman, activist and founder of
the Children's Defense Fund

Soon after the school shooting in Parkland, Florida, in 2018 that killed seventeen, sending our nation into mourning, my friend was talking to his high school daughter about it and wondering what feelings it had stirred up in her.

Was she angry? Was she upset? Well, of course, she was. But then he asked whether she was shocked by the attack.

"No, that's just how things are," she replied matter-of-factly. "You come to expect it."

His first reaction was to tell her, "No, that's not right! This type of thing *isn't* normal!" But then he realized she was completely right. This, sadly, was the new normal. It was an eye opener for my friend, just as it was for many parents and teachers. Adults grew up in a world where school shootings just weren't something that crossed our radar. But the Columbine school shooting was more than twenty years ago. A whole generation of children has grown up thinking that mass murder, including shootings inside a school, is something you "come to expect."

I'm not here to provide some magic cure for this spate of school shootings. But I do know that decreased empathy and poor social-emotional health in general are part of the cause. Adolescence is a challenging enough time for both teens and parents. It's a time when teens are striving for independence and creating their own identities, which can run counter to parents' efforts to keep their children safe, provide guidance, and inspire empathy. The blame for Columbine and Parkland, of course, belongs with the attackers. But in both cases, fellow students reported that these shooters were long-standing victims of both bullying and exclusion. If nothing else, these instances remind us how hurtful and pervasive bullying can be every day for some teenagers. In the extreme, pervasive peer rejection and constant feelings of isolation, perhaps exacerbated by mental health issues, can become ingredients for disaster.

Well-respected social psychologist Stanley Eitzen sheds light on these issues in a journal article published in 2004:

> [T]he consequences of this accelerating social isolation are dire. More and more Americans are lonely, bitter, alienated, anomic, and disconnected. This situation is conducive to alcohol and drug abuse, depression, anxiety, and violence. The lonely and disaffected are ripe candidates for membership in cults, gangs, and militias where they find a sense of

belonging and a cause to believe in, but in the process, they may become more paranoid and, perhaps, even become willing terrorists or mass murderers as were the two alienated adolescents who perpetrated the massacre at Columbine High School in a Denver suburb.[1]

There's another, more compelling reason to take empathy development seriously in your home: You can't rely on your teen's school. While some of us are lucky enough to have good schools with many resources for social-emotional learning, others are stuck with schools that lack the resources or the desire to teach it, or both. A report commissioned by the Collaborative for Academic, Social, and Emotional Learning (CASEL) forewarns that "few schools are meeting their students' needs and fostering the SEL [social-emotional learning] competencies that can help them build better relationships, deal with stress, handle difficult situations, learn how to empathize with others, and become more engaged and motivated learners."[2]

Teenagers might be lacking in empathy due to structural deficits in the brain. Clearly, says researcher Sara Jane Blakemore from University College-London Institute of Cognitive Neuroscience, such changes, in addition to massive hormonal shifts, affect teenagers' thinking.[3]

"We think that a teenager's judgment of what they would do in a given situation is driven by the simple question: 'What would I do?'" Blakemore says in relation to these findings. "Adults, on the other hand, ask: 'What would I do, given how I would feel and given how the people around me would feel as a result of my actions?'"[4]

I've hit you with a lot of disheartening news about the challenges that high schoolers face. Well, given that that there are millions of well-adjusted teenagers out there (raise your hand if you've heard glowing descriptions of your teenager from other parents that you'd never believe if you hadn't heard them yourself), the situation is far from hopeless. In fact, rumor has it that many teenagers grow up into adults who behave like, well, adults! So enough of the bad news; let's focus on what we can do to make things better.

Some would argue that efforts to improve empathy and anti-bullying initiatives are just a waste of time, especially those with a "man-up" philosophy.

Don't buy it! That's what Ugo Uche, a licensed professional counselor, says (as do I). Empathy is good for high schoolers. Empathetic kids are better able to avoid conflict in the first place by engaging in communication that involves the ability to see the other person's side. Uche's therapeutic approach, which involves the concept of empathy and teaching teens how to express their feelings, reaps results.[5]

"To date, every adolescent client of mine who has bought into this therapeutic approach [has] experienced the unintended but welcome side effect of improving their academic grades," Uche writes. "In every exit interview with these clients, they would report experiencing a desire to become more curious about others and the world around them, a departure from their previous sense of being self-centered and entitlement. One former client even referenced a Jimi [Hendrix] quote, '*I used to live in a room full of mirrors; all I could see was me. I take my spirit and I crash my mirrors, now the whole world is here for me to see.*'"[6] Talk about results!

Relationships and Belonging

When students are in high school, we still have the opportunity to improve empathy and other social-emotional skills so that our teens can learn to better respond to others and improve their life skills. We have the chance to counter bullying, cyberbullying, social media pressures, and more. We can thwart increasing social isolation, which can lead to alcohol and drug abuse, depression, anxiety, and violence. For years I have both read about and discussed the rising importance of "belonging" and "engagement for all kids." Belonging and empathy are vital parts of relationships. When teenagers (or anyone, for that matter) don't belong, things can get really dark.

"By high school, as many as 40% to 60% of students become chronically disengaged from school. . . . There is general agreement that engagement in learning is as important for success in school as it is elusive in the vast majority of traditional, bureaucratic school structures," write researchers Adena M. Klem and James P. Connell.[7]

The Columbine attackers Dylan Klebold and Eric Harris reportedly were not just bullied but also excluded. They did not belong. Not belonging was so painful in their eyes that they sought revenge, and twelve young people and one teacher died as a result. Ideally, a teenager imbued with bold empathy and empathetic action in the school could have reached out to them and included them in the students' activities. But this apparently did not happen.

Of course, we would think that if the warning signs were always that obvious, such tragedies would be more preventable. Dylan's mother wrote a book called A *Mother's Reckoning: Living in the Aftermath of Tragedy*, in which she explains how her son got to the breaking point without her knowledge. "I'll never know if I could have prevented my son's role in the terrible carnage that unfolded that day," Sue Klebold writes, "but I have come to see things I wish I had done differently."[8] I give her credit for having the courage to stand up and speak out to share "lessons learned" after an inexplicable tragedy. What guts she exemplifies by traveling the country talking and coaching parents on the power of empathy and belonging. She also started a foundation to help other families and parents.

Sometimes there are warning signs, such as your child turning inward and showing signs of depression. If you have suspicions, talk to your child, but also consult a professional. Trust, but verify.

Another example of a tragic loss of empathy is the story of Tyler Clementi, whom I first mentioned in chapter 1. Tyler, an eighteen-year-old student at Rutgers University with his entire life ahead of him, jumped to his death off the George Washington Bridge between New York and New Jersey in 2010 as a result of being humiliated online by his own roommate, who secretly filmed him via webcam kissing a man and then circulated the video online purely for laughs. In my opinion, just one person with empathy could have saved his life. This one hit home for me because the two students responsible for posting the video went to high school in my Central Jersey school district. If their parents or my school district had been better at inculcating empathy, Tyler might be alive today.

I can't speak for these young people's parents, but I do feel from personal knowledge that our school district failed them. Although the district does dabble in a few good character education programs (mostly non–evidence based), its priorities are academics, testing, and sports.

Tyler's parents, whom I had the pleasure to meet and honor as Kidsbridge humanitarians for starting a foundation to help other youth, issued this statement in his memory: "[O]ur hope is that our family's personal tragedy will serve as a call for compassion, empathy and human dignity."

These tragic losses can be used as inspiration for teaching empathy to parents, educators, and, of course, youth. Relevant points for discussion include

- decency, privacy, and invasion of privacy;
- what could have saved Tyler's or the lives of others who commit what is known as bullycide;
- what is good and not good about social media;
- desensitization and how media numbs us to kindness, civility, and respect; and
- why there is so much humiliation and exclusion shown on TV and online, often shown with a "laugh track" piped in.

A major difficulty in parenting is that sometimes there are things happening at school that you don't see at home. That's why it's important to support and advocate for programs that address empathy, inclusion, and belonging.

Self-Compassion and Mindfulness

Research experts agree that stress levels in youth have increased. The most common stressors for youth are (1) standardized tests; (2) hopelessness, leading to depression; (3) homework loads; (4) lack of sleep; and (5) excessive media use. That list doesn't even include a plethora of others, including body shaming, which leads girls to compare themselves to the unrealistic models they see on TV, in magazines, and online, leaving them with diminished self-esteem and even self-loathing.

I don't claim to have all the answers, but I'm here to do my best to help. Self-compassion and mindfulness can be powerful tools for any age, but especially for young teens. I discuss this subject in chapter 9 on the elementary school years, because the odds of success are much higher if you start early. It can still work, however, if your teen has the maturity and the desire to try; learning and practicing mindfulness and self-compassion strategies can have positive effects. Teens won't feel silly trying these strategies as they get older.

Mindfulness is an "in" thing among researchers, teachers, and even the media. More and more, research suggests that it helps students regulate emotions and manage stress. It's all about being aware and "living" in the present moment. We essentially observe our feelings, thoughts, and sensations and allow ourselves to accept them rather than playing "judge and jury" with what's going through our minds.[9]

In 1938, Dr. W. Randolph Lovelace invented the high-altitude oxygen mask.[10] I can't tell you when, but I know it wasn't long afterward that flight attendants were telling parents to put on their oxygen masks before putting them on their children in an emergency. Then it became a saying because it had other applications in life. *Put on your own oxygen mask first.* Students have to realize they are no good for others if they don't take care of themselves. "[I]f you don't meet your own emotional needs by giving yourself compassion, you will become depleted and less able to give," say Kristin Neff and Christopher Germer in *The Mindful Self-Compassion Workbook.*[11]

For readings on self-compassion, my go-to person is Neff. She has written numerous books on the topic, including a workbook for teens. Following are some additional resources, including another of her top books:

- *Self-Compassion: The Proven Power of Being Kind to Yourself,* by Kristin Neff (New York: Guilford Press, 2018), helps you "stop beating yourself up and leave insecurity behind."

- *The Self-Compassion Workbook for Teens: Mindfulness and Compassion Skills to Overcome Self-Criticism and Embrace Who You Are,* by Karen Bluth (Oakland, CA: Instant Help Books, 2017), helps teens stop being their own worst critics so they can feel compassion for themselves and others.

- *Mindful Games Activity Cards: 55 Fun Ways to Share Mindfulness with Kids and Teens,* by Susan Kaiser Greenland and Annaka Harris (Berkeley, CA: Shambhala, 2017), is a playful way to develop attention and focus and to regulate emotions.

Talk about Racial/Ethnic and Other Kinds of Bias or Empathy

A researcher at the University of Texas had an idea. She would do a study to learn whether children's videos with multicultural storylines have an effect on children's attitudes toward race. She divided her sample of children into three groups. One group was given multicultural videos, such as a relevant episode of *Sesame Street*, to watch at home. Another received the videos and the parents were asked to discuss interracial friendship, while the last group was asked to have a discussion but received no videos.[12]

The study had one wildly unexpected outcome. Five families abruptly dropped out. "We don't want to have these conversations with our child. We don't want to point out skin color," they told researcher Birgitte Vittrup, even though parents knew ahead of time they might be asked to do just that. This was a huge shame, because Vittrup found those conversations about interracial friendships to be highly effective in increasing kids' tolerance for those who were different.[13]

Many parents, especially those who are White, try to avoid talking about not only race but also gender, income level, and various other differences among people. They reason that if they don't discuss prejudice, then it won't suddenly appear in their children's attitudes.[14] (I guess these same parents wouldn't provide sex education, either.)

But research has shown that's not true. Even preschoolers see differences and hold biases.[15] When adults don't talk to children about prejudice, they can make things worse; children end up absorbing societal stereotypes from media or assuming they have touched on a taboo topic. Vittrup recommends you discuss bias openly with your tweens and teens.

Have the hard discussions, researchers say. Surprisingly, they *really* aren't that difficult. Bring up topics like race. Talk to your children about the fact that racism exists, that boys and girls haven't always been allowed to do the same things, that different families have different levels of resources, and that families are made up of different combinations of people.

Don't silence children when they remark on skin color or skip the parts in books in which characters face discrimination. These are learning moments. Instead, talk about discrimination and why it's wrong. If they make a comment in public, experts suggest saying something like "Yes, people come in all different skin colors, just like you and I have different hair colors."[16]

Claire Cain Miller of the *New York Times* has an excellent list of recommended books for dealing with topics on race and oppression:[17]

- *So You Want to Talk about Race*, by Ijeoma Oluo (New York: Seal Press, 2019).

- *The New Jim Crow: Mass Incarceration in the Age of Colorblindness*, by Michelle Alexander (New York: New Press, 2012).

- *The Making of Asian America: A History*, by Erika Lee (New York: Simon & Schuster, 2015).

- *The Indian World of George Washington: The First President, the First Americans and the Birth of the Nation*, by Colin G. Calloway (New York: Oxford University Press, 2018), explores the relationship between George Washington and Native Americans.

- *Heartland: A Memoir of Working Hard and Being Broke in the Richest Country on Earth*, by Sarah Smarsh (New York: Scribner, 2018), explores the relationship of growing up poor in the Midwest.

- *The New Negro: The Life of Alain Locke*, by Jeffrey C. Stewart (New York: Oxford University Press, 2018), examines the life of a key architect of the Harlem Renaissance.

High schoolers, approached in the right way, can be receptive to these kinds of books, which offer a twist on the assumptions that they might bring home or into their classrooms. Just think of the good that you can do by turning on your high schooler's radar to empathy toward those of a different religion, color, ethnicity, gender identity, and more.

I introduced "persons first" language in chapter 9, and it applies here as well. We are all "persons first," and the accoutrements of clothes, religion, the pigmentation of our skin, and so on are minor differences.

I want to leave this discussion by introducing you to the ultimate eye-opening book: *Rising Out of Hatred: The Awakening of a Former White Nationalist*, by Eli Saslow (New York: First Anchor Books, 2018). It tells of a former White nationalist whose views toward Jews were transformed by a series of Sabbath dinners with Orthodox Jewish students at his college.[18] The college students didn't judge; they listened with patience and empathy, and the White nationalist learned how wrong his prejudices were. There are quite a few books written by White supremacists who have turned their backs on hate; they make for great reading and family discussions. Turning away from hate is a difficult process, but worth the effort.

Try Out Someone Else's Life

Here I roll out some ideas to blow your teenager's mind, because what better way is there to grab their attention and hold it? When my kids were in high school, I managed to talk my family into taking an adventuresome vacation in Central America. It became one of our favorite trips. In Belize, we visited Mayan temple ruins, diverse communities, a zoo with jaguars and exotic birds, beaches, and jungle. But the trip also provided a glimpse of extreme poverty. On the way to the Mayan temple site of Tikal (located in nearby Guatemala), along a bumpy dirt road, we passed miles upon miles of poor people living in dire conditions, with no running water or plumbing. I noticed little children playing by the side of the road, which made me extremely nervous for their safety.

Through the miles, I actually did not have to say much; my kids' mouths were agape and their eyes wide open. These Third World nations revealed extreme poverty the likes of which they had never seen and have never forgotten. In future moments of high school entitlement, when they complained about "First World" problems such as slow downloads on the internet or having to decide at what restaurant they would like to eat, I would say, "Remember the road to Tikal." I could almost see them visualize the road as they became quiet or changed the subject. The seeds of empathy had sprouted! We had truly put the "walk" in "walking in someone else's shoes"!

You don't have to go to a foreign land to introduce an exotic new culture into your household. Perhaps your teen has the curiosity and excitement to participate in an exchange program. I knew plenty of  students in in my day who stayed with a family in Spain and had their high school counterpart come to America to stay with them. If a foreign land doesn't do it for you, perhaps you could do a different kind of exchange program—say, with someone of a different religion. Your child goes with that child's family to their house of worship, and then that child attends yours! When I was in middle school, I went with my friends to watch them take Communion in a beautiful Catholic church. It was amazing to watch, and I was grateful to be included.

Community Service versus Service Learning

We once had a "can't miss" idea for building empathy at Kidsbridge. We gathered youth from higherand lower-income families at the

Tolerance Center. They made sandwiches to be delivered to those in need and experienced an uplifting day of community service.

But the can't-miss idea *missed*.

We measured the students' empathy learning with preand post-activity surveys and *alas!* did not find any improvement whatsoever. Slowly, we realized where we went wrong. Children can make sandwiches for hungry people whom they don't see, but doing it *doesn't* provide any experience of what a hungry person goes through—that is, empathic concern.

Community service is a great thing, but it doesn't create empathetic human beings. Service learning does.[19] What is the difference? Service learning involves both discussion and evoking feelings for kids to understand what it feels like to be hungry, what it feels like to not know where their next meal is coming from, or what it feels like to be in a homeless shelter.

A truly meaningful program took place in 2018 when middle and high school students from Detroit and Rhode Island came together to distribute pure, safe water to residents of Flint, Michigan. This was service of the highest nature, based on the conviction that clean water should not be a privilege that can be lost by those in a poorer community.[20]

The Toughest, Most Rewarding Road to Empathy

The Harley School near Rochester, New York, has a program that is as fine an example of promoting empathy as I've ever seen for high schoolers. Participants have been visiting hospices for years as part of the school's empathy education program in an effort to teach compassion and increase listening skills. For students to be able to communicate with those at the end of life and find some meaningful way to make a difference is about as courageous and spirit building as you can get.[1]

Note

1. "Harley School Gives an Education in Empathy," Rochester Democrat and Chronicle, July 5, 2011.

High Schoolers and Disabilities

Speaking of creative ways to learn empathy, Ridgewood (NJ) High School found a way to tackle the issue of empathy for individuals with disabilities. Students were shown photos of young people with genetic disorders such as muscular dystrophy and various rare diseases. Then they wrote poems, blogged, created dance pieces, and more. It was all part of the Pearls Project about understanding others with disabilities in an effort to promote tolerance and empathy.[21]

"It was kind of shocking, because you felt yourself judging right away," said Madison Konner, age eighteen, a senior in philosophy and dance classes. "You say, 'There's a boy with a funny face, ha, ha.' But you find out later he can't help it."[22]

I don't expect every school to be able to duplicate such an intensive program. But your child's school can do something to teach empathy for those with physical and intellectual disabilities. If your school isn't doing it, you can do it in your own home.

It's easy for you to model appropriate behavior when you leave the house. Take special notice when you see or pass a person with a disability. And don't forget your "persons first" language. For example, you could express to your kids that the homeless man you pass in the street is possibly a veteran with post-traumatic stress disorder. The woman in that wheelchair has cerebral palsy and struggles to cross the street. Feel for them, but don't feel *sorry* for them. They don't want that. They want to be respected as persons.

Following are some things you can do with your children:

- When you pass a person in a wheelchair, say hi.

- When you see an old person struggling, ask if you can help.

- When you see a person with intellectual disabilities, observe your tween/teen and see whether he or she feels comfortable seeing or interacting with the individual. Discuss what you observed later.

- Ask your teens/tweens if they know of any persons with intellectual or physical disabilities in their school and ask them how such a person is treated. Perhaps you can get your teen to "walk in a person's shoes" and have a good discussion.

- Do you have a person with disabilities in your family? Share that person's struggle and challenges with your family. At the center, students love to share this experience with us; it feels good for them to discuss an aunt, uncle, cousin, or parent who is different and know that other kids have persons with disabilities in their families.

We shouldn't be afraid of people who are different than us
and it's ok to ask questions or to be curious about someone.
—Jessica, fifteen years old

Here's what I *don't* recommend: watch the movie *Tropic Thunder*, starring Ben Stiller, unless you're using it to teach kids what not to do and plan to discuss it *verrrrry* soon after watching it. My family convinced me to see it, but I felt trepidation going in and an even worse feeling going out. I explained to them that the movie upset me because it was making fun of people with intellectual disabilities.

I explained to them that the word *retarded*, used quite a bit in the movie, is regarded in the respectful educational community as the "R" word and that it would not ever be used in our house.

If you see a movie with your kids that ends violently or seems to be devoid of values and ethics, challenge your kids to "fix" the movie or create a better ending without disrespecting others. Could this movie have been just as entertaining without disparaging persons with mental disabilities? Would the movie have been compromised? How does it benefit our society to make fun of others? Why do human beings do this, and what does this say about our nature and our culture?

Role Models

In 1993, basketball star Charles Barkley, who to this day is a big media presence, made headlines when he recorded a commercial in which he said, "I'm not a role model. Just because I dunk a basketball doesn't mean I should raise your kids." Given the misbehavior rampant today among athletes, movie stars, and politicians, that sentiment may not have been the worst to share with kids. But the fact is, anyone with star power tends to wind up being a role model for tweens and teens, for better or worse.

However, the world is full of *real* role models whose stories can benefit our kids. With a little bit of research, we can find them. Unfortunately, real role models are competing with inappropriate, mean, and disrespectful media personalities who explode upon impressionable minds in our homes. If you search online for "role models," "teen heroes," or "tween heroes," you probably won't get good ones at first. Dig deeper. Perhaps you and your high schoolers can brainstorm a good role model if you search together.

When you notice people in the news who inspire you, text your kids a link to the article or screenshot it and share it with your tweens and teens. Let them know what it takes to be a good role model.

If you insist on having movie stars as role models, here are some of my suggestions: Natalie Portman supports an international self-sufficiency organization and recently visited lowland gorillas in Africa. Mia Farrow adopted Darfur in the Sudan as her cause and travels the globe to advocate for those torn by hunger and warfare. Rihanna volunteers to make clean water available to children around the world as a UNICEF ambassador. John Legend focuses on school lunches in low-income neighborhoods and America's criminal justice system. And here's an athlete who really shines: then Philadelphia Eagles football player Chris Long donated his entire $1 million salary in 2017 to scholarships and promoting educational equity.

Empathy for Our Planet

In the previous chapter I introduced a new empathy recipient: Earth. The *Guardian* has a good list of young adult climate science fiction.[23] This "cli-fi" genre is about youth struggling to survive climate change and other natural disasters. Your kids will have fun reading while hopefully being inspired to do something to help our planet. Following are a couple of books recommended in the *Guardian* that are appropriate for teens:

- *Breathe*, by Sarah Crossan (New York: Greenwillow Books, 2012), is about a place where there are no trees and no oxygen unless you pay for it.

- *Floodland*, by Marcus Sedgwick (London: Orion Children's Books, 2000), has a main character who seeks to live on an island amid high waters after climate change leaves England flooded.

In early 2019, the United Nations released a report stating that one million plants and species are on the verge of extinction. Those extinctions have major implications for human survival itself, including your children's and grandchildren's. Fires, floods, hurricanes:

How much more of a wakeup call do we need to have empathy for our planet?

Relationships, Dating, and Media Literacy for the High Schooler

High school students will often need lessons about how to treat their boyfriends or girlfriends on a date. About 9 percent of high school students reported being hit, slapped, or physically hurt on purpose by their boyfriends or girlfriends.[24] Many of the programs to prevent teen dating violence focus on changing knowledge, attitudes, and behaviors linked with dating violence while focusing on the skills needed to build healthy relationships.[25]

These concerning statistics are also related to an empathy deficit. Subconsciously, boys and girls may be modeling lack of respect, backstabbing, and "drama" that they see in movies or on TV. I have noticed the word *drama* creeping into the vocabulary of American youth, and it's not a good sign. Teenagers may know intellectually that the scenes are not real, but emotionally they just aren't sure.

A reflection by a tween named Marisol on a visit to the Tolerance Center underscored this idea after an activity on media literacy: "I didn't realize how influenced I was by television and social media. I think I need to work harder to figure out what the difference is between fantasy and reality."

Jobs, Employers, College, and Empathy

After high school graduation, you have one more precious summer with your children, and then off they go. Some leave the nest to depart for college, while others take their newfound independence and pursue other paths. If you follow some of my recommendations to flex their empathy muscles, you can rest assured that your children should see benefits, starting with their ability to make friends quickly.

In a survey about college freshmen, two researchers discovered that empathy fosters close relationships.[26] Think about it: They're in a new environment and need friends quickly. They need people they can trust and confide in. Those high in empathy not only make friends quickly, the researchers say, but also are at the center of their social networks based largely on the trust they engender.

What better reward is there for parents than the knowledge that when they send their child off into the world, their son or daughter has the character and social skills to develop meaningful relationships, a core requirement for happiness? As a mother, I can assure you that the saying "you're only as happy as your unhappiest child" is true. So, doing everything you can to have happy, successful, and compassionate children is the best present for them *and* you.

Empathy Helps with Getting a Job and Keeping It

It's not jobs, jobs, jobs anymore. It's relationships, relationships, relationships.

—David Brooks, *New York Times*[1]

The Empathy Advantage will help your child get a job *and* keep it! When kids are seeking their first jobs during or after high school, or after college, people skills are at the top of the list of what they'll need, particularly empathy. It is the foundation for success in interviewing, team building, and promotion.

When I network in my community, these are the types of complaints that I typically hear from employers and human relations professionals:

- "Job applicants don't look me in the eye."

- "Applicants shake hands like a droopy fish."

- "Applicants can't hold conversations."

In fact, I've seen some corporations so interested in improving these "soft skills" (as opposed to literacy and math, which are "hard skills") for future workers that they initiate programs for *middle schoolers*. They must think high school is too late!

Employers want to hear YES to the following questions:

- Can you be respectful online? Will you be a team player?
- Will you treat coworkers, customers, and the public fairly and with respect?
- Will you do your best to fit into our corporate culture?

When my son Jake was about to go on one of his first interviews, he was full of nerves. But I eased his mind by providing empathy strategies in my prep talk. How?

I shared the concept of the movie *Zelig* with him, suggesting that he observe the body posture of the interviewer and reflect it in some way. If the interviewer leaned in, he could lean in. If the interviewer talked slowly, he could slow down his speech, too. If the interviewer had sports paraphernalia in his office, he could try a couple of light questions about the particular sport.

Most of all—and most enticing to parents—is that empathy is key to *leadership*. Researchers Daniel Goleman, Richard Boyatzis, and Annie McKee argue in *Primal Leadership* that empathy outweighs cognitive skills and that leaders who use empathy create the most energizing, top-performing cultures.[2] When empathy is high, a leader better succeeds in both persuading and inspiring teamwork. So help your child become a leader. Teach empathy!

Notes

1. David Brooks, "It's Not the Economy, Stupid," New York Times, November 29, 2018, https://www.nytimes.com/2018/11/29/opinion/american-economy-working-class.html.

2. Daniel Goleman, Richard Boyatzis, and Annie McKee, Primal Leadership: Unleashing the Power of Emotional Intelligence (Boston: Harvard Business Review Press, 2013).

Do your kids know the difference between fantasy and reality? I suggest you watch some shows  together on TV or the internet. Quiz them about what is real and what is scripted. Discuss reality shows. Is this how people really act? Or are the so-called regular people playing it up for the cameras like actors?

twelve
empathy
critical for bullying prevention

[K]indness changes the brain by the experience of kindness.
Children and adolescents do not learn kindness by only thinking
about it and talking about it. Kindness is best learned by feeling
it so that they can reproduce it.
—Patty O'Grady, expert in neuroscience,
emotional learning, and positive psychology

In 2001, journalists Neil Marr and Tim Field wrote *Bullycide: Death at Playtime*, coining a word for when a child, seeing no other avenue of escape from bullying, commits suicide. The following year, a twelve-year-old special education student named J. Daniel Scruggs hanged himself in the bedroom closet of his Connecticut home, and the term took off.

The case gained notoriety because Daniel's mother was charged with and convicted of creating an unsafe home environment that prosecutors argued was a contributing factor in the boy's suicide. But courtesy of the mother's lawyer injecting the term into the case, it was also the first time that *bullycide* gained wide use. Daniel had missed forty-five days of school and been late on twenty-nine others, his mother told police, because he was afraid of bullies who had kicked and punched him. His classmates and teachers said that he smelled bad and that he had no friends. Daniel did live in a filthy house, although, in defense of his mother, she worked two jobs and was a single parent.[1] Sadly, Daniel was isolated from both belonging and others' empathy. If he'd been in a different home or a different school, Daniel *might* be alive today.

Sadly, bullying affects all genders, ages, religions, ethnicities, and heritages. It occurs in elementary, middle, and high school. It can even happen in preschool. At the Tolerance Center, job one is doing whatever we can to prevent bullying and the violence that can often result, but it's not easy.

When I became executive director of Kidsbridge, at the time it was a not-for-profit devoted to character education and diversity appreciation. But while we were helping kids with social-emotional skills, kindness, and respect, the tragic upswing in the number of children like Daniel killing themselves started gaining national attention. Children who weren't even old enough yet to understand what life was about lost all hope, deciding it was better to end their lives.

I couldn't stand by and do nothing. Kidsbridge had to pivot to help kids, parents, and educators address bullycide. We rapidly adjusted the curriculum, but as hard as we worked, we weren't gaining any traction. Our knowledgeable Kidsbridge Education Committee advised more empathy and empowerment activities. That proved to be the key to getting results. Our student and teacher surveys began to indicate these new strategies were hitting home, which I share with you later in the chapter.

It's easy to be complacent when you see your school district send home letters about anti-bullying policies and conducting assembly programs. This promotes the appearance that administrators have things under control. But don't fall into the complacency trap. Sadly, many schools sweep "bad things" under the rug. Another thing that schools do that irks me is applying a bandage to bullying, like a one-shot *ineffective* assembly program.

The Southern Poverty Law Center did a survey of ten thousand K–12 educators after the 2016 election; while the survey did not use a random sample, the flood of responses was impossible to ignore. They indicated that children of color, Muslim and Jewish kids, and LGBT youth were being teased and bullied more than in recent years. Hate speech and bias were on the rise for both students and adults. An overwhelming majority had seen a negative impact on students and increased instances of verbal harassment, the use of slurs and derogatory language, and cyberbullying. Incidents involving swastikas, Nazi salutes, and Confederate flags were on the rise as well. More than twenty-five hundred educators described specific incidents of bigotry and harassment that they felt were related to rhetoric from the election.[2]

Furthermore, a 2017 poll by the Institute for Social Policy and Understanding found that two in five Muslim families reported bullying of their children, with one-quarter of these incidents involving bullying *by a teacher*.[3] And one more statistic for you: a Public Religion Research Institute poll in 2017 found that two-thirds of Americans believe that bullying of gay, lesbian, and transgender teenagers is a major problem in our schools.[4]

Having worked with the best educators in New Jersey and studied the research, I have concluded that the path to reduce bullying starts with empathy. In a nutshell, would a child hurt another child physically or emotionally if he or she stopped for a moment to think how it would feel if that were happening to him or her?

In this chapter I first define what bullying is, then discuss the three types of individuals involved in bullying: those who bully or harm, those who get bullied (targets), and bystanders. Finally, I talk about cyberbullying and the special set of challenges it involves.

> ### Don't Label Someone a Bully!
> Labeling someone a bully is a bad idea. As discussed previously, labeling a child is the one of the worst things we can do. We all have strengths and weaknesses; we all have good behaviors and bad behaviors. Someone who bullies one day might be a victim the next. So you'll notice that I will talk about "those who bully or harm" rather than affix the word *bully* to individuals. Also, I avoid the word *victim*. The word *target* is now used more commonly by experts.

What Is Bullying?

Have you ever heard friends say that the issue of bullying is over-blown, that it's just kids being kids? Have you ever heard parents say that the only problem is that kids are babied and that what they really need is to learn to suck it up or have a thicker skin? When I hear that, I have a sudden urge to switch into *teaching moment* mode, and I say, "That might work for some kids, but some kids kill themselves!" Typically, the listener is dumbfounded and walks away sheepishly. It's the equivalent of a swift kick (not a literal one, lest I lose all credibility on this bullying issue!).

Sure, there are gray areas. We don't want to get to the point where innocent roughhousing or an exchange of name calling on the playground is viewed as a major incident. But being targeted by others, whether by being punched, shoved, belittled, or humiliated, on a *regular basis* is another. Such attacks can take multiple forms, including online harassment (cyberbullying) and purposeful exclusion and ostracism. That's bullying. Period.

My state, New Jersey, has one of the best bullying prevention laws in the land. However, we don't have the resources we need to enforce the law, although schools (not all, but for the most part) try to follow it in good faith, with nonprofit agencies like Kidsbridge trying to pick up the slack. A definition in our anti-bullying laws clarifies what bullying is, describing a standard of reasonableness as far as what happens on school grounds, focusing in particular on attacks related to race, religion, sexual orientation, and so on. It has three facets: (1) a reasonable person should know that the act will physically or emotionally harm a student or place him or her in fear of harm, (2) the act insults or demeans a student or group of students, and (3) it creates a hostile educational environment.[5] Check out the laws and policies in your state or for your school district. Check online, or ask the principal, a counselor, or (if your school has one) your anti-bullying or HIB (harassment, intimidation, and bullying) specialist.

Contrary to popular myth, bullying is unrelated to low self-esteem. It is related to power and popularity. Those who bully are aggressive attention seekers who enjoy an audience and tend to lack empathy. They tend to be strategic about it, too. They strike quickly, shoving another kid or dishing out their insults before adults can catch on and, in the case of a school setting, send them to the principal's office. Would it surprise you to learn that those who bully have already been bullied and felt powerless themselves?

Those who bully tend to be popular and respected, but also feared. That was a shocking revelation for me. How is it possible that the meanest and nastiest kids are also the most popular? But I suppose when you look at what's on phones, television, and the internet, maybe we shouldn't be surprised. In the media, backstabbing, competition, and gossip are glamorized. It's reasonable to assume that children are picking up the media messages and internalizing them.

General Parent Tips

Ken Rigby knows that your children are watching you very carefully. Rigby, an adjunct professor at the University of South Australia and a leading international researcher in the area of bullying in schools, has authored many books for parents. Some of Rigby's sage recommendations for the home pertaining to bullying and empathy are crystallized here:[6]

1. Don't act like a bully yourself. Your child is watching and learns by copying what he or she sees.

2. Promote empathic concern for others in your home and outside your home. This will help your children be more accepting of others and less inclined to bully or be a bystander.

3. Teach and practice the "Golden Rule." At the Tolerance Center, we have activities demonstrating that all religions basically have the same Golden Rule: "Do unto others as you would have them do unto you."

If your child exhibits bullying behaviors or attitudes, cut 'em off at the pass, as they say in old Western movies. Get in the way of that behavior before it gets away from your ability to easily corral it. Immediately put your child on a path of empathy. This strategy will get you further than discipline and punishment. I'm not saying that setting limits on aggressive behavior through consistent discipline is without merit, but it's not the most effective cure. With the power of empathy, you can do much better.[7]

- Show your children that they can get what they want without teasing, threatening, or hurting someone. Tell your children that the most successful adults in life have good people skills, including kindness and compassion.

- Talk to your children about how bullying hurts other children. Ask them to "walk in another child's shoes" and then how it felt to be on the other end of bullying or other mean behaviors.

- Be a positive role model and demonstrate peaceful resolution to conflicts. And when your children say, "Mom and Dad, you're always fighting," don't brush it off! Our children are our best mirrors.

- Use books, stories, and photos to teach your children about empathy for other people, whether real or fictional, and make sure that you schedule a time every week devoted to empathy. The sooner, the better.

Finger Wagging

We all wish we had a magic wand so we could fix the bullying problem for our children and our society. In fact, some people seem to act as if an outstretched finger *is* a magic wand. They'll finger wag 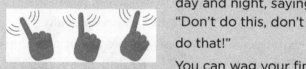 day and night, saying, "Don't do this, don't do that!"

You can wag your fingers until they drop off. You can try to tell your children not to bully, you can instruct them how to avoid being targets, you can encourage them to be UPstanders instead of bystanders. It doesn't

work! (I'm reminded of my elementary schoolteach-
ers saying, "Am I talking to a wall?!") Most children
know the right thing to do, but they don't do it, for
two reasons: (1) they might not know how because
they lack the strategies, or (2) they might have fears
about being excluded, not fitting in, losing friends,
and so on.

Also, it's not a good idea for your school to go into default
mode and use the regular old tools of suspension and detention.
Detention gives children a chance to sit around and do nothing
rather than learn from their troublesome behavior. Suspension is a
day off from school—what's the punishment in that for the child?
It's more of a punishment for the parents, who have to take off from
work or arrange care.

Those Who Bully
Risks for Children Who Exhibit Aggressive Behavior

The risks for children who bully are plenty. Having learned to
use power and aggression to control and victimize other children at
a young age—and often thinking of it as entertainment—they are
more likely to bully as an adult. Furthermore, they are more likely
to experience anxiety and depression and become entangled in drug
and alcohol abuse.[8]

As the years have flown by, I have watched proactive discipline
and treatment improve for addressing those who bully. Instead of
detention and suspension, I am seeing more talking, more therapy,
and more efforts to have them try to repair the harm they've done.
And yes, of course, I've seen more empathy. We figured out how to
do this at the Tolerance Center years ago because we know, considering that we educate thousands of kids, we will always come across
some who are mean and exclude others.

At the Tolerance Center, we conduct various activities to deliberately place all the children in the shoes of others who have been bullied and mistreated. One method is to "work behind the scenes," partnering with the children's teachers. This is how it works. When we do our conflict resolution skits, we strategize with the teacher to put the "child who bullies" in the role of the target or the role of the UPstander. This way, empathy is generated, and the person who bullies is put in the position of solving the problem or being the target.

The following week, the teacher might challenge the child and say something like "Remember how you solved this problem last week at Kidsbridge? I know you know how to solve this problem and you can do this again," or "How did it feel to be the target last week in the Kidsbridge skit?"

How to Encourage Empathy

Here are some great suggestions from a prevention website in Canada, centering on how to empower those who bully to redirect their negative energies into positive actions and remorse. These are so good for parents or teachers that I provide them verbatim:[9]

- Help your children identify and label feelings of shame, embarrassment, anger, fear, or sadness in themselves and in others.

- Have your children draw a picture of what they think it must feel like to be bullied. Talk about the feelings that children who are bullied might feel.

- Have your children talk with you, a sibling, or another adult about their bullying experiences and the impact it had on them.

- Have your children watch a movie about bullying (e.g., *Mean Girls, Back to the Future*) and encourage them to focus on the feelings of the victimized person. Help them to identify these feelings by looking out for facial expressions, body posture, and tone of voice.

- Have your children identify instances of bullying in the media (e.g., television, newspapers, radio, magazines, websites) and talk with them about their reactions to these instances.

- Talk with your children about their own strengths and weaknesses and how they can use power to help, not hurt, others.

I didn't realize I was a bully until after our Kidsbridge program ended. I sometimes do things that are mean or nasty. But now I know that this behavior won't help me and I will try harder to stop.
—Frank, seventh grade

Making Amends

When a child bullies, things have to be made right. While the child may not have the skills to repair a relationship, at least he or she can learn to respect others and understand others' right to feel safe.[10]

But if children can go further and are genuinely willing, sincere, and able to say they're sorry, you could have them write an apology. They could also give a specific apology, including stating how they'll do right by the victim from now on. If property was damaged or taken, have the child fix or replace it.[11]

Empowering with Kindness

Every child needs to know he or she has power in this world. But as they say in the Spiderman movies, "With great power comes great responsibility." OK, they don't have spider senses or cosmic powers and can't web-sling across the city, but they are able to make a positive change. Encourage your kids to perform acts of kindness and to observe compassion that they see in school or after school. Talk to them about what they see. To make a child who bullies feel powerful in a good way, have him or her do something constructive like coaching baseball or tutoring another or younger child. Those are great ways to redirect the child's energy.[12]

But whatever you do, do not deal with children who bully by being a bully yourself. You may think you're teaching a lesson, but that lesson may prove to be on how to be *more effective* at bullying. In fact, take the time to reexamine your own behavior. In talking to hundreds of teachers at the Tolerance Center, I have learned that more often than not, many mean and exclusive behaviors are learned at home or via the media.

If Your Child Is a Target

The first step in helping a child who is the target of a bully is to find out that it's happening. Often kids are too embarrassed to admit they've been shoved or made to feel ashamed on the playground because of their religion or skin color or have been humiliated in the high school cafeteria for something as simple as what they eat for lunch. It's a perfectly understandable reaction. As a child, I did not confide in my parents and wanted to solve all my problems by myself, so I understand that some of your kids will not share everything with you. But sometimes children will drop hints, so be perceptive and ask questions. Make them comfortable with the idea that it's OK to come to you.

Once I was bullied for my weight. People used to call me fatty and pig.
They used to whisper when I walked by and would push me around.
—Dominique, fourth grade

> *People were laughing at my friend because*
> *he had glasses and they called him a nerd.*
> —Taquan, sixth grade

Try to make your questions open ended: ask about their day, their interests, and their afterschool activities without demanding too many details. Always keep the lines of communication open and let them know you care. If you were bullied or teased at their age, now's a good time to share *your* story with them so they know they are not alone. Have your spouse or significant other share his or her stories, too.

Here's some additional advice, courtesy of Rigby, for parents of targeted and bullied youth:[13]

- If you sense something has happened and your child won't let on, keep in touch with school to see if something's going on.

- Don't tell your child to "man up" and stand up to the bully.

- Don't say you'll work it out for them with a perpetrator's parent. That tends to backfire (think about whom the other child may have learned bullying behavior from).

- Work with the school to see whether administrators and teachers can help. Give them time, but escalate the problem to superiors if need be. If you have to pull your children from school, tell them why.

Hopefully your school will be proactive and solve the problem, but, sadly, I've heard many stories over more than eighteen years about school administrators, counselors, or teachers not doing their jobs. In extreme cases, I've heard of parents demanding a transfer to another school or even moving to another school district. This may sound drastic, but consider this as an option if your school fails you and your child. I know many parents who wished they had done this earlier. Your child's well-being and self-esteem are at stake.

Dave Yeager, an associate professor of developmental psychology at the University of Texas at Austin, recommends an intervention by adults in which teenage bullied kids learn about how the brain and personality change over time. This incremental approach, he asserts, reduces youths' tendencies to retaliate aggressively. Yeager states, "By teaching teenagers that people can change, it makes them feel less like they need to escalate things if they're bullied."[14] Interesting advice to follow.

Victims/targets need a foundation of self-empathy to solve this problem. They need to understand that they don't deserve to be bullied, teased, excluded, or called a name. This concept is covered thoroughly in chapter 14, which deals with self-compassion and self-empathy.

One of the best pieces of advice I can provide is to make sure your kids have a network of friends *outside* of school. Whether in sports, youth clubs, Boy Scouts/Girl Scouts, faith-based clubs, or some other group, it is critically important that they have friends somewhere. And when I say friends, I mean those near enough to see face to face, because friends online are not adequate, and online acquaintanceships can lead to further isolation.

When advocating for your child at school, empathy is a great tool to use with the teachers and administrators as well. Tell them you understand how difficult their jobs can be. Don't go into the meeting with the teacher, counselor, or principal if you are upset. Take a breath. Then share your feelings, the pain your child is going through, and the challenges.

It's a good idea to request an action plan—with dates—from the administration before you leave. That way the school won't get the impression that they can ignore you. It lets them know you are serious and won't stop until your child gets respect, safety, and justice. If in the end you don't get satisfaction, you need to be the "squeaky wheel" and persist until your child has no contact with the child who is bullying and a proactive action plan is seriously considered. Some parents of bullied children hire lawyers who are experts in protecting such children.

> *If someone is mean, be an UPstander. Even though someone is a different size, religion or color, you should still be respectful of that person.*
> —Olivia, age eight

How to Promote Empathy in Bystanders

The majority of kids in a classroom, on sports teams, or in any youth group are neither bullies nor targets; they are bystanders. We live in a bystander society that trickles down to our children. We've all heard these messages in daily life: "Don't get involved. Don't stick your neck out. Don't be a snitch." Sometimes we might be telling our kids to intercede for a friend, but another time we might tell them the opposite. Understandably, they are confused and don't know what to do as a result.

> *I remember when I was in 3rd grade and we had a new girl. She was Puerto Rican so nobody in my class wanted to be friends with her. I didn't either at first, but then I started feeling about her feelings. So I started to talk to her and now—me and her are still friends now.*
> —Melody, seventh grade

"Those Who Bully" Can Be Bullied, Too

It's true! When bullied kids are in pain, sometimes they can flip to being bullies themselves. They seek revenge and want to retaliate.

Research has a term for these kids: *bully/victims*. They can go back and forth: being in pain and causing pain. They tend to be characterized by poor problem-solving skills. They also tend to fare poorly academically, feel isolated, are rejected and isolated by peers, and tend to be negatively influenced by those with whom they do interact.[1]

Note

1. American Psychological Association, "Who Is Likely to Become a Bully, Victim or Both?" July 8, 2010, https://www.apa.org/news/press/releases/2010/07/bully-victim.

Let me remind you that those who bully are actually in the minority. Bystanders can control the culture and take over when they transform into UPstanders (a word coined almost twenty years ago). Proportionally, bystanders are the largest portion of any group or classroom activity. That is why we must teach them to take charge of the culture and stop those who bully and harm. When bystanders take action, they transform themselves into UPstanders.

UPstanders, changemakers, or allies can be sensitive to others' emotional states and are empathetic. UPstanders have the courage to help a target and feel they can make a difference. Sometimes they are courageous; sometimes they are not. But most of them take great comfort in serving as helpers and feel good about doing the right thing. UPstanders are *practiced* young persons with strategies to understand that when safety is involved, it's time to involve an adult.

Occasionally, children might see someone being targeted and, feeling empathetic, might get emotional, yet not take action. But then later, they *do* take action. This is a good step. If this kind of child gets practice in school, he or she might grow up to be the kind of person who improves our system and makes the world a kinder and more respectful place.

What Is Cyberbullying?

Cyberbullying tends to consist of five characteristics: electronic forms of contact, an aggressive act, intent, repetitiveness, and harm to the target.[15] The results can be quite serious, and even deadly. In chapter 11, which covers empathy for high school children, I discuss the example of Rutgers University student Tyler Clementi, who was driven to jump off the George Washington Bridge when a roommate circulated a video of him kissing another man.

It's difficult to imagine anyone thinking cyberbullying is a minor matter anymore. In fact, a survey in 2019 found that 60 percent of kids ages fourteen to eighteen had been cyberbullied.[16] Such high numbers are easy to imagine when we realize how simple it is to bully from the safety of a computer screen as opposed to in front of someone's face.

To combat cyberbullying, I like to recommend some tips offered by Tchiki Davis, an expert on well-being technology. She approaches cyberbullying etiquette from an empathetic point of view and points out that much of what constitutes cyberbullying can result from misunderstandings stemming from miscommunication in both texts and emails.[17]

1. **Assume good intentions.** Don't assume the worst. It's hard to know what people mean if we can't see their faces or hear their tone of voice. Detecting the emotion or intent behind the written word is tricky, especially given how short and incomplete these messages tend to be.

2. **Cultivate awareness of unconscious biases.** We may have preconceived notions of what a person is trying to communicate and let them cloud our understanding. Be careful.

3. **Explore the emotional undertones of the words themselves.** Is a person being serious or sarcastic? Is he or she complimenting you by saying you worked hard on a task, or is it an insult meant to insinuate the opposite? Weigh all the possibilities.

4. **Seek out more information.** The bottom line? Don't guess! Ask questions and be empathetic as you do.

The most important thing I learned was that being an UPstander is important. Now if I know someone is being bullied I can help them.
—Zain

One important thing that I learned at Kidsbridge is being an UPstander for myself. One thing I will do differently is taking care of the situations that I see. For example, going to an adult for help.
—Samantha

The most important thing I learned was not to exclude!
—Aidan, age nine

Kids get made fun of for who they are and when I see this discrimination I stand up for the victims. It's okay to be different.
—Johan, seventh grade

Additional Resources

Edginton, Shawn Marie. *The Parent's Guide to Texting, Facebook, and Social Media: Understanding the Benefits and Dangers of Parenting in a Digital World.* Dallas, TX: Brown Books, 2011.

PACER Center. "What If Your Child IS the One Showing Bullying Behavior?" 2005, 2015. www.pacer.org/parent/php/PHP-c109.pdf.

US Department of Health and Human Services. "Stop Bullying on the Spot." N.d. www.stopbullying.gov.

thirteen
what parents want

Parents can only give good advice or put them on the right paths, but the final forming of a person's character lies in their own hands.
—Anne Frank

In the beginning of parenthood, there is sheer panic. They send you home from the hospital with your precious little newborn and the realization hits you over the head: this kid doesn't come with an instruction book! Suddenly, you're on your own. You start with simple problems such as whether to throw the binky into the dishwasher if it hits the floor or simply give it a quick rub with your shirtsleeve; did you realize that first-time parents tend to answer that one *verrrrry* differently than parents who've had two children or more (i.e., the famous five-second rule that eventually takes over the household)? As the kids get bigger, the problems do, too.

When my kids were growing up, I did not feel confident that I could handle all situations and sought input from others. My husband, who commuted from Central Jersey to New York City every day, was typically not home until 9:00 p.m., when the kids were almost in bed, leaving me a greater share of the responsibility. I read as many parenting books as I had time for, but I also asked friends for their advice when we encountered situations in which we weren't sure what to do.

In the end, you weave together what you've learned through life experiences and the advice you've receive from friends, family, and books. Put it all together, and you find you have woven a tapestry of your own set of parenting values.

Let's explore what you want for your children contrasted to what most parents want for their children. It might be the same thing, but it might differ.

What Do Parents Want?

In the beginning of this book, I asked you to rank the top nine things you want for your children. Now I want you to rank them again to see whether your priorities have changed after reading more than half of this book and trying some of my recommendations. This time, I want to steer you away from the obvious things like a good education, a job, high SAT scores, marriage, career, and so on. Think about core child-rearing values.

Now, compare your selections to the intrinsic characteristics listed in a national Pew Research Center survey in 2014 as those that will make your child a success. This is your chance to see how you compare. These are the values listed in the survey (in no specific order):[1]

- Hard work
- Independence
- Empathy

- Good social-emotional skills
- Tolerance
- Learn responsibility
- Religious faith
- Being well mannered
- Help others

Notice what has changed in your rankings and discuss the changes with your spouse or significant other. If you're feeling bold, you can even discuss this with your entire family.

action tips

So, what do parents want? The Pew Research Center asked parents in the survey what is "especially important to teach children."[2] Pew surveyed 3,243 adults on the traits that are most important to teach children, finding that an overwhelming 94 percent said it is important for children to learn responsibility, 92 percent agreed that hard work is important to teach, and 86 percent responded that helping others is significant. Being well mannered was rated fourth. Other traits rated as important, although not as high as the first four, were independence (79 percent), creativity (72 percent), empathy (67 percent), and tolerance (62 percent). That's a number seven ranking for empathy, closely followed by tolerance (which today really means "acceptance"). See figures 13.1–13.3.

Pew then compared the responses across age groups, looking at what's considered important for tots, tweens, and teens. Not surprisingly, parents' viewpoints toward empathy and other values were fairly similar regardless of the child's age.[3]

But if we contrast married mothers with single moms, the rankings are shaken up a bit.[4] Married mothers were more likely than single mothers to say it is important to teach children empathy (81 percent of married mothers versus 60 percent of single mothers). In my opinion, single mothers are trying to survive and in some cases may not feel they have the luxury of teaching empathy.

In most cases, however, married and single mothers view child-rearing values similarly. For instance, overwhelming percentages of both groups (96 percent each) say it is important for children to be taught responsibility, and about half (50 percent of married mothers, 55 percent of single mothers) view it as "most important" to teach their children accountability.

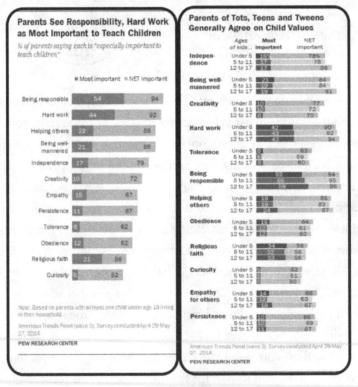

Figure 13.1 and 13.2
"Families May Differ, But They Share Common Values on Parenting,"
Pew Research Center, Washington, D.C., September 18, 2014.
https://www.pewresearch.org/fact-tank/2014/09/18/families-may-differ-but-they-share
-common-values-on-parenting/

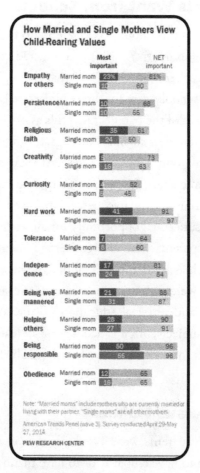

Figure 13.3
"Families May Differ, But They Share Common Values on Parenting." Pew Research Center,
Washington, D.C., September 18, 2014. https://www.pewresearch.org/
fact-tank/2014/09/18/families-may-differ-but-they-share-common-values-on
-parenting/

The *New York Times* conducted an online survey of newspaper subscribers, asking parents to rank the most important attributes for children: (1) funny, (2) healthy, (3) kind, (4) rich, (5) smart, (6) strong, or (7) unique. I was thrilled to see that "kind" won first place at 47 percent. Go kindness![5]

What Parents Want from Schools

What do parents want schools to contribute to their children's education and development? A survey conducted for the American Federation of Teachers found in 2017 that the highest priority that parents held for schools were for their children to be safe and secure. Sixty-eight percent of the parents rated this as extremely important.[6] In these days of senseless school shootings, this finding makes sense.

Parents also want schools to develop their children's knowledge and academic skills: 63 percent of the participants voted this extremely important. Sixty-two percent believed it was extremely important to ensure equal opportunity for all students.

Of course, parents were also concerned about evolving trends in education such as local and federal budget cuts, but among their other concerns were cutbacks in nonacademic areas such as art, music, libraries, and physical education (78 percent). Considering classes in these subjects, often called "specials," foster teamwork and superior social-emotional skills, we, too, should be fearful when they are cut.

Empathy versus Manners

In another study, parents were asked whether it was more important for children to have empathy or to have manners. More parents chose manners: 58 percent. (Yikes, please rush out and buy them a copy of this book!) Said Jennifer Kotler Clarke, who blogged about the study for the Joan Ganz Cooney Center, "If the surface behaviors involved in manners is seen as more important than truly understanding where other people are coming from and how they might feel, we . . . have a lot of work to do."[7] I couldn't have said it any better.

Clarke, who works for Sesame Workshop, recommends that parents take the *Sesame Street* "K Is for Kind" survey.[8] Sesame Workshop conducted a national survey, and as you answer the questions, you will simultaneously be able to see how other parents rated kindness. I urge you to take the survey and hang on through the last page, which gives tips on how to teach kindness, including telling your children how "kindness is being a friend"; "kindness is giving, speaking, and doing"; and "kindness is being thankful." By taking the survey, not only will you have learned more about life skills, empathy, and kindness, but you will have been educated on how most other parents value them as well.

As you go on through parenthood, you will find your self-confidence in your skills growing. But knowing how your values fit in with those of others—and knowing how empathy and kindness count—can only bolster the benefits!

fourteen

self-compassion and self-empathy

Knowing that we can be loved exactly as we are gives us all the best opportunity for growing into the healthiest of people.
—Fred Rogers (Mister Rogers)

[t]rue empathy is always free of any evaluative or diagnostic quality. This comes across to the recipient with some surprise. "If I am not being judged, perhaps I am not so evil or abnormal as I have thought. Perhaps I don't have to judge myself so harshly."
—Carl R. Rogers

It's hard to imagine that a singer as famous as Rihanna, who has multiple Grammys to her credit and was named the world's richest female musician by *Forbes* magazine in 2019—raking in more dollars than even Beyoncé and Madonna—ever had self-esteem issues. She seems to be the epitome of someone with confidence in her abilities and beauty. But it's true.

In 2012, just before a London performance for which she was being paid $1 million, Rihanna enrolled in sessions for "confidence counseling." "I just had to face my fear," she said. "You always find something wrong, you always find something you're uncomfortable with, and one thing turns into another and you get embarrassed and self-conscious about it—you feel like everybody can see what you see."[1]

She's far from the only one. Superstars such as Sandra Bullock, Will Smith, and even arguably the greatest actress who ever lived, Meryl Streep, have admitted to bouts of self-doubt and low self-esteem. Streep once said, "I have varying degrees of confidence and self-loathing." Imagine that!

I know I'm not alone when I tell you I've experienced the same thing. I used to spend so much time beating myself up, wasting sadness and energy. I can't think of one benefit from being mired in the depths of despair for the "sin" of failing to be perfect. I know no parent wants his or her child to go through this.

One of the best ways to address low self-esteem is through self-compassion. Research indicates there are many benefits for those with self-compassion, which refers to being kind to yourself. It is a great way to improve your mental health and the well-being of those around you. And you will not be surprised when I say that the way to increase self-compassion is, yes, empathy! I extol empathy for others, but first you need to be empathetic to yourself.

Self-compassion is a great treatment plan for low self-esteem. "[S]elf-compassion and treating yourself with the same kindness and care you treat a friend" is what Kristen Neff, a professor of educational psychology at the University of Texas at Austin, recommends. Another approach is to be "kind and understanding toward one's self in instances of pain or failure rather than being harshly self-critical."[2]

Self-esteem is a judgment about how valuable you are, but self-compassion sidesteps this inner critical dialogue of woe. When a child develops self-compassion, motivation shifts. This dovetails nicely with the "growth mindset" that I have discussed at length in this book. You perform better out of a place of kindness for yourself than from a place of self-criticism and fear, according to Neff. "When we are self-compassionate, we remind ourselves: 'I am a human and the human condition is imperfect for all of us,'" she says.

Following are Neff's tips on how parents and teachers can help children learn self-compassion:[3]

- **Remind yourself that we're all human**: If we can be supportive of others, we can give ourselves permission to treat ourselves with equal kindness.

- **Trade criticism for supportive feedback**: If your child comes home with low grades on tests and report cards, take advantage of the teachable moment. Mistakes are an opportunity to learn more.

- **Model compassionate self-talk**: Let your kids see you be self-compassionate, too. If you encounter failure, demonstrate how you acknowledge that everyone makes mistakes and move on to solving the problem instead of beating yourself up and taking your problems out on others.

- **Be a good friend to yourself**: Children understand the concept of friendship by age seven. So when children feel frustrated or upset, teach them to ask themselves, "What would you say to a friend in this situation?"

- **Try deep breathing and mindfulness**: Teach your kids not to give in to the spike of adrenaline and anxiety that can accompany making mistakes. Tell them to take deep breaths to slow down their respiration while putting their hands on their hearts.[4]

Teens

Stress is exponentially increased today for teens, whose lives are complicated by, among other things, the pressures involved in trying to live in a social media world. Fortunately, there are programs on self-compassion targeted at high schoolers. One such program—the Inward Bound mindfulness program—encourages teens to analyze stress and cultivate self-compassion. In this program, teens are encouraged to focus on their breathing and asked to repeat, "May I be happy, may I be safe, may I be at ease." Then the teens are asked to extend that phrase to loved ones and even people they don't like. They are first creating self-acceptance and then using that love from within to extend outward with empathy toward others.

"May I be happy" and similar phrases are a nice way to open or close family meetings. Together, you can make up a new self-compassion mantra unique to your family. Or how about having each family member invent his or her own personal mantra? Have fun with it and be creative! I suggest phrases such as "I am still learning," "Who can I ask for help?" "I am resilient," "I will do better next time," and, of course, "Everyone makes mistakes."

> *Little by little we human beings are confronted with situations*
> *that give us more and more clues that we are not perfect.*
> —Fred Rogers

By reducing the physical symptoms of stress, tweens and teens take a big step forward. But of course we are addressing mental health, too. Responding to personal failures with kindness rather than criticism contributes to improved emotional well-being for adolescents. Self-compassion helps teens realize that they're not alone in their struggles; they are "part of the larger human experience" and less isolated, says Neff. Furthermore, Neff's research indicates that self-compassion is positively correlated with less depression and anxiety.[5]

The better our children handle stress, the better they can handle academic and other pressures.

In one study conducted by the University of California, Berkeley, researchers found a surprising way to increase self-compassion: acting compassionately toward others. The researchers asked one group of participants in a study to provide support to another person, such as writing down suggestions to make a friend feel better after he or she had caused a car accident. The other group was just asked to recall a fun time with a friend or to read about others enduring suffering. The support-giving group wound up giving themselves a higher grade for self-compassion than the other group.[6] The implications of this finding are tremendous for the Empathy Advantage: empathy engenders self-compassion. They go together like macaroni and cheese.

"There was a unique benefit to giving support—the benefit wasn't just from feeling connected or realizing that others had problems, too," said Juliana Breines, who performed the study with fellow researcher Serena Chen.[7]

Self-Compassion in Schools

Why can't our schools teach self-compassion? This is a good question. They should! With pressure from parents on grades and testing, many schools are giving scant attention to social-emotional learning (SEL). In a workshop I attended, teachers were complaining about the low status in schools of social-emotional skills, which include self-compassion.

Interestingly, there is no shortage of programs for SEL overall—a review of eighty-two school-based SEL programs in 2018 found them to be effective, with lasting benefits—yet programs on self-compassion as well as on compassion for others were noticeably absent. Such programs were found to exist for adults, but not kids. The data show that they *could* be used to teach compassion, but they're not being used with small children, teens, or young adults.[8] So there's a lot more that can be accomplished at home and in classrooms.

Feelings Vocabulary

Teachers at the Tolerance Center who work with preschool and elementary children have shared that young children are less able to express how they are feeling. Although they understand, anger, happiness, sadness, and other basic emotions, they are less able to express the subtler feelings and emotions: anxiety, fear, sympathy, guilt, and so on.

Karen E. Gerdes, an associate professor in the School of Social Work at Arizona State University, says self-compassion can help in that regard: "A lot of kids don't have self-soothing behaviors nor know how to manage their feelings." However, self-compassion improves individual ability to articulate feelings. "It provides a vocabulary," she says.[9]

Collecting and Self-Compassion

Since elementary school, I have loved to collect and share my collections of dolls (let's hear it for Barbie and Ken!), clothes, retro hats/hat pins, photos, handwritten letters, report cards, favorite birthday cards, theater playbills, scrapbooks, and other memorabilia with my family. A hoarder, you say? I think that's pretty typical for my generation, actually.

I did a report on snowy owls in fifth grade and have been in love with them ever since. Five years ago I started collecting owl tchotchkes (knick-knacks). It wasn't a conscious decision. It just made me feel happy, so now I have twenty owls made of glass, stone, clay, and acrylic.

Objects that we treasure evoke priceless memories, allowing us to hold on to the past. They're gateways into self-compassion, making us feel good about ourselves and our personal history. They trigger recollections of good times and good friends.

Peter Funt, writing in the *New York Times*, noticed this as well. Postcards, printed photos, and the biggest endangered species—the handwritten letter—are going the way of home milk delivery. Emails and digital photos just don't elicit memories the same way. They don't have that touch and feel. And that's a real loss.[10]

Mark B. McKinley, a psychologist who teaches at Lorain Community College (and the author of many books on collections), told Funt that collections can "serve as a means of control to elicit a comfort zone in one's life . . . calming fears, erasing insecurities." Funt theorizes that collecting things is "critical to the mental and emotional development of kids." Not to mention, he added, will your kids frame their first paycheck, or will it be paid by direct deposit?[11]

Share your collections with your kids! Next, create a self-compassion box for each of them. Have them select only things that evoke great memories and  good times, such as special greeting cards, small gifts or toys, or perhaps something from nature. Then put them in the special box (at least shoebox size) and work with your kids on decorating those boxes (you could make one each year when they enter a new grade).

When your child feels low or lonely, sit down with him or her and open that treasured self-compassion box. Revisit good times and favorite things, allowing your child to regenerate self-worth.

We Do It at the Tolerance Center

A few years ago at the Tolerance Center we did an analysis of our empathic concern learning scores. We discovered that our efforts at teaching empathy were not as successful as we had thought. Scouring the research, we learned that we had failed at teaching self-compassion. How could we ask kids to help others and take action if they were feeling bad about themselves? Asked another way, how could they be UPstanders for others if they were not standing up for themselves?

Back to the drawing board we went, making self-compassion our target. Our new, engaging exercises added self-compassion and mindfulness, teaching youth that you can help others more effectively when you first prize yourself as a person who should not be teased or bullied, who is deserving of asking adults for intervention and help, and who is worthy of respect and kindness.

fifteen
active listening

Simply listening very attentively was an important way of being helpful
. . . listen for the feelings and emotions behind the words.
—Carl R. Rogers

or Queen Elizabeth II, active listening apparently is something to keep behind palace doors. But three cheers for Prince William and Duchess of Cambridge Kate, who have withstood pressure from their royal granny, persisting in using active listening with their own children.

In June 2016, William knelt down to talk to Prince George on the balcony of Buckingham Palace during a display by the Royal Air Force—an excellent example of active-listening technique, as being at eye level demonstrates to a child that you're paying attention. The queen, however, wasn't a fan. She tapped William on the arm and uttered words that could plainly be made out on video. "Stand up,

William," she reprimanded him.[1] But royal observers have observed that William continues to use his active listening. The headline in *People* about the incident was perfect: "Why Every Parent Should Copy Prince William's Special Dad Move with Prince George."[2] In fact, a few months later, when the royal couple landed for a visit in Canada, Kate, with Princess Charlotte at her side, was caught on camera kneeling down to be face to face at eye level with her son in active listening mode as well. She clearly wasn't bowing to the queen's protocol on active listening, either.

"Active listening is one of the most important ways you can send the message *you're important to me*," child development expert Gill Connell writes in *A Moving Child Is a Learning Child*. "Get down on the child's level, lean in and make eye contact. Hang on his [or her] every word. React with positive verbal and nonverbal cues such as nodding, smiling, and hugging."[3]

In 1957, Carl Rogers and another psychologist coined the term *active listening*. This term has endured for more than sixty years. Active listening is another strategy for increasing empathy. It communicates that you care about what is being shared and requires that you

1. ask open-ended questions,

2. reflect another's feelings (show understanding for how they feel),

3. clarify, and

4. summarize what you hear.[4]

One of the earliest books on empathy I discovered was by David A. Levine, *Teaching Empathy: A Blueprint for Caring, Compassion, and Community*. Levine is a teacher, author, facilitator, and musician and has been working with students, teachers, and parents across the United States and abroad since 1984. He is the founder and director of Teaching Empathy, a training, development, and research group that is devoted to creating emotionally safe learning communities. He emphasizes musical expression, social skills development, leadership training, community building initiatives, and, of course, active listening.

Active listening is an important commitment for you to make to your family members because you are valuing what each person has to say. It will help in all relationships, including with friends, family members, and colleagues, as well as in job interviews and team and career skills.

Among the tips for an effective listener, according to Levine, are those used by William and Kate: good eye contact and good listening posture.[5] Part of that is having your kids put their phones down, I'd add (don't be surprised by pushback!). Active listening is not a multitasking sport.

That goes for you, too, as parents. I know we're all busy between work, activities, and taking care of the kids, but if you're on your phone or busy with other things, such as making dinner or posting on Instagram, you are unfocused and distracted. Just take five to ten minutes to stop and really listen. I promise you will reap the benefits for years to come. Active listening will be role modeled by your children and will lead to greater people skills and success in all their relationships and future job interviews.

At the Tolerance Center, we sometimes recommend engaging in Pair Shares (simply, two persons working together) to practice respect and instill empathy. You can do this in your home with a child, spouse, or friend:

1. While face to face, one person talks, and the other demonstrates both attentiveness and good eye contact.

2. Reflect back what you heard *or* ask related questions about what the person expressed.

3. Occasionally agree or do "The Nod."

I learned about "The Nod" from an article in the *New York Times* by Adam Bryant. Bryant is a respected and noted expert on executive leadership, whose work includes columns in newspapers, coaching CEOs, and many books on leadership.

Here's his advice: lean in, nod your head, and keep nodding. "Use body language to add energy to the conversation," he writes. "Even if you are listening intently, you have to *show* people you are listening to them."[6]

Another tip from Bryant: Don't cross your arms or appear like you don't care. "Listening, done well, is an act of empathy," he writes. "You are trying to see the world through another person's eyes, and to understand their emotions. That's not going to happen if you are judging the other person as they're talking. It will dampen the conversation, because you will be sending all sorts of subtle nonverbal cues that you have an opinion about what they're saying. If you go into the discussion with the main goal of understanding their perspective, free of any judgment, people will open up to you, because they will feel they can trust you to respect what they are saying."[7]

Other best advice on active listening is offered by the Relationship Foundation,[8] which really gets both empathy and listening, providing individuals with communication skills that empower them to express confidence, leadership, and empathy in all of their relationships. The foundation refers to empathy as the "Art of Listening." For example, if someone says, "I'm so tired, I couldn't get any work done," the foundation advises *not* doing the following because these actions cause distance and disconnection, blocking empathy:

- One-upping: "I'm so tired myself. I couldn't get any work done either."

- Advising/fixing: "Maybe you should get more sleep."

- Educating: "There's a good book you should get on sleep and productivity."

- Analyzing: "You know, this seems to be a pattern of yours."

- Consoling: "That's too bad. I'm sure tomorrow things will go better."

- Discounting: "Okay, but shouldn't you just be glad you have a job?"[9]

Have a discussion with your family to review typical responses you use, and then shift to practice some of the following suggestions from the foundation:

- "I hear you." Said with sincerity, this meets a person's need to be heard.

- "Tell me more." Said with sincerity, this shows you are really interested.

- "Wow." Said softly, this gives the speaker a sense you are listening.

- "I don't even know what to say right now, I'm just grateful you told me."[10]

I also like these listening tips from the *Positivity Blog*:

1. Keep in mind: listening is win/win.

2. Tell yourself that you'll tell someone else about this conversation later on.

3. Ask instead of trying to mind read.

4. Consider sharing what you have done in a similar situation.[11]

Tweens, Teens, and Active Listening

Although previous chapters discussed tweens and teens, it's worth reminding you that both middle and high schoolers really want to "be heard" despite any protests to the contrary suggesting they don't want to talk. Adolescence can reshape happy, talkative children into sullen and moody kids, caught in the whirlpool of academic and social pressures.[12] Active listening and empathy are keys to winning them back—at least to some extent. The older kids get, the less useful discipline may be. Active listening is an important addition to your survival toolkit, one that you can learn through dedication to practicing what you have learned here.

Make some time for active listening, as I did with my kids. Honestly, sometimes while listening I was wincing inside. Fortunately, I was a good actress. Hearing about the challenges happening all around them—including about sex and drugs—can be trying, but I strengthened my relationships with both of my kids as a result. I listened and did not judge (unless there was a safety issue). My reward is that I get to be a "listening board" (as opposed to a "sounding board") for my millennial children even today.

Active Listening Done Right

Close attention demonstrates to the speaker that you care about what he or she has to say. Consider what your body is doing. Look in the mirror. Is there a better way to position yourself to demonstrate you are really listening? Do you have your own technique to share with your family? Maybe your kids have some ideas to share.

One other friendly reminder. In the words of Stephen R. Covey, "Most people do not listen with the intent to understand; they listen with the intent to reply." If we only focus on what we are saying next, we are not listening and not engaged empathetically. Case closed.

The Empathy Guy

One of my favorite active listeners is Edwin Rutsch, widely known as the Empathy Guy. Rutsch tweets regularly about empathy and has a website chock-full of empathy resources, including experts, history, quotations, and interesting interviews, as well as information on books and conferences. He is fostering meet-ups called empathy circles, at which people meet face to face to have conversations, sometimes even difficult ones. He strives to build a culture more infused with empathy. Guru that he is, I have to wonder why he hasn't written a book yet. Follow him on Twitter as I do: I think you will find him inspiring.

Kidsbridge Activity

Of course, we practice what we preach. At the Tolerance Center, we integrate active listening into our Ice Breakers (the first activities) and throughout our program in Pair Shares (two kids face to face together). During Ice Breakers, students are encouraged to be respectful and listen to each person talking; if there is too much chat, we stop the activity and ask whether it is important that each and every voice be heard. Of course they agree, but it is important that we model that students should not talk over one another. We emphasize that honing their listening skills will serve them well in the future.

Sometimes something as simple as a stick can help teach active listening. At Kidsbridge, we occasionally use a "talking stick." Anything can serve as a talking stick: a marker, a spoon, or a toy. We even

245

have a fake sponge microphone in the center
for fun.

- Share that in many Native
  American tribes, people
  used "talking sticks" to
  make sure that each person
  in the tribe had a turn
  to speak.
- Whoever has the stick gets to talk, and others
  have to listen respectfully, modeling the tips out-
  lined in this text.
- You can also use this activity for conflicts
  between siblings (try testing it for conflicts between spouses and let me know how
  that works!).

Before I conclude this chapter, I want to share my theory that great artists are great listeners. Whether they're involved in art, literature, theater, or philosophy, artists are carefully listening to reflect on the cultures they inhabit. Your kids might not grow up to be great artists, but your family can still be inspired by the following quotes, one from the great storyteller Ernest Hemingway and one from the ancient Greek philosopher Epictetus:

> *I like to listen. I have learned a great deal*
> *from listening carefully. Most people never listen.*
> —Ernest Hemingway

> *Nature gave us one tongue and two ears*
> *so we could hear twice as much as we speak.*
> —Epictetus

Reading Up

Active listening can be fun. After you read a book together or practice some activities, reward your partners with some silly, fun books. The following are a few you might want to try. A good book on listening for teens is also listed.

Picture Books for Younger Kids

- *Crunch, the Shy Dinosaur*, by Cirocco Dunlap, illustrated by Greg Pizzoli (New York: Random House Books for Young Readers, 2018), helps young readers learn to socialize and pick up social cues via a bashful brontosaurus.

- *Strega Nona*, by Tomie dePaola (New York: Aladdin Paperbacks, 1975), is about Big Anthony, who nearly destroys the whole town because he can't listen when the magical Strega Nona tells him not to touch the pasta pot.

- *Listen and Learn*, by Cheri J. Meiners (Minneapolis, MN: Free Spirit Publishing, 2003, 2017), is a colorful book to show the importance of listening at school.

Elementary-Age Kids

- *Is Your Child Really Listening? One Minute Games to Help Kids Focus*, by Rhea Farbman (n.p.: CreateSpace, 2015), includes short, snappy activities to get your child to focus and listen.

Teens

- *Communication Skills for Teens: How to Listen, Express, and Connect for Success*, by Michelle Skeen, Matthew McKay, Patrick Fanning, and Kelly Skeen (Oakland, CA: Instant Help Books, 2016), teaches about active listening, assertiveness, compassion, and more.

sixteen
empathy and gender

Kindness and gentleness never had a gender, and neither did empathy.
—Rebecca Solnit

my daughter is a grown-up, successful woman putting in twelve hours a day doing something she is passionate about: working for an entrepreneurial startup that brings organic food to young people. I am very proud of her.

Having buttered her up a bit, I hope she won't want to kill me when she reads what's next. Sometimes I think back to a time when I was frustrated and didn't know how to curb her annoying habit of looking in the mirror. She was obsessive about her appearance when she was about eight years old. I knew this obsession came in large part from mass media, with the constant and overwhelming barrage of messages through advertisements and TV shows to girls about looks, makeup, and clothes. These messages brainwash them to care only for their appearance, not about social-emotional skills like kindness or leadership or about academic skills such as math or science.

I would ask her to stop looking in the mirror or try to shift her attention in some other direction, but to no avail. My point is that if our daughters are staring at their mirrors (or the newest craze—using their smartphones' cameras as mirrors), that leaves less time for face-to-face skills and empathy. I don't know anyone who can learn empathy while staring at themselves. My son never seemed to have this problem. In other words, issues with empathy can vary by gender.

What's Going On with Girls?

In 2011, I was stopped dead in my tracks by the results of an excellent (yet alarming) study by the Girl Scouts, which makes it clear that girls think reality shows are real life. Seriously? The study also says these shows promote negative behavior. Following are some of the detailed findings about girls' viewpoints, those who watch reality shows as opposed to those who don't:[1]

- Gossip is a normal part of relationships between girls (78 percent of reality-show viewers vs. 54 percent of nonviewers).
- It's girls' nature to be catty and competitive (68 percent vs. 54 percent).
- It's difficult to trust other girls (63 percent vs. 50 percent).

Also, girls in the survey were more likely to think people have to lie to get what they want (37 percent vs. 24 percent) and that being mean earns someone more respect (28 percent vs. 18 percent).[2]

Yikes, these findings are empathy killers! In one blow, that survey reinforced my commitment not only to increase Kidsbridge's efforts to teach kindness at the Tolerance Center but also to double our efforts to teach empathy. With empathy, girls could walk in the shoes of another girl, trust that girl, not be catty or competitive, and prize friendship with others.

Claire Cain Miller, who writes about gender issues for the *New York Times*, argues that girls are getting mixed messages. On the one hand, they are getting some good, powerful messages from society that they can succeed in areas traditionally dominated by boys, such as science and sports. But on the other hand, she says, they're hearing that "[w]hat they look like matters more than" anything.[3]

Furthermore, she says, boys are somewhat stuck in the roles dictated by traditional gender norms. Girls feel free to vent their feelings by crying, screaming, or talking about them. But boys are still expected to be strong, athletic, and stoic. When they are sad or scared, they feel pressured to suppress those feelings.[4] They need to broadcast that they are tough and strong. Sadly, "man-up" philosophies were and still are prevalent.

These kinds of stereotypical feelings on both sides are empathy inhibitors and reinforce the urgency of your duty as a parent or teacher to counteract the dictates of culture and our society.

What's Going On with Boys?

Two decades ago, the psychologist William Pollack theorized that boys start out sensitive but, through a "shame hardening process," are told to stop crying and stop showing emotions.[5] This must be so confusing for boys.

Moises Velasquez-Manoff, a *New York Times* contributing writer and author of *An Epidemic of Absence: A New Way of Understanding Allergies and Autoimmune Disease*, is spot on when he says, "We learn to wear masks." What a perfect metaphor. Velasquez-Manoff goes on to advise parents, "Take off your mask. Don't shame your son. Treat women well." He also advises parents to talk to their boys about what a healthy relationship looks like.[6]

Jackson Katz, the author of *The Macho Paradox*, whom I heard speak a few years ago, is really on the mark on how to counsel boys. He recommends that parents expose boys early to discussions about feelings and help them develop a vocabulary for talking about feelings.

Barbara Risman, sociology professor at the University of Illinois at Chicago, told Miller what boys are up against: "I call it boys policing each other to be boyish, particularly when showing emotions or wanting to do something considered feminine, like volleyball or ballet. Boys have the sense that they can't stray a bit."[7]

Peggy Orenstein, a longtime reporter and author of books including *Girls and Sex*, surprised herself and her fans by deciding that after decades of writing about girls, it was time to write about teenage boys' lives. Her new book, *Boys & Sex: Young Men on Hookups, Love, Porn, Consent, and Navigating the New Masculinity*, encourages parents to talk to their sons about relationships. "We're asking boys to navigate contradictory messages about what it means to be male," said Orenstein, "to on the one hand be better men, to behave with integrity and responsibility in intimate relationships, to value mutuality and egalitarianism, while that's in direct conflict with some pretty entrenched messages guys get, telling them that being a 'real man' means exactly the opposite."[8]

If we let boys learn through what they see in the media, and they learn about sex and consent via pornography, empathy in their future relationships is doomed.

Interestingly, folk wisdom indicates that girls are more empathetic than boys. But there is the distinct possibility that culture is making a majority of the difference, says one scientist, Gwen Dewar. Experiments have shown that while females report greater empathy, such as when kids look at animated clips of people getting hurt, the physiological signs that reveal empathy (such as cerebral blood flow) show no differences.[9]

A Primatologist Weighs In

Across the world, women do have more empathy than men, according to renowned primatologist Frans de Waal. Anthropologists have surmised that from the beginning of our species, women needed more empathy than men to focus on infants and toddlers. Girls are more prosocial than boys in the following ways:[10]

- They are better readers of expressions.

- They are more attuned to voices.

- They are more remorseful after hurting someone.

- They are measured to be better at taking another's perspective.

Research also says boys are less attentive to others' feelings, more action oriented, and rougher in play than girls. Not differing too much from Dewar, de Waal says there is some physiological basis baked in, but it's not all about hardwiring.[11]

De Waal comments on the variations in empathy related to age: "The first sign of emotional contagion—one baby crying when it hears another baby cry—is already more typical of baby girls than baby boys ... gender differences usually follow a pattern of overlapping bell curves: Men and women differ on average, but quite a few men are more empathic than the average woman, and quite a few women are less empathic than the average man. With age, the empathy levels of men and women seem to converge."[12]

Going back to Homo sapiens' hunter-and-gatherer days, I feel it makes sense that evolution would produce females with higher levels of empathic concern. Mothers were the gatherers of fruits and vegetables and the face-to-face responders to children while the males were out hunting for meat and other resources. But I wasn't there, so I won't go out on a limb and say that's for certain.

I want to point out one other study, this one about adolescents and empathy. It found that girls' empathic abilities ramp up during their teens. It also found that more physically developed boys showed less empathy than those who were less physically developed.[13] It's fascinating that boys who are physically mature report less concern for others. I would chalk that up to the societal "macho" culture. Boys who don't have the stereotypical macho physique have more leeway to lean into empathy.

Breaking Gender Stereotypes at Kidsbridge

At Kidsbridge, we teach activities that raise the level of empathy as well as stereotype awareness, achieving attitude improvements that are confirmed by our research. When we taught the same activities to both boys and girls, improvement varied from question to question between boys and girls. Sometimes it was the same, but typically girls' responses were slightly different.

We have a fabulous gender activity at the Tolerance Center that encourages all children to be respectful and kind to any person, regardless of gender or gender identity. In this fun interactive activity, called Gender Game, we line up stereotypical objects, such as a football or lacrosse stick for boys, and put it next to a long column of things girls are known to like, such as makeup and shoes with high heels.

After that sinks in, we surprise the kids with a third category, called "other." Slowly, we challenge every child to participate by asking them to consider, for example, whether a girl characteristic such as long hair might be something enjoyed by a boy. Most typically say yes. Then we take a boy characteristic like playing football and ask whether a girl might want to play the sport, and most usually say yes again.

Two characteristics that are a little tougher to address come at the end of the activity: high heels and automotive repair. But by the end of the game, they really get it. They understand that boys and girls can do whatever they want. This activity leaves them, staff members, and me on a high. I feel that the kids are relieved to find out they can do and be anything they want.

This activity has been measured to also increase empathy. It teaches the kids that it's OK for a girl to be a tomboy or work on cars and for a boy to play the flute or put on ballet shoes.

Do Girls Have More Empathy?

Yes, girls do tend to have more empathy. But the question still not answered by research is whether girls are genetically born with more empathy, develop it because of our culture, or both.

I have read all the research I can focus my inquiring mind on and have reached my own unshakeable conclusion: the subject needs more study. What do *you* think?

Who has more empathy in your home? In your extended family? In the neighborhood? What a great discussion to have with your family! At any age, each family member will have unique experiences to share with you. What will the consensus be? Ask for specific examples. Who wins at empathy? I bet you're curious to see where the opinions lie in your own household!

The Best Gender Advice

Some of the best advice I have read about the path to embracing all gender expressions is in Karla McLaren's *The Art of Empathy*.

McLaren suggests that we create an empathy sanctuary in our homes and teach our children gender roles as a part of dramatic play. If your daughter is a tomboy, reinforce this behavior and tell her she's OK. If your son wants to take a ballet class, support him as well.[14]

What's novel about McLaren's advice is that she suggests you let your children know that some people will give them a hard time. *Forewarned is forearmed.* Some peers will tease a tomboy, and some peers will make fun of a boy who is passionate about ballet. If your children are prepared, she maintains, they will be able to anticipate the bullying and teasing that inevitably comes and be ready with strategies to handle it.[15] McLaren goes on to point out that you can have fun with gender in your home by proactively buying costumes and toys that are fun for any gender and inviting your children to play with them.[16]

One year for Halloween, I had my kids wear outfits that did not theoretically go with their gender. My son wore a princess outfit, and my daughter wore a tough-guy outfit. We had fun and a lot of laughs. As far as I can judge, they emerged unscathed.

Good News on Gender

Today's youth don't want to be boxed in by gender, and that's a great thing. They want to express themselves as persons. It's a confusing time for us older folks, but society is progressing.

Gender identity education is evolving, and I am happy to say that we now have many new tools to educate both boys and girls in self-compassion, respect, and mindfulness. There are many books, websites, and classes that can help you parent your way through gender using the Empathy Advantage. Use them to *your* advantage!

seventeen
empathy's cousins
social-emotional skills

The good news is the social and emotional learning
movement has been steadily gaining strength.
—David Brooks, *New York Times*, January 17, 2019

given that the title of this book is *The Empathy Advantage*, it's not a heavy lift to figure out that I have a soft spot for social-emotional learning (SEL), the set of skills necessary to help you empathize and learn how to manage your emotions.

I'm glad, as the quote from David Brooks notes, that parents and educators are increasingly learning to appreciate these empathy cousins. But their motivation isn't necessarily what it ought to be. Experts say that parents and educators view SEL as a means to achieve better classroom discipline rather than as a foundation for better academic and career outcomes over time.

In 2011, esteemed researcher Joseph Durlak conducted the mother of all meta-analyses (an evaluation of studies on 213 school-based programs involving 270,000 K–12 students). It showed that those who received high-quality SEL instruction had achievement scores that were, on average, 11 percentage points higher than students who did not.[1]

In 2017, Durlak participated in additional research that showed school-based SEL led to higher graduation rates and safer sexual behavior, even eighteen years after the program. Yes, learning how to control your emotions, as opposed to letting your emotions control you, has real, measurable results. As a parent, who wouldn't want that?[2]

The Collaborative for Academic, Social, and Emotional Learning (CASEL) has identified five core skills that are widely recognized as critical social-emotional skills:[3]

- **Self-awareness:** the ability to recognize your emotions and understand the links between emotions, thoughts, and behaviors

- **Self-management:** the ability to regulate emotions, thoughts, and behaviors

- **Social awareness:** the ability to take other's perspectives and demonstrate empathy

- **Relationship skills:** the ability to build and maintain healthy relationships

- **Responsible decision-making:** the ability to make good choices about your behavior and interactions with others

Many studies have been done with doctors to see if health outcomes can be improved using social-emo-  tional learning. One radiologist had the idea for a study to see how other radiologists, who generally don't interact with the individuals getting X-rayed or scanned, would treat their patients' cases if a photo of the individual were attached to the patient file. Dr. Yehonatan N. Turner of Shaare Zedek Medical Center in Jerusalem had tried this technique on himself initially before studying how other radiologists would react, saying that he thought "having a photo of the patient would help me relate in a deeper way."[1]

The result? Radiologists provided longer, more detailed reports for files that had a photo attached than for those that didn't. Apparently, feeling some sort of connection to patients has dividends.[2]

Notes

1. Dina Kraft, "Radiologist Adds a Human Touch: Photos," New York Times, April 6, 2009, https://www.nytimes.com/ 2009/04/07/health/07pati.html.

2. Ibid.

Gratification

I was in an art museum with my twelve-year-old daughter, wanting to share with her some of my favorite pieces of art. As we toured, I couldn't keep up with her. She was practically running through the museum, probably wanting to get back to her phone or friends. This wasn't the only time I couldn't keep my kids' attention. When they were younger, they loved family nature hikes, but I found as they got older, they became bored. At the time, my husband and I didn't know how to solve the problem, but after a while, we identified the issue. *Delayed gratification* was not something my kids could tolerate anymore. With phones, rewards are immediate. With arts and nature, that's not the case.

The granddaddy of youth psychological experiments was conducted in the 1960s by Walter Mischel at Stanford University. No book touching on social-emotional skills would be complete without discussing it. Mischel presented a dilemma to preschool and school-age participants. They could have a marshmallow now, or they could have a reward (such as two marshmallows, cookies, pretzels, and so on) if they waited, alone, for up to twenty minutes. What did he find? "The more seconds they waited at age four or five, the higher their SAT scores and the better their rated social and cognitive functioning in adolescence."[4]

The researchers continued to follow up with the children over the next several decades. They found the ability to employ delayed gratification was a gift that kept on giving. Over the years, the children who had "passed" the marshmallow test developed the following characteristics:[5]

- had a lower body mass index (BMI)
- had a better sense of self-worth
- pursued goals more effectively
- had better emotional coping skills

Fortunately, there are better methods for teaching delayed gratification than saying, "Wait … wait … WAIT!!" And, most definitely, I won't be doing any finger wagging here. Instead, I leave you with a fistful of strategies. The credit here goes to Sarah Ramirez, a writer specializing in parenting research.[6]

Avoidance

"Out of sight, out of mind" is more than just a saying. It works. When researchers covered the marshmallows, the temptation to eat them was less because the kids couldn't see them. So if there's a bowl full of Hershey Kisses that seems to call your child's name, just remove it.

De-Emphasis of Rewards

Don't make delayed gratification all about the reward. Do your best not to tell your child, "You can have a cone of ice cream after we're done shopping if you're patient." (Quick therapy session: Yes, we've all bribed our children. So don't beat yourself up over a moment of weakness.) Find other ways to motivate your child, and don't provide a reward only in response to good behaviors.

Positive Distraction

Researchers find thinking "fun thoughts" can be an effective way to get a child to wait. Have the child sing a song, tell knock-knock jokes, or engage in some other fun distraction. This works *waaay* better than threats of punishment.

Abstraction

Children in the study were able to wait longer when told to think of a marshmallow in an abstract way, as if it were a cloud, for example, rather than how scrumptious it is. Getting their intellectual capacities in gear can reduce the temptation. Have them go on a scavenger hunt for other items that are marshmallow shaped, for example.

Self-Directed Speech

Researchers found that children who engaged in self-directed speech (yes, I'm telling you to let your children talk to themselves) were able to wait longer. Successful participants repeated phrases to themselves like "I have to wait, so I can get two marshmallows." And it helped them wait.

Ramirez also had a multipronged action plan. She emphasized examining your children's self-control issues and using one of the five delayed-gratification strategies to address them. On the heels of that should come examining *your own* self-control issues. Do you have to see a movie on the first day it comes out, or are you able to wait a bit and see it when the theater is less crowded and you can get in at a discounted price? If you're the can't-wait type, maybe you're modeling the wrong things. Always evaluate your strategies, and if some of them backfire, that's OK. This is both an art *and* a science.

I've got my own toolkit, which you're welcome to try for teaching about delayed gratification:

- Have an older sister or brother mentor a younger sibling.
- At family meet- 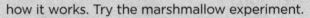 ings, have a parent or child teach an example of how delayed gratification can be rewarding. Model how it works. Try the marshmallow experiment.
- Assign family members to go on a spy mission, trying to find examples of people practicing delayed gratification in school, sports, religion, the internet, or online games, and report back to the family in a week.

Gratitude

I have been running a "youth competition for helping others" for Kidsbridge for years, and this year I received a lovely thank-you note from a winner. I was at first teary-eyed but then dumbfounded. Why was this the first thank-you note I had received? Why had Kidsbridge not received any thank yous in the previous six years? Why don't we ask our kids to express gratitude anymore?

Yes, I battled my kids to write notes after birthdays and life events, but before I proffer advice, I want to share one of my favorite thank-you notes written by my son:

> *Dear Uncle Morty and Aunt Jeanie,*
> *Thank you for the money. It really helped my money sitch [situation].*
> *Love,*
> *Jacob*

After I saw his draft, I explained to my son why he needed to try again. But I had to control myself from laughing as I did it. I held onto that draft and smile every time I glance at it. It's a keeper.

Why should we care about gratitude? It gives us an appreciation of life that we would not otherwise have. We can get lost in the wilderness of life, never feeling grateful for the simplest gifts in our world, such as trees, sunlight, or a glimmering ocean. We can also get lost in not appreciating what others do to make us happy. A 2012 poll found that 59 percent of those surveyed thought most people today are "less likely to have an attitude of gratitude than 10 or 20 years ago." The youngest group (ages eighteen to twenty-four) was the least likely to express gratitude (just 35 percent) and most likely to have self-serving reasons ("it will encourage people to be kind or generous to me").[7]

The worst thing we can do is cater to our children's every whim and not expect any kind of gratitude. That just creates entitlement. But it's never too late to work on gratitude!

Activity 1: If Jimmy Fallon can do thank-you notes on the *Tonight Show* every week for laughs, your child can do it after a birthday or special occasion for gratitude. Before you rush out to buy your child a beautiful box of Hallmark thank-you notes, how about having your child design thank-you cards himself or herself? Photocopy the design, and then have your child write a short personal note on each one.

Activity 2: What if you walked together in the shoes of the gift giver? Explain it like this: *Grandma spent a lot of time buying this present. First she asked me what you wanted. Then she had to get someone to take her to the store. Then she went to a second store. Then she had to wrap it.* You get the idea. Share that buying presents is not as simple and easy as one, two, three.

Emotional Intelligence

A friend of mine who's a fan of the Philadelphia Eagles was telling me how emotional intelligence has increased in the esteem of fans of the football team. The Eagles were in the market for a new coach after a disastrous season under a coach who could not relate to his players. The owner, Jeffrey Lurie, had fans rolling their eyes, laughing, or both when he hired coach Doug Pederson in 2016 in large part because of his "emotional intelligence." Well, no one was laughing when Pederson was holding a trophy during a parade attended by hundreds of thousands after his second season. The Eagles had won their first Super Bowl ever.

So what is emotional intelligence (EI)? A little bit of every-thing. In *The Heart of Parenting*, one of the authors, John Gottman weighs in on EI: "For parents, this quality of 'emotional intelligence' means being aware of your children's feelings, and being able to empathize, soothe, and guide them. For children, who learn most lessons about emotion from their parents, it includes the ability to control impulses, delay gratification, motivate themselves ... and cope with life's ups and downs."[8] Gottman advocates for parents to be emotion coaches. Even babies can learn from how parents handle stress, anger, and fear. "Family life is our first school for emotional learning," he writes.[9]

Three books by EI expert Daniel Goleman can help you learn more about this important subject: *Emotional Intelligence* (New York: Bantam Book, 1995), *Working with Emotional Intelligence* (New York: Bantam Book, 1995), *and Social Intelligence* (New York: Bantam Book, 2006).

What is the difference between SEL and all those other emotional terms?

Don't get caught up in semantics! For all intents and parenting purposes, *life skills, social-emotional skills, emotional intelligence*, and *social intelligence* can be used interchangeably unless you are a scholar, professor, author, or tolerance center director.

FAQ

eighteen
teaching empathy
through documentary films, storytelling, and photos

Shared joy is a double joy, shared sorrow is half a sorrow.
—Swedish proverb

C able news shows, newspapers, and other types of media often have a way of leaving us feeling beaten up by all manner of bad news. But if you pick your programs and surf YouTube the right way, you can find media sources that can actually make you and your child feel better. There is a wealth of wonderful documentaries, stories, and images to light up your child with compassion, enthusiasm, and curiosity.

This chapter discusses ways you can encourage your children to make use of stories to generate empathy. Not only will this reduce the concept of "the other," but, in an organic way, it will also create empathy for the hardships that others face.

Documentary Films

When you want your children to walk in others' shoes, discuss what news or historical events interest them, because passion will drive them toward learning, curiosity, and epiphanies. They could focus on the victims of a hurricane or any natural disaster. It could be a homeless person they passed on the street. It could be the burning of the Amazon rainforest in Brazil or fires in Australia, which hurt us all. Help them along the way by going to the library or sitting down with them to search online for documentary films that make individual stories come alive.

There are also children's film festivals around the country. Take your family to one of these festivals or check their websites for resources. PBS Learning Media also offers a large selection of free educational videos and resources for your family.[1]

Most middle and high schoolers have cell phones and are *waaaaay* more adept than the average adult at creating a film of their own. Have the children make their own documentary based on empathy. Have a few ideas ready, such as a neighbor who saves stray cats or a girl who cuts her hair and donates it to Locks of Love for those who have lost theirs due to health crises.

action **tips**

Storytelling

Storytelling is the oldest form of teaching (all you need to do is take one look at cave drawings, and you'll know what I mean). It is one of the most fun, creative, and enriching things you can do.

At the Tolerance Center, we ask teachers to share stories about when they were bullied, excluded, or called a name. Of course, students' expressions are rapt, and we can hear a pin drop when teachers share their personal experiences. When the teachers are shy, sometimes I share my own stories. I start out something like this: "When I was your age, kids would make fun of my middle name by teasing me, singing a song about it, and making me cry." I do this so kids and youth visiting the Tolerance Center know that there is nothing shameful about being teased and that it's OK to feel a variety of emotions, including sadness.

Share stories that you have heard from your parents or your grandparents. Perhaps you can share tales of the obstacles that your ancestors experienced as immigrants to this country. You might reveal how you helped others, or perhaps how others helped you and how you were affected. The objective for all such stories is to have your children "walk in your shoes" or in the shoes of others who have less than they do.

According to Karla McLaren, whom we met in chapter 4 on defining empathy, good storytelling teaches children how to feel and recognize emotions, helping children, tweens, and teens develop their emotional vocabularies and skills. In fact, she says, no matter how old you are, "You live in a social world of stories" that teach you how you fit in from everything to your family to your school to your country.[2] "In stories, we learn how to feel, how to empathize, how to approach huge emotions like terror and grief, how to interact in love and during conflict, and how to become social and moral beings," she says. "Yet this learning doesn't end in childhood, because no matter how old you get, stories continue to provide you with basic emotional and empathic training."[3]

The structure for good storytelling technique can be complicated, but we can condense the lesson plan into two parts (can't get any more doable than that!):

1. Describe an obstacle.

2. Share whether there was a solution.

Don't feel that you have to have a happy ending to every story. As we all know, life is sometimes like that.

Photos

Photos have been very powerful in my life and a useful teaching tool at the Tolerance Center. One of the most effective ways to generate empathy is showing photos of children or adults suffering around the world. At the Tolerance Center we have to be discreet when sharing photos of distressed families in Darfur, an area of the South Sudan in Africa. We make sure the photos are developmentally appropriate for the age group we are teaching.

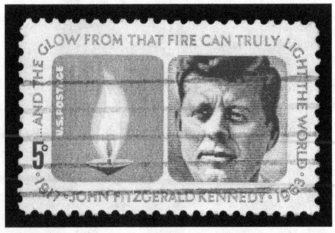

A postage stamp to honor President John F. Kennedy; images of the assassination shook me to the core. I was in fifth grade. Photo 69929854 © Maxironwas | Dreamstime.com

Going back in time to when I was a young girl in fifth grade, I can still replay the footage in my mind of President John F. Kennedy getting shot. It was the coming-of-age moment for TV, marking the first time such a major breaking news story was shown with ongoing live coverage. The TV stations showed the film over and over again, and I remember how he looked, and Jackie Kennedy's pink dress stained with his blood. Those are images I will never forget.

Other disturbing images that I will carry with me forever are of a three-year-old Syrian boy whose lifeless body washed up on the beach in 2015 when a boat full of refugees sank in the Mediterranean; a Vietnamese girl crying in pain, dripping in napalm (a defoliant meant to deprive Viet Cong soldiers of cover from trees during the Vietnam War); and children starving during a civil war in Nigeria. Why were adults letting this happen? I just couldn't understand it. Even more inconceivable is that children are dying today in war zones and families are still starving around the world.

How is this little boy in a refugee camp feeling? Heartbreaking images can be used to create empathy at appropriate ages. Photo 99429520 © Zatletic | Dreamstime.com

Sadly, with more than twenty million refugees around the world with no country, no resources, and no home, we will never have a shortage of such photos that give us the opportunity to understand suffering.

With strategy, photos of distress and concern can be used to grow your child/student's empathy. Ask them to describe that they see and to surmise how these people are feeling.
Photo 28552578 © Cpenler | Dreamstime.com

Shifting to a positive note, photos of courage and heroism can be both inspirational and a lesson in empathy. Show your children the picture of the man who stood in front of a column of Chinese tanks in Beijing in 1989 after troops had suppressed protests in Tiananmen Square. That is an image I will never forget. Who was that brave person, and where did he go? Would your children dare to walk in his shoes?

"Photographs . . . offer a direct effect of experience that spawns empathy. They help [children] reach out to distant times and circumstances, seeing the human beings who inhabit worlds unlike their own, as people like themselves, rather than abstractions," write Joan Skolnick, Nancy Dulberg, and Thea Maestre, social studies teachers who authored *Through Other Eyes*.[4] Don't forget to include some historical photos. "The almost palpable impact, for example, of a photograph showing would-be gold miners lined up for miles waiting to ascend a steep ridge—some of them giving in to exhaustion and frostbite and sliding back down the mountain—puts a human face on our textbook knowledge of the Alaska-Klondike gold rush," note Skolnick, Dulberg, and Maestre.[5]

So, as a parent or teacher, make use of these resources to cultivate a motivation to learn and develop empathy. Let those photos stir questions about what individuals in an image are thinking or feeling. A picture truly is worth a thousand words, if not more, when it comes to sparking empathy.

nineteen
pets and empathy

I think people should be accustomed, from their cradles,
to be tender to all sensible creatures.
—John Locke, English philosopher

a fall landed my mother in the hospital a couple of years ago. She was in pain, feeling bruised and battered both physically and emotionally. Lying in the hospital is enough to sour anyone's mood, and she was no different. She was impatient with me. She was impatient with the doctors. But then a therapy dog came into the room, guided by a nice older woman.

Miraculously, my mother transformed into a new person. She petted the dog, started calling it affectionate names, and asked the volunteer lots of questions. Suddenly, she wasn't noticing the pain. I asked the volunteer to stay longer, and she hung around for a good ten minutes before she had to go visit other patients. My mother wasn't cured, obviously, but her mood lightened for a little while, something for which I was most grateful.

Therapy dogs reached new levels of attention in February 2018 after a mass shooting at Marjory Stoneman Douglas High School left seventeen dead and shuttered classes for two weeks. When classes resumed, a group of therapy dogs greeted everyone, helping to lift the spirits of students, staff, and others in the school community as they tried to find their routines again. The dogs stayed around and even returned after summer vacation. Fourteen of them, outfitted in ribbons, bows, and anything else that constitutes a doggie's finest, were photographed and given a group page in the school yearbook.

"They provide comfort for us. They just make it really happy," teacher and yearbook adviser Sarah Lerner said on NBC's *Today* show. "They are on campus every day. The students can go pet them and spend time with them at lunch. Some of the dogs go into the classes. I sometimes have them come into my English class."[1]

What is it about therapy dogs? Well, in a nutshell, they know how to give empathy and teach us about giving it. They bring comfort and joy in hospitals and elsewhere, lifting the spirits of the elderly and others dealing with sickness and disease. We also recognize their worth for autistic children, helping children with disabilities calm down and focus more.

We know intuitively that when children are feeling calm and more confident, they can learn better in school and can focus on social skills. For some children with disabilities, pets can help them gain confidence and decrease anxiety.

It's not surprising that some kids with lagging social skills will gravitate to an animal or a pet. We see this often at the Tolerance Center. In one of our small-group activities, we ask kids to create a support team composed of both peers and adults to help prepare them for future challenges.

One of the most common questions asked by younger kids

during the activity is if they can add their pet cat, dog, or even guinea pig to the team. It's a reminder of the value of a safe "friend" who always listens and is always loving. Sadly, some of these kids do not mention any person—not one adult or peer as a friend (this situation is dealt with confidentially by informing the child's teacher)—but at least some have a pet they adore and trust.

Denise Daniels, a child development and parenting expert who specializes in social and emotional development, learned on Christmas Eve in 1989 about the unmistakable love that a pet can give. Her family's house was on fire, and their Newfoundland dog kept running back toward the house to make sure all the children were out and to make sure everybody was safe. "It was the most selfless, unconditional act of love I'd ever witnessed," she writes.[2]

So, it's no surprise that she offers this simple advice for raising empathetic kids: get them a pet. Studies indicate that children who interact with animals have high levels of empathy as well as better self-esteem and social skills. Pets can be invaluable in teaching children empathy, enhancing their social-emotional skills. There is a correlation between attachment to a pet and higher empathy scores, Daniels says. The reason is obvious: caring for a pet forces a child to focus attention on the animal rather than on himself or herself. It shifts the priority to "What are [the pet's] needs and what can I do to help?"[3] That kind of emotional learning is priceless and worth all those visits to the vet.

I can hear some parents' protest that they can't cram a pet into their busy lives. Well, if there's a will to connect your child with an animal friend, there's a way. Head down to an animal shelter and volunteer. My sister Karen chairs a local no-kill shelter. She tells me that these kinds of shelters always need walkers and groomers. Or consider temporarily fostering an animal. (Call before you go to see whether the shelter has a minimum age for volunteers.)

Alternatively, consider donating a pet to your child's elementary school (such as a hamster, goldfish, turtle, or lizard). It won't be just your child's pet, as it will belong to the whole class, but your child will be the proudest big brother or sister ever! Since pets don't speak, children need to focus on nonverbal cues. A dog might have one type of bark for wanting to go outside, another to ask for food, and another for the poor soul delivering the mail. A pet's demeanor and body language need to be interpreted, and this new skill set can be easily extrapolated to understanding humans.

A recent study about autistic children's interactions with guinea pigs showed how guinea pigs can help these children display more interactive social behavior and become less anxious. Autistic youths smiled and laughed more and frowned and cried less.[4] So if you don't like cats or dogs, guinea pigs might be an option.

Research on parrots indicates that they react the same way to trauma as humans do. And parrots, too, respond to treatment. Parrots dwelling at a garden called Serenity Park, at the West Los Angeles Veterans Administration Medical Center, administer their own special brand of therapy when being cared for by veterans with post-traumatic stress disorder.[5] After spending time with these parrots, the veterans become quite attached to them, and many of these ex-military men and women begin to heal. If you don't mind the chirping, consider parrots, cockatoos, or other kinds of intelligent birds as an option.

Need I suggest that the earlier you get a pet, the better? Children as young as four can help walk a dog and feed animals. What wouldn't a parent give to calm down a child who's anxious and can't seem to relax? Daniels also conducted research at the National Childhood Grief Institute and measured blood pressure of both dogs and children when they interacted; the experience lowered the blood pressure of the dogs as well as the children.[6]

Have a pet handy? Here are some "feelings" prompts to get your kids "walking in their pet's paws":

- How do you think Rover is feeling?
- What does a wagging tail mean?
- What if the tail is droopy?
- How can we tell if our kitty is happy or sad? Hungry? Tired of playing?

action tips

In the short term, they'll learn to take better care of their pets. In the long term, social-emotional skills will grow.

Stressed kids should be encouraged to read out loud to an animal. Knowing that animals don't judge, children are instantly comfortable. I recommend that any child at an early age be urged to read out loud to cats, dogs, or other animals. Little ones can also show picture books to animals and invent stories.

There is no shortage of research on the benefits of companion animals to children's emotional development. One wide-ranging review of the research found a clear association between pet ownership and increased self-esteem and decreased feelings of loneliness.[7] Other research points to reductions in fear and anxiety, believed to be related to increased levels of oxytocin in the brain.[8]

Yes, pets can be challenging for families with two busy parents. But the payoff is big: increased empathy for your child. Your children will tune in to an animal's wants, needs, and acceptance, translatable into people skills later in life. Not to mention that a fuzzy, cuddly, buddy who listens to Mom and Dad is a pretty good deal, too!

twenty
heroes and more heroes

the world is full of real adult role models of empathy, but there is no shortage of kids, teens, and tweens as well who may stun you with their adult-like maturity, persistence, and grace. With a little bit of research and help from your kids, you will find these role models. Following are two of my favorites who empathize with other people or causes.

Greta Thunberg, Climate Activist

At only sixteen years old, Greta was on the verge of tears, demanding that world leaders at the 2019 UN Climate Summit take climate change seriously and do something to stop a global warming trend that will affect all of the world's children in the future.

"You all come to us young people for hope," the young Swede said. "How dare you? You have stolen my dreams and my childhood with your empty words, and yet I'm one of the lucky ones. People are suffering. People are dying. Entire ecosystems are collapsing."

"This is all wrong," she said in her concluding remarks. "I shouldn't be up here. I should be back in school, on the other side of the ocean."

I watched her, riveted. How can a sixteen-year-old have the confidence to say what most others are thinking? "How dare you?" she asks. Citing more than thirty years' worth of scientific studies about climate change, Thunberg criticized adults for not developing solutions and strategies to confront global warming. She is my hero number 1.

Swedish climate activist Greta Thunberg speaks worldwide demanding urgent action on responding to climate change. She started when she was 15. Photo 232794576 / Greta Thunberg © Per Grunditz | Dreamstime.com

Haile Thomas, Nutrition Advocate

Everyone has heard about Alex's Lemonade Stand and the famous girl who started it to raise money for cancer. But have you heard of Haile Thomas?

Starting at age twelve, Haile founded an organization to address the need for health through plant-based nutrition. Now eighteen, she is an international speaker, health activist, vegan food and lifestyle influencer, the youngest certified integrative nutrition health coach in the United States, and the CEO of the nonprofit HAPPY (Healthy Active Positive Purposeful Youth). Haile gives back by focusing on culinary education in underserved/at-risk communities.

Haile Thomas speaks onstage during WE Day UN 2018 at Barclays Center on September 26, 2018 in New York City. Photo by Bryan Bedder/Getty Images for WE Day.

When you search "role models for kids," "kid heroes," "teen heroes," or "tween heroes" on the internet, search engines return inspiring stories about heroes, change makers and UPstanders. A role model is defined as "a person whose behavior, example, or success is or can be emulated by others, especially by younger people." The word to focus on is *person*. A character in a sitcom or reality show is not a person. Do not look for role models on TV; turn it off and grab your laptop, or pick up a scissors and look in a newspaper or magazine.

Discuss with your children what it takes to be a real role model. Go online and visit some of our favorite hero/role model websites, such as https://myhero.com/ or https://www.giraffe.org/, which features a Kids Only section for people who "stick their neck out." Go to the library to check out books on role models and heroes and read them to your kids. Librarians can help. To find children, tweens, or teens who are real role models and otherwise doing good things to emulate, search the library database for keywords like "heroes," "role models," and "community service."

When you notice people in the news who inspire you, print or cut out the articles and share them with your children; do a search online on a laptop sitting side by side. Explore and discover together.

action tips

If you insist on choosing movie stars as role models, there are some goodies. Natalie Portman supports an international self-sufficiency organization and has visited lowland gorillas in Africa. Mia Farrow has adopted war-ridden Darfur as her cause and travels the globe to advocate for aid. Shaquille O'Neal is in the Superman Hall of Heroes (https://www.supermanhallofheroes.com/). Shaq teamed up with the Boys & Girls Clubs of America in 1992. His relationship to the group dates back to his youth in Newark, New Jersey. He has put on many events for the Boys & Girls Clubs, including Shaq-A-Claus, Shaqs-giving, and Toys for Tots.

— top ten —
heroes / sheroes

Top Ten: Lynne's Favorite Adult Empathy Heroes/Sheroes

Hopefully you and your child have explored your top empathy heroes. Now it's my turn. I discuss here the top ten individuals who have in my eyes set an example as the ultimate in empathy givers.

You will notice I am especially in awe of empathetic and courageous journalists. I love the way David Finkel, national enterprise editor for the *Washington Post*, affirms that empathy is vital to the reporting process. "When you're underway and you're immersing yourself, that's when empathy really starts," he says. "I genuinely am interested, I don't have an agenda, I'm curious about something, I want to understand something. That's empathy all the way."[1]

WORLD
MALALA
DAY

MALALA
YOUSAFZAI

"When the whole world is silent,
even one voice becomes powerful."

Kid heroes, 'sheroes' and youth Upstanders come in all shapes and sizes. Online, search for kids making a difference with your children/students. Newspapers and magazines can be a great source also. Illustration 189914613 © Amar Tanveer | Dreamstime.com

Daniel Coronell, Colombian Journalist

Coronell, president of news for Univision in the United States, had to flee Colombia with his family after exposing links between the government and drug gangs, resulting in threats to his family. A brave journalist. Instead of thinking of himself or his family, Coronell walked in the shoes of his fellow Colombians in search of social justice. He gave back by being a journalism professor in Colombia.

Berta Caceres, Honduran Human Rights Activist

In the small mountain town of La Esperanza, the courageous Caceres spent years fighting on behalf of her indigenous people for their land rights; eventually she was assassinated.

Irv Refkin, US Spy

A daring spy for the United States and Britain, Refkin smuggled explosives to the French Resistance in Paris, infiltrated Nazi Germany to kill specific targets, and sabotaged train tracks before Europe was liberated. We can safely surmise that as a Jew, he knew that hundreds of thousands of Jews, gypsies, gay persons, and others were being murdered and felt he had to do everything in his power to win the war. Refkin was awarded the Bronze Star and other medals. He died at age ninety-six in California.

Lt. Sayed Basam Pacha, Afghan Police Lieutenant

Face to face with a suicide bomber, Pacha hugged the bomber to protect others. Although he died along with thirteen other people, and eighteen were wounded, more would have perished without his heroic act.

Anna Politkovskaya and Arkady Babchenko, Russian Journalists

Standing up for real news and the truth about Vladimir Putin and the Chechen conflict, Politkovskaya was arrested by the Russian military and poisoned, but she persevered until her eventual murder.

Babchenko, too, persisted in criticizing both Russia and Putin. He famously faked his death, working with officials to arrest Ukrainian assassins. While journalism is a reporting profession, ultimately it is also a listening profession, especially when journalists interview their sources face to face. These empathetic journalists cared deeply about their communities and countries, risking their lives.

Samuel Snipes, Lawyer

Back in 1957, this White lawyer represented an African American family that wanted to be the first to move into the new development of Levittown, Pennsylvania. Despite pushback, threats, and a mob of protestors, the courageous Snipes said he felt that the Myers family had every right to live there, and so they did. Snipes was a Quaker peace activist.

Liu Xiaobo, Chinese Human Rights Activist

Liu was a dissident who won the Nobel Peace Prize while jailed in China. He circulated petitions calling for democracy and an end to censorship in China. For putting others first, Liu was awarded the prize for "his long and non-violent struggle for fundamental human rights in China." His famous statement, "I have no enemies," expressing his devotion to peace, love, and justice, is worth reading with your family.[2] Bring a box of tissues to share.

Loujain al-Hathloul, Saudi Women's Rights Activist

This fighter for women's rights bravely defied the ban on women driving cars in Saudi Arabia by not only driving but also filming herself at the wheel and posting her videos on YouTube. After the driving ban was lifted, Hathloul and other activists were put in jail anyway. As of the printing of this book, she is still in jail for the crime of driving a car.

Susan Fowler, Sexual Harassment Whistleblower

Having heard that Uber was a woman-friendly workplace,

Fowler was excited to work there, but she found out firsthand that the company wasn't what it purported to be. She proceeded to blow the whistle after experiencing sexual harassment and retaliation. The CEO was subsequently forced to resign. She was among five women (along with actress Ashley Judd) named Person of the Year by *Time* in 2017 for helping to spark the #MeToo movement as her fight benefited women across America.

Joe Howlett, Whale Rescuer

Joe Howlett spent years untangling whales from fishing lines, feeling empathy for the trapped animals, and with his Campobello Whale Rescue Team, he probably saved at least one hundred whales off the tiny New Brunswick island in the Bay of Fundy. He died in 2017 on a rescue voyage. It's is so exhilarating to watch humans cutting whales free; check this out by searching "Joe Howlett" online.

Group Heroes: Grupo Especializado de Fiscalização (Specialized Inspection Group)

Better known as GEF (pronounced JEFF), this groups operates in some of the most remote areas of the Amazon River basin— places so remote that it takes days to reach them by riverboat or truck—in an effort to preserve it. GEF is needed more than ever, with deforestation increasing, caused in large measure by thousands of fires set by farmers and ranchers. The Amazon forest serves to cool the planet and reduce global warming and is home to thousands of unique species. GEF operates as part of Brazil's environmental protection agency, patrolling in helicopters and using satellite images to detect deforestation as well as combat animal smuggling and other activities. One of the squad members was shot in the shoulder, but that didn't stop him.

twenty-one
empathy and paying it forward

Citizens are not born, but made.
—Baruch Spinoza, philosopher

the path to becoming the first Black woman to win the Nobel Prize in literature opened for author Toni Morrison when she came to this realization: "If there is a book that you want to read, but it hasn't been written yet, you must be the one to write it." I'm no Toni Morrison (Who is? Sadly we recently lost her after eighty-eight golden years), but her epiphany resonates with me. When I could not find a parent/teacher-friendly book on empathy, I had to write it. If I can make headway in getting parents and educators to see the importance of empathy and teach it to their children/students, it will have been well worth the effort.

Here's another quotation that strikes a chord for me: Aristotle's

"We become what we practice." Considering we are born with limited and varying amounts of empathy, how motivating it is that we have the freedom and resources to increase it! If we strategize and practice, we can build this critical social skill. I want to help put empathy on the map to confront increasing name-calling, bias, and discrimination incidents across the country. Kids are suffering from increased bullying and cyberbullying, and I can't understand why we don't show that we care about each and every one of our children. I feel their pain every day.

Often we don't see their pain until it's too late. In 2017, a Cincinnati mother named Cornelia Reynolds came home one day after school to find her son Gabriel had hung himself with a necktie in his bedroom, and she subsequently sued the school district for failing to tell the family of a bullying incident two days earlier. He was eight years old. Eight! And he's not the youngest child to have killed himself, with suicides reported at as young as age five. Yes, suicide is on the rise, and it occurs even among our youngest children.[1] And yet if one child had had empathy for Gabriel and supported him, and if one college student had had empathy for Tyler Clementi and supported him (see chapter 1), maybe they would both be here today. Empathy can save lives.

There has been an accompanying increase in depression among our youth. It has been on the rise for more than half a century, with psychologist Peter Gray finding that "rates of anxiety and depression among children and adolescents were far lower during the Great Depression, World War II, the Cold War, and the turbulent 1960s and early '70s than they are today."[2] There was a 63 percent increase in major depressive episodes among adolescents aged twelve to seventeen from 2009 to 2017.[3] I mention these alarming and startling stats not to depress you but to provide hope. Armed with the new tools of empathy and mindfulness, teachers, parents, and caregivers can be smarter and more successful in reducing these alarming trends.

However, the challenges are significant. Empathy is on the decline among college and high schoolers, and in the pipeline behind them, middle and elementary school youth are at risk of being damaged even more. Teachers and parents complain that kids are increasingly narcissistic and have diminished face-to-face and interpersonal skills. Teachers want to educate and nurture, but they often run up against kids with broken moral compasses and complain that they lack the support and guidance to deal with them. An *Education Week* survey found that "while most teachers say it's important for them to teach these skills, many still don't feel equipped to help students manage their emotions—especially when it comes to the children who are facing the greatest hurdles."[4]

But parents and educators have the ability to do something about this problem. This book is just one example of the type of support that's out there for them. It's time for them to step up. Many are doing it already, and they'd love to have your company!

The Empathy Advantage Payoff: Beyond Family to Society Itself

I believe empathy is the most essential quality of civilization.
—the late Roger Ebert, film critic

Although times are challenging, the research is clear. Kids with better empathy and related social-emotional skills are kinder and more respectful, perform better academically, and experience greater success. As someone working with other professionals in the SEL sphere, I believe the field is gaining momentum, will permeate schools in the future, and can start to turn the tide.

Our society can be strengthened when we empathetically care about others—not only our family and our tribe (those closest to you) but also our community, our country, and our world.

Former *CBS News* anchor Dan Rather and coauthor Elliot

Kirschner wrote a book on patriotism in 2017. Titled *What Unites Us: Reflections on Patriotism*, it devotes an entire chapter to empathy, which I find validating and inspiring. My favorite quote in the empathy chapter is this: "When we live in a self-selected bubble of friends, neighbors, and colleagues, it is too easy to forget how important it is to try to walk in the shoes of others."[5]

In the book, Rather reminisces about how he learned about empathy. Raised in a poor family, when he asked his mother why they gave Christmas gifts to other families, his mother responded, "We do not feel sorry for them, we understand how they feel." Wow! Rather reflects that "my parents taught me about the importance of empathy through their words and deeds."[6]

Rather also looks to history for insights, saying that a "sweep of empathy continued after the war [World War II]. One of the best foreign policy efforts in American history was to help rebuild Europe and Japan. Our enemies became our friends through an acknowledgment of the common bonds of humanity."[7] Empathy makes for wise foreign and domestic policy.

In his book, evolutionary biologist David Sloan Wilson writes that "people nurturing other people" is key in life. You can be surrounded either by people who, through empathy, help your goals or by those who are indifferent or hostile to them.[8]

The Treasure We All Share

My last shout-out is for the jewel we share: Earth. Since college I have waited for its citizens to overwhelmingly appreciate, revere, and treasure what we have. Although I see pockets of hope (mostly made up of young people), I also see greed and a lack of empathy toward our planet reigning today. Climate change and pollution continue to exact a toll.

Last summer I took a walk on the beach in New Jersey. I saw small pieces of plastic wrap, nylon rope, and balloons. When I was a kid, we didn't have all this plastic littering our sands. (Have you seen the photos of autopsied whales and dolphins with their stomachs filled with plastic, which killed them?) I knelt down and picked up what I could. I figured that for every single piece of plastic I picked up, I would be saving a life—the life of a turtle, crab, or fish.

I got such a sense of satisfaction, but, sadly, there's only so much one person can do. Teaching others to clean up our beaches, parks, and other public spaces will in turn educate more individuals, bringing even greater hope. When my daughter was little, we picked up plastic while visiting a beach in Florida, and she arranged all the pieces in a rainbow of colors. Ironically, it turned into art and was somewhat beautiful as an abstraction, and we took photographs of it. (This could be a fun activity with your kids. Make it into a contest!) Don't forget to immerse your children in the miracle of this planet that we take for granted every day. Wilson uses a sailing metaphor: "Get anyone to imagine the whole earth as like a single ship, and that person will start regarding the whole earth as the appropriate moral circle."[9] It is one planet that we share, isn't it?

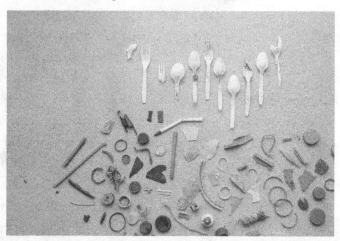

Art created by my daughter Rachel as a child from plastic cleaned up from the beach. You will have to imagine how she arranged the items into a rainbow of colors.

Empathy and Democracy

Joel Westheimer, a university research chair in democracy and education at the University of Ottawa in Ontario, has written an article on educating our children ("What Kind of Citizens Do We Need?") that focuses on the common good. He recommends[10]

- teaching your children to question
- exposing your kids to multiple perspectives
- focusing on others, both locally and nationally

I especially love this advice from Westheimer: "Students should also examine controversial *contemporary* issues. Students are frequently exposed to past historical controversies—such as slavery, Nazism, or laws denying voting rights to women—that are already settled in the minds of all but a small fringe minority. But those same students are too often shielded from matters that require thoughtful engagement with *today's* competing ideas. Yet that kind of engagement is exactly what democratic participation requires."[11] Yes, while Westheimer doesn't say it explicitly, the ability to truly hear other's ideas is best built on a foundation of empathy. The next time you're in a heated discussion, take a breath, think about what must be going on inside the other person's head, and empathize! Listen before you speak.

Even throughout history, we can see how democracy and empathy have intertwined. Alexis de Tocqueville, a famous French political thinker and sociologist, visited America in 1835. Writing in his renowned classic, *Democracy in America*, de Tocqueville observed that "habits of the heart" were what allowed Americans to maintain their democratic republic in spite of the highly individualistic values upon which the country was founded. He said its founding principle of social equality was *preserved* by the compassion that its citizens had for one another.

final thoughts

In these trying times of decreasing empathy, I am constantly inspired and fueled by the wisdom of Mother Teresa: "If you can't feed a hundred people, feed just one." That's what I do at home with my family and how we teach every day at the Kidsbridge Tolerance Center. This statement spells out a strategy on how to not be overwhelmed and discouraged. We can't tackle everything and empathize every minute of every day; it would be exhausting. But we can teach our own children empathy. We can teach entire classrooms of kids empathy to create caring communities. That's doable. It's within reach.

And like a stone when it's thrown into a pond, the effects of our actions can ripple out into the world. You just never know. Martin Luther King Jr. may have been the leader of the civil rights movement, but his partner was empathy.

When citizens watched the news and saw fire hoses and German shepherds turned on courageous African American protesters in the 1960s, the empathy in the hearts of individuals across the nation turned into a force for social change that altered the course of history. Likewise, Harriet Beecher Stowe's novel *Uncle Tom's Cabin* helped to stop slavery by encouraging empathy for all human beings. You just never know what will happen.

So get started and enjoy the small pleasures as you do it. Take your children to diverse neighborhoods and different parts of your state and let them see people and places they haven't seen before. Read to them about kids in countries that are far away but from whom they can appreciate diversity while learning about unknown multicultural ethnic groups. Have them try foods from all over the world—everything from taquitos to sushi to couscous—to get a taste of a different culture. Take the time for family meetings so your kids can understand what's going on inside you, and you can understand what's going on inside them. Help them to understand that when they see a schoolmate being bullied or excluded, they can make a difference in that child's life by standing up for him or her.

And here's one more bit of inspiration for you to teach empathy. In a recently published book, Stanford University psychology professor Jamil Zaki says the fight to build empathy is bigger than all of us. He reminds us that empathy is a gift that we can give to our children that can go on and on: "Our empathy is the legacy we leave generations to come, who must live in the world we leave behind."[1]

Teaching empathy works, and it will be worthy of the time you invest. I'll make you a promise: every time you do teach empathy, you'll feel a little enchantment in your heart. So let's start creating that legacy. Let's start paying it forward! You will never regret for a single moment trying to change a child—and our world—for the better.

about the author

Lynne Azarchi is the executive director of Kidsbridge Tolerance Center outside of Trenton, New Jersey, a nonprofit organization dedicated to fostering bullying prevention, diversity appreciation, empathy, and empowerment for youth. She is a tireless advocate for improving the lives of at-risk youth in communities across New Jersey. Kidsbridge is the only evidence-based tolerance center in the United States dedicated to youth, with more than twenty-three hundred preschool, elementary, and middle school students improving their social-emotional skills each year. Visiting youth divide into small groups to discuss strategies for addressing bullying, cyberbullying, stereotypes, media literacy, UPstander strategies, bias, diversity appreciation, and other related topics.

Azarchi graduated from Penn State University (BA in anthropology) and has an MBA in marketing/marketing research from Columbia University. She has won many awards and been published in both newspapers and academic journals. She is a frequent speaker at major educational group meetings, including the American Alliance of Museums, National Association for Media Literacy Association, and National Association for the Education of Young Children. She lives with her husband in Princeton Junction, New Jersey. To give back, she volunteers for many nonprofits in her community.

bibliography

Alexander, Jessica. "America's Insensitive Children?" *Atlantic*, August 9, 2016. https://www.theatlantic.com/education/archive/2016/08/the-us-empathy-gap/494975/.

Alexander, Jessica, and Iben Sandahl. *The Danish Way of Parenting: What the Happiest People in the World Know about Raising Confident, Capable Kids*. New York: TarcherPerigee, 2016.

American Psychological Association. "Who Is Likely to Become a Bully, Victim or Both?" July 8, 2010. https://www.apa.org/news/press/releases/2010/07/bully-victim.

Andari, Elissar, Jean-René Duhamel, Tiziana Zalla, Evelyn Herbrecht, Marion Leboyer, and Angela Sirigu. "Promoting Social Behavior with Oxytocin in High-Functioning Autism Spectrum Disorders." *PNAS* 107, no. 9 (2010): 4389–94. https://www.pnas.org/content/107/9/4389.full.

Anderson, Leigh, "Bullying: Can Schools Teach Kids Empathy." *Newsweek*, December 15, 2010. https://www.newsweek.com/bullying-can-schools-teach-kids-empathy-68795.

Arkin, Monica. "School-Based Mindfulness Programs Can Help Students Cope with Stress." Child Trends, April 16, 2019. https://www.childtrends.org/school-based-mindfulness-programs-help-students-cope-with-.

Astor, Maggie. "Dove Drops an Ad Accused of Racism." *New York Times*, October 8, 2017. https://www.nytimes.com/2017/10/08/business/dove-ad-racist.html.

Barnwell, Paul. "Students' Broken Moral Compasses." *Atlantic*, July 25, 2016. https://www.theatlantic.com/education/archive/2016/07/students-broken-moral-compasses/492866/.

Baron-Cohen, Simon. *Zero Degrees of Empathy: A New Theory of Human Cruelty and Kindness*. London: Penguin Books, 2012.

Beetz, Andrea, Kerstin Uvnäs-Moberg, Henri Julius, and Kurt Kotrschal. "Psychosocial and Psychophysiological Effects of Human-Animal Interactions: The Possible Role of Oxytocin." *Frontiers in Psychology* 3 (2012). https://doi.org/10.3389/fpsyg.2012.00234.

Benson, P. L. *All Kids Our Kids: What Communities Must Do to Raise Caring and Responsible Children and Adolescents*. 2nd ed. San Francisco: Jossey-Bass, 2006.

Bhanoo, Sindya N. "For Prairie Voles, a Furry Shoulder to Cry On." *New York Times*, January 22, 2018. https://www.nytimes.com/2016/01/26/science/for-prairie-voles-a-furry-shoulder-to-cry-on.html.

Bilton, Nick. "Looking at Link between Violent Video Games and Lack of Empathy." *New York Times*, June 15, 2014. https://bits.blogs.nytimes.com/2014/06/15/looking-at-link-between-violent-video-games-and-lack-of-empathy/.

Bischoff, Paul. "Almost 60 Percent of Parents with Children Aged 14 to 18 Reported Them Being Bullied." *VPN & Privacy* (blog), May 8, 2019. https://www.comparitech.com/blog/vpn-privacy/boundless-bullies/.

Bloom, Paul. *Against Empathy: The Case for Rational Compassion*. New York: Ecco, 2016.

Blum, Robert Wm., and Heather P. Libbey. "Executive Summary." *Journal of School Health* 74, no. 7 (2004). https://onlinelibrary.wiley.com/toc/17461561/2004/74/7.

Borba, Michele. *Building Moral Intelligence: The Seven Essential Virtues That Teach Kids to Do the Right Thing*. San Francisco: Jossey-Bass, 2001.

———. "Teen Narcissism Is Worse: Is Social Networking the Cause?" *PediatricSafety: One Ouch is Too Many*, March 14, 2016. https://www.pediatricsafety.net/2016/03/teen-narcissism-is-worse-is-social-networking-the-cause/.

Bosacki, Sandra L., Zopito A. Marini, and Andrew V. Dane. "Voices from the Classroom: Pictorial and Narrative Representations of Children's Bullying Experiences." *Journal of Moral Education* 35, no. 2 (2006): 231–45. https://doi.org/10.1080/03057240600681769.

Bowman, Sarah Lynne. *The Functions of Role-Playing Games: How Participants Create Community, Solve Problems and Explore Identity*. Jefferson, NC: McFarland, 2010.

Brazelton, T. Berry, and Stanley I. Greenspan. "Why Children Need Ongoing Nurturing Relationships." *Early Childhood Today* 21, no. 1 (2006). https://eric.ed.gov/?id=EJ745704.

Brody, Jane E. "How to Foster Empathy in Children." *New York Times*, December 10, 2018. https://www.nytimes.com/2018/12/10/well/live/how-to-foster-empathy-in-children.html?fbclid=IwAR0bCHOazAGUio3Uu2Nqmhzdp-LaO7U_lkDnZ4F4NMfPf1ZyNBGuYtykl3Do.

Bronfenbrenner, Urie. "The Origins of Alienation." *Scientific American* 251 (1974): 53–64.

Bronson, Po, and Ashley Merryman, "Even Babies Discriminate: A NurtureShock Excerpt." *Newsweek*, September 4, 2009. https://www.newsweek.com/even-babies-discriminate-nurtureshock-excerpt-79233.

Brooks, David. "It's Not the Economy, Stupid." *New York Times*, November 29, 2018. https://www.nytimes.com/2018/11/29/opinion/american-economy-working-class.html.

Brown, Jennings. "Former Facebook Exec: 'You Don't Realize It But You Are Being Programmed.'" Gizmodo, December 11, 2017. https://gizmodo.com/former-facebook-exec-you-don-t-realize-it-but-you-are-1821181133.

Bryant, Adam. "How to Be a Better Listener." *New York Times*, n.d. https://www.nytimes.com/guides/smarterliving/be-a-better-listener.

Bui, P. Kim. "The Empathetic Newsroom: How Journalists Can Better Cover Neglected Communities." American Press Institute, April 26, 2018. https://www.americanpressinstitute.org/publications/reports/strategy-studies/empathetic-newsroom/single-page/.

Burkett, James P., Elissar Andari, Zachary V. Johnson, Daniel C. Curry, Frans B. M. de Waal, and Larry J. Young. "Oxytocin-Dependent Consolation Behavior in Rodents." *Science* 351, no. 6721 (2016): 375–78. https://doi.org/10.1126/science.aac4785.

Carr, Nicholas. "How the Internet Is Making Us Stupid." *Telegraph*, August 27, 2010. https://www.telegraph.co.uk/technology/internet/7967894/How-the-Internet-is-making-us-stupid.html.

———. *The Shallows: What the Internet Is Doing to Our Brains.* New York: W. W. Norton, 2011.

Center for Parenting Education. "Freeing Your Child from Disabling Labels." n.d. https://centerforparentingeducation.org/library-of-articles/self-esteem/freeing-your-children-from-disabling-labels/.

Centers for Disease Control. "Understanding Teen Dating Violence." Fact sheet, 2014. https://www.cdc.gov/violenceprevention/pdf/teen-dating-violence-2014-a.pdf.

Certain, Laura K., and Robert S. Kahn. "Prevalence, Correlates, and Trajectory of Television Viewing among Infants and Toddlers." *Pediatrics* 109, no. 4 (2002): 634–42. https://www.ncbi.nlm.nih.gov/pubmed/11927708.

Character Counts.org. "2012 Report Card on the Ethics of American Youth." Josephson Institute, 2012. https://charactercounts.org/national-report-card/2012-report-card/.

Christakis, Dimitri A., Frederick J. Zimmerman, David L. DiGiuseppe, and Carolyn A. McCarty. "Early Television Exposure and Subsequent Attentional Problems in Children." *Pediatrics* 113, no. 4 (2004). http://pediatrics.aap-publications.org/content/113/4/708.short.

Christakis, Erika. "The New Preschool Is Crushing Kids." *Atlantic*, January/February 2016. https://www.theatlantic.com/magazine/archive/2016/01/the-new-preschool-is-crushing-kids/419139/.

Clarke, Jennifer Kotler. "Diversity: Brought to You by the Letter E; Exposure & Empathy." Joan Ganz Cooney Center, Sesame Workshop, *Blog*, July 11, 2017. https://joanganzcooneycenter.org/2017/07/11/diversity-brought-to-you-by-the-letter-e-exposure-empathy/.

Connell, Gill, and Cheryl McCarthy. *A Moving Child Is a Learning Child.* Minneapolis, MN: Free Spirit Publishing, 2014.

Cortés, Carlos. *The Children Are Watching: How the Media Teach about Diversity.* New York: Teachers College Press, 2000. https://www.tc.columbia.edu/articles/2000/november/the-children-are-watching-how-the-media-teach-about-diversi/.

Daniels, Denise. "Want to Raise Empathetic Kids? Get Them a Dog." *Washington Post*, April 14, 2015. https://www.washingtonpost.com/posteverything/wp/2015/04/14/want-to-raise-empathetic-kids-get-them-a-dog/?noredirect=on&utm_term=.7454002585a3.

Davis, Carol M. "What Is Empathy and Can Empathy Be Taught?" *Physical Therapy* 70, no. 11 (1990): 707–11. https://doi.org/10.1093/ptj/70.11.707.

Davis, Mark H. *Empathy: A Social Psychology Approach*. Boulder, CO: Westview Press, 2018.

Davis, Tchiki. "6 Tips for Decoding Emotions in Text Messages." *Psychology Today*, October 11, 2017. https://www.psychologytoday.com/us/blog/click-here-happiness/201710/6-tips-decoding-emotions-in-text-messages.

De Waal, Frans. *The Age of Empathy: Nature's Lessons for a Kinder Society*. New York: Harmony, 2009.

———. "The Evolution of Empathy." *Greater Good Magazine*, September 1, 2005. https://greatergood.berkeley.edu/article/item/the_evolution_of_empathy.

"Dear Reader: Would You Rather Raise a Child to Be . . . ?" *New York Times Magazine*, January 6, 2019.

Denham, Susanne Ayers, Hideko Hamada Bassett, and Todd Wyatt. "The Socialization of Emotional Competence." In *Handbook of Socialization: Theory and Research*, edited by Joan E. Grusec and Paul D. Hastings. New York: Guilford Press, 2015. https://www.researchgate.net/publication/232535707_The_Socialization_of_Emotional_Competence.

DePaoli, Jennifer L., Matthew N. Atwell, John M. Bridgeland, and Timothy P. Shriver. *Respected: Perspectives of Youth on High School & Social and Emotional Learning*. Chicago: Collaborative for Academic, Social, and Emotional Learning, 2018. https://casel.org/wp-content/uploads/2018/11/Respected.pdf.

Dewar, Gwen. "The Case for Teaching Empathy: Why Empathy Doesn't 'Just Happen.'" *Parenting Science*, 2009–2013. https://www.parentingscience.com/teaching-empathy.html.

Doty, James R. *Into the Magic Shop: A Neurosurgeon's Quest to Discover the Mysteries of the Brain and the Secrets of the Heart*. New York: Avery, 2016.

Dryfoos, Joy G. "The Prevalence of Problem Behaviors, Implications for Programs." In *Issues in Children's and Families' Lives*. Vol. 8, *Healthy Children 2010: Enhancing Children's Wellness*, edited by Roger P. Weissberg, Thomas P. Gullotta, Robert L. Hampton, Bruce A. Ryan, and Gerald R. Adams, 17–46. Thousand Oaks, CA: Sage Publications, 1997.

Durlak, Joseph A., Roger P. Weissberg, Allison B. Dymnicki, Rebecca D. Taylor, and Kirston B. Schellinger. "The Impact of Enhancing Students' Social and Emotional Learning: A Meta-Analysis of School-Based Universal Interventions." *Child Development* 82, no. 1 (2011): 405–32. https://www.casel.org/wp-content/uploads/2016/01/meta-analysis-child-development-1.pdf.

Eaton, Danice K., Laura Kann, Steve Kinchen, Shari Shanklin, James Ross, Joseph Hawkins, William A. Harris, et al. "Youth Risk Behavior Surveillance—United States, 2007." *Morbidity and Mortality Weekly Report. Surveillance Summaries* 57, no. 4 (2008): 1–131.

Edberg, Henrik. "How to Become a Better Listener: 10 Simple Steps." *The Positivity Blog*, updated March 4, 2019. https://www.positivityblog.com/better-listener.

Eitzen, D. Stanley. "The Atrophy of Social Life." *Society* 41, no. 6 (2004): 12–16.

Elias, Maurice. "Developing Empathy in Kids Ages 8–11." *Parent Toolkit* (blog). n.d. https://www.parenttoolkit.com/social-and-emotional-development/advice/social-awareness/developing-empathy-in-kids-ages-8-11.

"Empathy: The Art of Listening." n.d. https://therelationshipfoundation.org/images/pdfs/empathy-art-of-listening.pdf.

Erickson, Elizabeth. "Effects of Storytelling on Emotional Development." Masters of Arts in Education Action Research Papers. St. Paul, MN: St. Catherine University, 2018. https://sophia,stkate,edu/cgi/viewcontent,cgi?article=1258&context=maed.

Feeley, Jef, and Christopher Palmeri. "Fortnite Addiction Is Forcing Kids into Video-Game Rehab." *Bloomberg*, November 27, 2018. https://www.bloomberg.com/news/articles/2018-11-27/fortnite-addiction-prompts-parents-to-turn-to-video-game-rehab.

"Food Taboos: It's All a Matter of Taste." *National Geographic News*, April 19, 2004. Reprinted at Digital Chalkboard. https://www.mydigitalchalkboard.org/portal/default/Resources/Viewer/ResourceViewer;jsessionid=2gUm-2FLZUEY61Ilg37CacA**?action=2&resid=35179&discussion.ascdesc=descending&discussion.listtype=chronological.

Funt, Peter. "Does Anyone Collect Old Email?" *New York Times*, April 5, 2019. https://www.nytimes.com/2019/04/05/opinion/memory-collections.html.

Gelles, David. "Mindfulness for Children." *New York Times*, n.d. https://www.nytimes.com/guides/well/mindfulness-for-children.

Gewertz, Catherine. "Principals Dealing with Hostility and Division in the Age of Trump, Survey Shows." *Education Week*, March 13, 2019. https://blogs.edweek.org/edweek/high_school_and_beyond/2019/03/hostility_and_division_schools_in_the_age_of_trump.html.

Gillespie, Noreen. "Mother Receives Suspended Sentence in Son's Suicide." Associated Press, May 14, 2004. http://www.nbcnews.com/id/4979447/ns/us_news-crime_and_courts/t/mother-gets-suspended-sentence-sons-suicide/#.XsgzsGhKjIU.

Ginsburg, Kenneth R., and Martha M. Jablow. *Building Resilience in Children and Teens: Giving Kids Roots and Wings*. Elk Grove, IL: American Academy of Pediatrics, 2011.

Gold, Claudia M. "Adverse Childhood Experiences (ACE) Study: Beyond Screening in Pediatrics." *Child in Mind* (blog), December 14, 2017. http://claudiamgoldmd.blogspot.com/2017/.

Goleman, Daniel, Richard Boyatzis, and Annie McKee. *Primal Leadership: Unleashing the Power of Emotional Intelligence*. Boston: Harvard Business Review Press, 2013.

Goodwin, Doris Kearns. *Leadership: In Turbulent Times*. New York: Simon & Schuster 2018.

Gottman, John, and Joan DeClaire. *The Heart of Parenting: How to Raise an Emotionally Intelligent Child*. London: Bloomsbury Publishing, 1997.

Goudarzi, Sara. "Study: Why Teens Don't Care." *Live Science*, September 7, 2006. https://www.livescience.com/7151-study-teens-care.html.

Grant, Adam. "How to Create a Creative Child, Step One: Back Off." *New York Times*, January 30, 2016. https://www.nytimes.com/2016/01/31/opinion/sunday/how-to-raise-a-creative-child-step-one-back-off.html.

———. *Originals: How Non-Conformists Move the World*. New York: Viking, 2016.

———. "Raising a Moral Child." *New York Times*, April 11, 2014. https://www.nytimes.com/2014/04/12/opinion/sunday/raising-a-moral-child.html.

Gray, Peter. "The Decline of Play and Rise in Children's Mental Disorders." *Psychology Today*, January 26, 2010. https://www.psychologytoday.com/us/blog/freedom-learn/201001/the-decline-play-and-rise-in-childrens-mental-disorders.

Gross, Gail. "Violence on TV and How It Can Affect Your Children." *The Blog*. *HuffPost*, October 15, 2013. https://www.huffpost.com/entry/violence-on-tv-children_n_3734764.

Hanna, Jason. "Suicides under Age 13: One Every 5 Days." CNN, August 14, 2017. https://www.cnn.com/2017/08/14/health/child-suicides/index.html.

"Harley School Gives an Education in Empathy." *Rochester Democrat and Chronicle*, July 5, 2011.

Harmon, Joanie. "Why Critical Media Literacy Should Be Taught in Schools." Phys.org, June 4, 2019. https://phys.org/news/2019-06-critical-media-literacy-taught-schools.html.

Hart Research Associates. *Public School Parents on the Value of Public Education*. Washington, DC: Hart Research Associates, September 2017. https://www.aft.org/sites/default/files/parentpoll2017_memo.pdf.

Hill, Erin. "Why Every Parent Should Copy Prince William's Special Dad Move with Prince George." *People*, July 21, 2016. https://people.com/royals/prince-williams-special-dad-move-with-prince-george/.

Hochman, Anndee. "How Do You Celebrate 'Day of the Dead' and Other Questions N.J. Classroom Asks Kids around the World." Philly.com, March 26, 2019. https://www.inquirer.com/news/empatico-webcam-wedgwood-elementary-classroom-kind-kathi-kersznowski-20190326.html.

Hockett, Jessica A., and Kristina J. Doubet. "Empathy through Academic Inquiry: A 'Controversial' Approach." *Learning with Empathy* 13, no. 1 (2017). http://www.ascd.org/ascd-express/vol13/1301-hockett.aspx.

Hoerr, Thomas R. "Steps and Strategies for Developing Empathy." *Learning with Empathy* 13, no. 1 (2017). http://www.ascd.org/ascd-express/vol13/1301-hoerr.aspx.

Hoffman, Martin L. "Psychological and Biological Perspectives on Altruism." *International Journal of Behavioral Development* 1 (1978): 333.

Hogan, Robert. "Development of an Empathy Scale." *Journal of Consulting and Clinical Psychology* 33, no. 3 (1969): 307–16.

Holding, Sarah. "Sarah Holdings Top 10 Cli-Fi Books." *Guardian*, April 23, 2015. https://www.theguardian.com/childrens-books-site/2015/apr/23/sarah-holdings-top-10-cli-fi-books.

Holpuch, Amanda. "Alaskan Village Threatened by Rising Sea Levels Votes for Costly Relocation." *Guardian*, August 18, 2016. https://www.theguardian.com/us-news/2016/aug/18/alaska-shishmaref-vote-move-coastal-erosion-rising-sea-levels.

"How to Encourage Empathy." PREVNet, n.d. https://www.prevnet.ca/bullying/parents/how-to-encourage-empathy.

Hu, Winnie. "Learning Empathy by Looking Beyond Disabilities." *New York Times*, June 21, 2011. https://www.nytimes.com/2011/06/22/nyregion/at-nj-school-learning-not-to-look-away-from-the-disabled.html.

Hüther, Gerald. *The Compassionate Brain: How Empathy Creates Intelligence*. Boston: Trumpeter, 2013.

Institute for Social Policy and Understanding. *American Muslim Poll 2017*. https://www.ispu.org/american-muslim-poll-2017/.

Jacobson, Linda. "Pre-to-3: New 'Baby PISA' Study to Include US 5-Year-Olds." *Education Dive*, March 8, 2019. https://www.educationdive.com/news/pre-to-3-new-baby-pisa-study-to-include-us-5-year-olds/549810.

Jahme, Carole. Review of *Zero Degrees of Empathy* by Simon Baron-Cohen. *Guardian*, April 14, 2011. https://www.theguardian.com/science/blog/2011/apr/14/zero-degrees-empathy-baron-cohen.

Jazaieri, Hooria. "Compassionate Education from Preschool to Graduate School: Bringing a Culture of Compassion into the Classroom." *Journal of Research in Innovative Teaching & Learning* 11, no. 1 (2018). https://www.emeraldinsight.com/doi/full/10.1108/JRIT-08-2017-0017.

Jones, Dan. "The Power of Mind." *New Scientist* (March 12, 2016), 29–31.

"Karen Gerdes & Edwin Rutsch: Dialogs on How to Build a Culture of Empathy." Center for Building a Culture of Empathy, n.d. http://cultureofempathy.com/References/Experts/Karen-Gerdes.htm.

Klebold, Sue. *A Mother's Reckoning: Living in the Aftermath of Tragedy*. New York: Broadway Books, 2017.

Klem, Adena M., and James P. Connell. "Linking Teacher Support to Student Engagement and Achievement." *Journal of School Health* 74, no. 7 (2004): 262. https://onlinelibrary.wiley.com/doi/epdf/10.1111/j.1746-1561.2004.tb08283.x.

Kounang, Nadia. "Watching Cute Cat Videos Is Instinctive and Good for You—Seriously." CNN, January 20, 2016. https://www.cnn.com/2016/01/20/health/your-brain-on-cute/index.html.

Kraft, Dina. "Radiologist Adds a Human Touch: Photos." *New York Times*, April 6, 2009. https://www.nytimes.com/2009/04/07/health/07pati.html.

Krakovsky. Marina. "Self-Compassion Fosters Mental Health." *Scientific American*, July 1, 2012. https://www.scientificamerican.com/article/self-compassion-fosters-mental-health/?redirect=1.

Kris, Deborah Farmer. *How Self-Compassion Supports Academic Motivation and Emotional Wellness*. KQED News, MindShift, January 14, 2019. https://www.kqed.org/mindshift/52854/how-self-compassion-supports-academic-motivation-and-emotional-wellness.

Kristof, Nicholas. "Save the Darfur Puppy." *New York Times*, May 10, 2007. https://www.nytimes.com/2007/05/10/opinion/10kristof.html.

Krznaric, Roman. *Empathy: Why It Matters, and How to Get It*. New York: Penguin Random House, 2014.

Lakoff, George. *Ten Lectures on Cognitive Linguistics*. Leiden, Netherlands: Brill, 2018.

Lanier, Jaron. *Ten Arguments for Deleting Your Social Media Accounts Right Now*. New York: Henry Holt, 2018.

Larratt, Stephanie. "1 Year after Parkland School Shooting, Therapy Dogs Get Special Yearbook Honors." *Today*, May 17, 2019. https://www.today.com/pets/marjory-stoneman-douglas-honors-its-therapy-dogs-yearbook-photos-t154344.

Levine, David A. *Teaching Empathy: A Blueprint for Caring, Compassion, and Community*. Bloomington, IN: Solution Tree, 2005.

Linesch, Debra. "Art Therapy at the Museum of Tolerance: Responses to the Life and Work of Friedl Dicker-Brandeis." *Arts in Psychotherapy* 31, no. 2 (2004): 57–66. http://dx.doi.org/10.1016/j.aip.2004.02.004.

Long, Emily. "3 Ways to Teach Empathy with Media Literacy." *Huffington Post*, June 29, 2016. https://www.huffpost.com/entry/3-ways-to-teach-empathy--w_b_10595740.

Lundy, Brenda L. "Service Learning in Life-Span Developmental Psychology: Higher Exam Scores and Increased Empathy." *Teaching of Psychology* 34, no. 1 (2007). https://doi.org/10.1080/00986280709336644.

Mackey, Robert. "Jailed Chinese Dissident's 'Final Statement.'" *New York Times*, October 8, 2010. https://thelede.blogs.nytimes.com/2010/10/08/jailed-chinese-dissidents-final-statement/.

Maxwell, Ryan. "When Character Is Center Stage, Teens Rise Up." *Schools Teens Need* 14, no. 26 (2019). http://www.ascd.org/ascd-express/vol14/num26/when-character-is-center-stage-teens-rise-up.aspx?utm_source=ascdexpress&utm_medium=email&utm_campaign=Express%2014-26.

"Maurice Elias: A View on Emotional Intelligence and the Family." *Edutopia*, February 22, 2001. https://www.edutopia.org/maurice-elias-emotional-intelligence-and-family.

McElroy, Molly. "Game Played in Sync Increases Children's Perceived Similarity, Closeness." University of Washington, news release, April 8, 2015. https://www.washington.edu/news/2015/04/08/game-played-in-sync-increases-childrens-perceived-similarity-closeness/.

McLaren, Karla. *The Art of Empathy: A Complete Guide to Life's Most Essential Skills*. Boulder, CO: Sounds True, 2013.

———. "Einfühlung and Empathy: What Do They Mean?" (blog). https://karla-mclaren.com/einfuhlung-and-empathy/.

Meleen, Michele. "Listening Activities for School." lovetoknow, n.d. https://teens.lovetoknow.com/listening-activities-middle-school.

Miller, Claire Cain. "How to Be More Empathetic." *New York Times*, n.d. https://www.nytimes.com/guides/year-of-living-better/how-to-be-more-empathetic.

———. "Many Ways to Be a Girl, But One Way to Be a Boy: The New Gender Rules." *New York Times*, September 14, 2018. https://www.nytimes.com/2018/09/14/upshot/gender-stereotypes-survey-girls-boys.html.

Mischel, Walter. *The Marshmallow Test: Mastering Self-Control*. New York: Little, Brown, 2014.

Moodie, Clemmie. "Rihanna Receiving 'Confidence Counselling' and Help from a Life Coach to Combat Low Self-Esteem Issues." *Daily Mirror*, May 13, 2014. https://www.mirror.co.uk/3am/celebrity-news/rihanna-getting-confidence-counselling-help-3537117.

Morell, Virginia. "It's Time to Accept that Elephants, Like Us, Are Empathetic Beings." *National Geographic*, February 23, 2014. https://news.nationalgeo-graphic.com/news/2014/02/140221-elephants-poaching-empathy-grief-extinction-science/.

Morelli, Sylvia A., Desmond C. Ong, Rucha Makati, Matthew O. Jackson, and Jamil Zaki. "Empathy and Well-Being Correlate with Centrality in Different Social Networks." *PNAS* 114, no. 37 (2017): 9843–47. https://www.pnas.org/content/114/37/9843.

Morin, Amanda. "8 Social Situations to Role-Play with Your Middle-Schooler." Understood, n.d. https://www.understood.org/en/friends-feelings/common-challenges/following-social-rules/social-situations-to-role-play-with-your-middle-schooler.

Mueller, Steve. "Developing Empathy: Walk a Mile in Someone's Shoes." *Planet of Success* (blog), March 31, 2017. http://www.planetofsuccess.com/blog/2011/developing-empathy-walk-a-mile-in-someone%E2%80%99s-shoes/.

Murphy, Tia, and Deborah Laible. "Attachment and Empathy: The Mediating Role of Emotion Regulation." *Merrill-Palmer Quarterly* 58 (2012): 1–21. https://www.researchgate.net/publication/236670743_Attachment_and_empathy_The_mediating_role_of_emotion_regulation

Nathanson, Amy I., and Joanne Cantor. "Reducing the Aggression-Promoting Effect of Violent Cartoons by Increasing Children's Fictional Involvement with the Victim: A Study of Active Mediation." *Journal of Broadcasting & Electronic Media* 44, no. 1 (2000): 125–42. https://doi.org/10.1207/s15506878jobem4401_9.

Neff, Kristin. "The Space between Self-Esteem and Self Compassion: Kristin Neff at TEDxCentennialParkWomen." February 6, 2013. https://www.youtube.com/watch?v=IvtZBUSplr4.

———. "The Development and Validation of a Scale to Measure Self-Compassion." *Self and Identity* 2 (2003): 223–50.

Neff, Kristin, and Christopher Germer. *The Mindful Self-Compassion Workbook: A Proven Way to Accept Yourself, Build Inner Strength and Thrive.* New York: Guilford Press, 2018.

"New Girl Scouts Research Exposes the Impact of Reality TV on Girls." *gsblog*, October 13, 2011. http://blog.girlscouts.org/2011/10/new-girl-scouts-research-exposes-impact.html.

O'Haire, Marguerite E., Samantha J. McKenzie, Alan M. Beck, and Virginia Slaughter. "Social Behaviors Increase in Children with Autism in the Presence of Animals Compared to Toys." *PLOS ONE*, February 27, 2013. https://doi.org/10.1371/journal.pone.0057010.

Orlans, Michael, and Terry M. Levy. *Healing Parents: Helping Wounded Children Learn to Trust and Love.* Washington, DC: CWLA Press, 2006.

PACER's National Bullying Prevention Center. *Cyberbullying* (blog), n.d. https://www.pacer.org/bullying/resources/cyberbullying/.

Parker, Kim. "Families May Differ, But They Share Common Values on Parenting." *FactTank* (blog), September 18, 2014. Pew Research Center. http://www.pewresearch.org/fact-tank/2014/09/18/families-may-differ-but-they-share-common-values-on-parenting/.

Pinker, Susan. *The Village Effect: How Face-to-Face Contact Can Make Us Healthier, Happier, and Smarter.* New York: Spiegel & Grau, 2014.

Planta, Robert C., Jay Belsky, Nathan Vandergrift, Renate Houts, and Fred J. Morrison. "Classroom Effects on Children's Achievement Trajectories in Elementary School." *American Educational Research Journal* 45, no. 2 (2008). https://doi.org/10.3102/0002831207308230

Pollet, Thomas V., Sam G. Roberts, and Robin I. Dunbar. "Use of Social Network Sites and Instant Messaging Does Not Lead to Increased Offline Social Network Size, or to Emotionally Closer Relationships with Offline Network Members." *Cyberpsychology, Behavior and Social Networking* 14, no. 4 (2011): 253–58.

Poole, Carla, Susan A. Miller, and Ellen Booth Church. "How Empathy Develops: Effective Responses to Children Help Set the Foundation for Empathy." *Scholastic Early Childhood Today* 20, no. 2 (2005): 21–25.

Powe, Julian. "The Practice of Empathy." *Forbes*, September 11, 2012. https://www.forbes.com/sites/trustedadvisor/2012/09/11/the-practice-of-empathy/#4ca289be58d6.

"Prince William and Kate Middleton Are the New Faces of This Parenting Technique." *Time*, September 26, 2016. http://time.com/4507607/kate-middleton-prince-william-active-listening/.

Public Religion Research Institute, prod. *PRRI Survey, February 2017.* US-PRRI.031017.R07C. Ithaca, NY: Cornell University, Roper Center for Public Opinion Research, iPOLL (distrib.), 2017.

Purewal, Rebecca, Robert Christley, Katarzyna Kordas, Carol Joinson, Kerstin Meints, Nancy Gee, and Carri Westgarth. "Companion Animals and Child/Adolescent Development: A Systematic Review of the Evidence." *International Journal of Environmental Research and Public Health* 14, no. 3 (2017): 34. https://dx.doi.org/10.3390/ijerph14030234.

Ramirez, Sarah. "5 Easy Ways to Teach Kids Self-Control and Delayed Gratification." *A Fine Parent* (blog), n.d. https://afineparent.com/emotional-intelligence/delayed-gratification.html.

Raphelson, Samantha. "Grieving Mother Orca Carries Dead Calf for More Than a Week, Over Hundreds of Miles." NPR, July 31, 2018. https://www.npr.org/2018/07/31/634316124/grieving-mother-orca-carries-dead-calf-for-more-than-a-week-over-hundreds-of-mil.

Rather, Dan, and Elliot Kirschner. *What Unites Us: Reflections on Patriotism.* New York: Algonquin Books, 2017.

Reiney, Erin, and Susan P. Limber. "Why We Don't Use the Word 'Bully' to Label Kids." October 23, 2013. https://www.stopbullying.gov/blog/2013/10/23/why-we-dont-use-word-bully-label-kids.html.

Riess, Helen. *The Empathy Effect: 7 Neuroscience-Based Keys for Transforming the Way We Live, Love, Work, and Connect across Differences.* Boulder, CO: Sounds True, 2018.

Rigby, Ken. "What If Your Child Is Being Bullied at School?" *What Parents Can Do* (blog), n.d. http://www.kenrigby.net/13-If-your-child-is-bullied.

———. "What Parents Can Do to Prevent Their Child from Being Involved in Bullying at School?" *What Parents Can Do* (blog), n.d. http://www.kenrigby.net/12-Prevention.

Rosati, Alexandra G., Lauren M. DiNicole, and Joshua W. Buckholtz. "Chimpanzee Cooperation Is Fast and Independent from Self-Control." *Psychological Science* 29, no. 11 (2018): 1832–45. https://doi.org/10.1177/0956797618800042.

Sagi, Abraham, and Martin L. Hoffman. "Empathic Distress in the Newborn." *Developmental Psychology* 12, no. 2 (1976): 175–76. https://doi.org/10.1037/0012-1649.12.2.175.

Scholastic. *Kids & Family Report*. 7th ed. 2019. https://www.scholastic.com/read-ingreport/home.html.

Schumann, Karina, Jamil Zaki, and Carol S. Dweck. "Addressing the Empathy Deficit: Beliefs about the Malleability of Empathy Predict Effortful Responses When Empathy Is Challenging." *Journal of Personality and Social Psychology* 107 (2014): 475–93. https://doi.org/10.1037/a0036738.

Schwartz, Sarah. "Teachers Support Social-Emotional Learning, But Say Students in Distress Strain Their Skills." *Education Week*, July 16, 2019. https://www.edweek.org/ew/articles/2019/07/17/teachers-support-social-emotional-learning-but-say-students.html.

"Self Compassion." February 1, 2016. https://www.youtube.com/watch?v=-kfUE41-JFw&feature=youtu.be.

Serani, Deborah. "Bullycide" (blog). *Psychology Today*, June 2, 2018. https://www.psychologytoday.com/us/blog/two-takes-depression/201806/bullycide.

Shafer, Leah. "Summertime, Playtime." *Usable Knowledge Blog*. Harvard Graduate School of Education, 2018. https://www.gse.harvard.edu/news/uk/18/06/summertime-playtime.

Share, Jeff. *Media Literacy Is Elementary: Teaching Youth to Critically Read and Create Media.* New York: Peter Lang Publishing, 2009.

Shenfield, Tali. "How to Communicate with Your Teen through Active Listening" (blog), October 16, 2017. http://www.psy-ed.com/wpblog/communicate-with-teen/.

Siebert, Charles. "What Does a Parrot Know about PTSD?" *New York Times*, January 28, 2016. https://www.nytimes.com/2016/01/31/magazine/what-does-a-parrot-know-about-ptsd.html.

Skolnick, Joan, Nancy Dulberg, and Thea Maestre. *Through Other Eyes: Developing Empathy and Multicultural Perspectives in the Social Studies.* New York: Pippin Publishing, 2004.

Smith, Adam. *The Theory of Moral Sentiments*. 1759. http://knarf.english.upenn.edu/Smith/tms111.html.

Southern Poverty Law Center. "The Trump Effect: The Impact of the 2016 Presidential Election on Our Nation's Schools." November 28, 2016. https://www.splcenter.org/20161128/trump-effect-impact-2016-presidential-election-our-nations-schools.

Stitt, Elisabeth. "Building the Consistency Muscle: An Introduction." *Joyful Parenting Coaching* (blog), November 2, 2014. http://www.elisabethstitt.com/past-newsletters-and-other-musings/joyful-musings-a-weekly-blog/2014/11/2/november-newsletter-building-the-consitency-muscle.

Swick, Kevin J., and Nancy K. Freeman. "Nurturing Peaceful Children to Create a Caring World: The Role of Families and Communities." *Journal of Childhood Education* 81, no. 1 (2004): 8. https://doi.org/10.1080/00094056.2004.10521284.

Szalavitz, Maia, and Bruce D. Perry. "Born for Love." *Psychology Today*, May 28, 2010.

Taylor, Rebecca D., Eva Oberle, Joseph A. Durlak, and Roger P. Weissberg. "Promoting Positive Youth Development through School—Based Social and Emotional Learning Interventions: A Meta—Analysis of Follow—Up Effects." *Child Development* 88, no. 4 (2017). https://doi.org/10.1111/cdev.12864.

Tesh, Miki. "How to Teach Self-Compassion to Children." National Institute for Trauma and Loss in Children, January 6, 2012. https://tlcinstitute.wordpress.com/2012/01/06/mindful-self-compassion-for-kids/.

Tiedt, Pamela, and Iris Tiedt. *Multicultural Teaching—A Handbook of Activities, Information and Resources*. London: Pearson, 2009.

Trei, Lisa. "New Study Yields Instructive Results on How Mindset Affects Learning." Stanford University, news release, February 7, 2007. https://news.stanford.edu/news/2007/february7/dweck-020707.html.

Turkle, Sherry. *Reclaiming Conversation: The Power of Talk in a Digital Age*. New York: Penguin Books, 2015.

Twenge, Jean M., A. Bell Cooper, Thomas E. Joiner, Mary E. Duffy, and Sarah G. Binau. "Age, Period, and Cohort Trends in Mood Disorder Indicators and Suicide-Related Outcomes in a Nationally Representative Dataset, 2005–2017." *Journal of Abnormal Psychology* 128, no. 3 (2019): 185–99. http://dx.doi.org/10.1037/abn0000410.

Uche, Ugo. "Empathy Promotes Emotional Resiliency." *Psychology Today*, May 18, 2010. https://www.psychologytoday.com/us/blog/promoting-empathy-your-teen/201005/empathy-promotes-emotional-resiliency,

Van Berkhout, Emily Teding, and John M. Malouff. "The Efficacy of Empathy Training: A Meta-Analysis of Randomized Controlled Trials." *Journal of Counseling Psychology* 63, no. 1 (2016): 32–41.

Van der Graaff, Jolien, Susan Branje, Minet De Wied, Skyler Hawk, Pol Van Lier, and Wim Meeus. "Perspective Taking and Empathic Concern in Adolescence: Gender Differences in Developmental Changes." *Developmental Psychology* 50, no. 3 (2014): 881–88. http://dx.doi.org/10.1037/a0034325.

VanClay. Mary. "The Caring Child: How to Teach Empathy (Ages 3 to 4)." Babycenter, March 2017. https://www.babycenter.com/0_the-caring-child-how-to-teach-empathy-ages-3-to-4_65717.bc.

Velasquez-Manoff, Moises. "Real Men Get Rejected, Too." *New York Times*, February 25, 2018. https://www.nytimes.com/2018/02/24/opinion/sunday/real-men-masculinity-rejected.html?smid=tw-nytopinion&smtyp=cur.

Vishton, Peter M. *Scientific Secrets for Raising Kids Who Thrive: Course Guidebook.* Chantilly, VA: Teaching Company, 2014.

Wallace, Jennifer Breheny. "How to Raise More Grateful Children." *Wall Street Journal*, February 23, 2018. https://www.wsj.com/articles/how-to-raise-more-grateful-children-1519398748.

Watson, Amy. "Children and Media in the U.S." Statista, March 8, 2019. https://www.statista.com/topics/3980/children-and-media-in-the-us/.

Westheimer, Joel. "What Kind of Citizens Do We Need?" In "Citizens in the Making." Special issue, *Educational Leadership* 75, no. 3 (2017): 12–18. http://www.ascd.org/publications/educational-leadership/nov17/vol75/num03/What-Kind-of-Citizens-Do-We-Need%C2%A2.aspx?utm_source=ascdexpress&utm_medium=email&utm_campaign=Express%2014-29.

Williams, Mari-Jane. "A New Report Shows Reading for Fun Declines between Ages 8 and 9. How Can We Stem the Tide?" *Washington Post*, March 20, 2019. https://www.washingtonpost.com/lifestyle/2019/03/20/new-report-shows-reading-fun-declines-between-ages-how-can-we-stem-tide/?utm_term=.0e17a5e81599.

———. "6 Ways Parents Can Help Kids Strike a Balance between Screen Time and the Real World." *Washington Post*, February 11, 2019. https://www.washingtonpost.com/lifestyle/on-parenting/6-ways-parents-can-help-kids-strike-a-balance-between-screen-time-and-the-real-world/2019/02/11/09e941f8-1a87-11e9-88fe-f9f77a3bcb6c_story.html?noredirect=on&utm_term=.9f1e8c7d967d.

Williford, Anne, Aaron J. Boulton, Shandra S. Forrest-Bank, Kimberly A. Bender, William A. Dieterich, and Jeffrey M. Jenson. "The Effect of Bullying and Victimization on Cognitive Empathy Development during the Transition to Middle School." *Child & Youth Care Forum* 45, no. 4 (2016): 525–41.

Wilson, Edward O. *The Social Conquest of Earth*. New York: Liveright Publishing, 2012.

Wollan, Malia. "How to Get Preschoolers to Share." *New York Times Magazine*, January 6, 2019.

Zack, Jessica. "Penny Orenstein Wants You to Talk with Your Boys about Sex." *San Francisco Chronicle*, January 17, 2020. https://datebook.sfchronicle.com/books/peggy-orenstein-wants-you-to-talk-about-sex-with-your-boys.

Zaki, Jamil. *The War for Kindness: Building Empathy in a Fractured World*. New York: Crown, 2019.

———. "What, Me Care? Young Are Less Empathetic." *Scientific American Mind*, January 1, 2011. https://www.scientificamerican.com/article/what-me-care/.

Zero to Three. "Talking to Toddlers about Differences." Parenting Resource, n.d. https://www.zerotothree.org/resources/1539-talking-to-toddlers-about-differences.

Zimmerman, Frederick J., Dimitri A. Christakis, and Andrew N. Meltzoff. "Television and DVD/Video Viewing in Children Younger Than 2 Years." *Archives of Pediatrics and Adolescent Medicine* 161, no. 5 (2007): 473–79. https://doi.org/10.1001/archpedi.161.5.473.

index

endnotes

Chapter 1. Why YOU Should Care about Empathy

1. Simon Baron-Cohen, *Zero Degrees of Empathy: A New Theory of Human Cruelty and Kindness* (London: Penguin Books, 2012), 14.

2. Michele Borba, "Teen Narcissism Is Worse: Is Social Networking the Cause?" *PediatricSafety: One Ouch Is Too Many*, March 14, 2016, https://www.pediatricsafety.net/2016/03/teen-narcissism-is-worse-is-social-networking-the-cause/.

3. Michele Borba, *Building Moral Intelligence: The Seven Essential Virtues That Teach Kids to Do the Right Thing* (San Francisco: Jossey-Bass, 2001).

4. Josephson Institute of Ethics, *2012 Report Card on the Ethics of American Youth* (Los Angeles: Josephson Institute, 2012), https://charactercounts.org/wp-content/uploads/2014/02/ReportCard-2012-DataTables.pdf.

5. Quoted in Paul Barnwell, "Students' Broken Moral Compasses," *Atlantic*, July 25, 2016, https://www.theatlantic.com/education/archive/2016/07/students-broken-moral-compasses/492866/.

6. Robert Wm. Blum and Heather P. Libbey, "Executive Summary," *Journal of School Health* 74, no. 7 (2004).

7. P. L. Benson, *All Kids Our Kids: What Communities Must Do to Raise Caring and Responsible Children and Adolescents*, 2nd ed. (San Francisco: Jossey-Bass, 2006).

8. Urie Bronfenbrenner, "The Origins of Alienation," *Scientific American* 251 (1974): 53–64.

9. Joy G. Dryfoos, "The Prevalence of Problem Behaviors, Implications for Programs," in *Issues in Children's and Families' Lives*, vol. 8, *Healthy Children 2010: Enhancing Children's Wellness*, ed. Roger P. Weissberg, Thomas P. Gullotta, Robert L. Hampton, Bruce A. Ryan, and Gerald R. Adams (Thousand Oaks, CA: Sage Publications, 1997), 17–46; Danice K. Eaton et al., "Youth Risk Behavior Surveillance—United States, 2007," *Morbidity and Mortality Weekly Report: Surveillance Summaries* 57, no. 4 (2008): 1–131.

10. Mark H. Davis, *Empathy: A Social Psychology Approach* (Boulder, CO: Westview Press, 2018).

11. James R. Doty, *Into the Magic Shop: A Neurosurgeon's Quest to Discover the Mysteries of the Brain and the Secrets of the Heart* (New York: Avery, 2016), 260–61.

12. Daniel Goleman, Richard Boyatzis, and Annie McKee, *Primal Leadership: Unleashing the Power of Emotional Intelligence* (Boston: Harvard Business Review Press, 2013).

Chapter 2. Empathy CAN Be Taught

1. Carol M. Davis, "What Is Empathy and Can Empathy Be Taught?" *Physical Therapy* 70, no. 11 (1990): 707–11, https://doi.org/10.1093/ptj/70.11.707.

2. Paul Bloom, *Against Empathy: The Case for Rational Compassion* (New York: Ecco, 2016).

3. Nicholas Kristof, "Save the Darfur Puppy," *New York Times*, May 10, 2007.

4. Emily Teding van Berkhout and John M. Malouff, "The Efficacy of Empathy Training: A Meta-Analysis of Randomized Controlled Trials," *Journal of Counseling Psychology* 63, no. 1 (2016): 32–41.

Chapter 3. The Science and Biology of Empathy

1. "Wounda's Journey: Jane Goodall Releases Chimpanzee into Forest," posted by Jane Goodall Institute of Canada, December 17, 2013, https://www.youtube.com/watch?v=YzC7MfCtkzo.

2. Frans de Waal, "The Evolution of Empathy," *Greater Good Magazine,* September 1, 2005, https://greatergood.berkeley.edu/article/item/the_evolution_of_empathy.

3. Alexandra G. Rosati, Lauren M. DiNicole, and Joshua W. Buckholtz, "Chimpanzee Cooperation Is Fast and Independent from Self-Control," *Psychological Science* 29, no. 11 (2018): 1832–45, https://doi.org/10.1177/0956797618800042.

4. Susan Pinker, *The Village Effect: How Face-to-Face Contact Can Make Us Healthier, Happier, and Smarter* (New York: Spiegel & Grau, 2014), 251.

5. Thomas V. Pollet, Sam G. Roberts, and Robin I. Dunbar, "Use of Social Network Sites and Instant Messaging Does Not Lead to Increased Offline Social Network Size, or to Emotionally Closer Relationships with Offline Network Members," *Cyberpsychology, Behavior and Social Networking* 14, no. 4 (2011): 253–58.

6. Sindya N. Bhanoo, "For Prairie Voles, a Furry Shoulder to Cry On," *New York Times,* January 22, 2018, https://www.nytimes.com/2016/01/26/science/for-prairie-voles-a-furry-shoulder-to-cry-on.html.

7. James P. Burkett et al., "Oxytocin-Dependent Consolation Behavior in Rodents," *Science* 351, no. 6721 (2016): 375–78, https://doi.org/10.1126/science.aac4785.

8. Virginia Morell, "It's Time to Accept That Elephants, Like Us, Are Empathetic Beings," *National Geographic*, February 23, 2014, https://news.nationalgeographic.com/news/2014/02/140221-elephants-poaching-empathy-grief-extinction-science/.

9. Samantha Raphelson, "Grieving Mother Orca Carries Dead Calf for More Than a Week, Over Hundreds of Miles," NPR, July 31, 2018, https://www.npr.org/2018/07/31/634316124/grieving-mother-orca-carries-dead-calf-for-more-than-a-week-over-hundreds-of-mil.

10. Gerald Hüther, *The Compassionate Brain: How Empathy Creates Intelligence* (Boston: Trumpeter, 2013), 56.

11. Frans de Waal, *The Age of Empathy: Nature's Lessons for a Kinder Society* (New York: Harmony, 2009).

12. Martin L. Hoffman, "Psychological and Biological Perspectives on Altruism," *International Journal of Behavioral Development* 1 (1978): 333.

13. Edward O. Wilson, *The Social Conquest of Earth* (New York: Liveright Publishing, 2012), 44 (emphasis added).

14. Hüther, *Compassionate Brain*, 55–56 (emphasis added).

15. George Lakoff, *Ten Lectures on Cognitive Linguistics* (Leiden, Netherlands: Brill, 2018), 122.

16. Quoted in Jane E. Brody, "How to Foster Empathy in Children," *New York Times*, December 10, 2018, https://www.nytimes.com/2018/12/10/well/live/how-to-foster-empathy-in-children.html?fbclid=IwAR0bCHO-azAGUio3Uu2NqmhzdpLaO7U_lkDnZ4F4NMfPf1ZyNBGuYtykl3Do.

17. Elissar Andari et al., "Promoting Social Behavior with Oxytocin in High-Functioning Autism Spectrum Disorders," *PNAS* 107, no. 9 (2010): 4389–94, https://www.pnas.org/content/107/9/4389.full.

18. T. Berry Brazelton and Stanley I. Greenspan, "Why Children Need Ongoing Nurturing Relationships," *Early Childhood Today* 21, no. 1 (2006).

19. Pinker, *The Village Effect*, 156.

20. Frederick J. Zimmerman, Dimitri A. Christakis, and Andrew N. Meltzoff, "Television and DVD/Video Viewing in Children Younger Than 2 Years," *Archives of Pediatrics and Adolescent Medicine* 161, no. 5 (2007): 473–79, https://doi.org/10.1001/archpedi.161.5.473.

21. Dimitri A. Christakis et al., "Early Television Exposure and Subsequent Attentional Problems in Children," *Pediatrics* 113, no. 4 (2004), http://pediatrics.aappublications.org/content/113/4/708.short.

22. Nicholas Carr, *The Shallows: What the Internet Is Doing to Our Brains* (New York: W. W. Norton, 2011).

23. Nicholas Carr, "How the Internet Is Making Us Stupid," *Telegraph*, August 27, 2010, https://www.telegraph.co.uk/technology/internet/7967894/How-the-Internet-is-making-us-stupid.html.

24. See https://evolution-institute.org/the-evolution-of-darwinian-empathy/.

Chapter 4. Empathy 101: Defining How Empathy Fits in with Other Emotional Skills

1. Adam Smith, *The Theory of Moral Sentiments* (1759), http://knarf.english.upenn.edu/Smith/tms111.html.

2. Karla McLaren, "Einfühlung and Empathy: What Do They Mean?" (blog), https://karlamclaren.com/einfuhlung-and-empathy/.

3. "Maurice Elias: A View on Emotional Intelligence and the Family," *Edutopia*, February 22, 2001, https://www.edutopia.org/maurice-elias-emotional-in-telligence-and-family. His Social-Emotional and Character Development lab's website has excellent resources as well (www.secdlab.org).

Chapter 5. Empathy, Media, and Social Media

1. Jaron Lanier, *Ten Arguments for Deleting Your Social Media Accounts Right Now* (New York: Henry Holt, 2018), 18.

2. Jennings Brown, "Former Facebook Exec: 'You Don't Realize It But You Are Being Programmed,'" Gizmodo, December 11, 2017, https://gizmodo.com/former-facebook-exec-you-don-t-realize-it-but-you-are-1821181133.

3. Lanier, *Ten Arguments*, 76.

4. Ibid., 80.

5. To learn more, see Amy Watson, "Children and Media in the U.S.," Statista, March 8, 2019, https://www.statista.com/topics/3980/children-and-media-in-the-us/.

6. Quoted in Nick Bilton, "Looking at Link between Violent Video Games and Lack of Empathy," *New York Times*, June 15, 2014, https://bits.blogs.nytimes.com/2014/06/15/looking-at-link-between-violent-video-games-and-lack-of-empathy/.

7. Ibid.

8. Jeff Share, *Media Literacy Is Elementary: Teaching Youth to Critically Read and Create Media* (New York: Peter Lang, 2009), 2, 56.

9. Joanie Harmon, "Why Critical Media Literacy Should Be Taught in Schools," Phys.org, June 4, 2019, https://phys.org/news/2019-06-critical-media-liter-acy-taught-schools.html.

10. Jamil Zaki, *The War for Kindness: Building Empathy in a Fractured World* (New York: Crown, 2019), 195.

11. Ibid., 153.

Chapter 6. Parent Tips: Strengthening Moral Compasses

1. CharacterCounts.org, "2012 Report Card on the Ethics of American Youth," Josephson Institute, 2012, https://charactercounts.org/wp-content/uploads/2014/02/ReportCard-2012-DataTables.pdf.

2. D. Stanley Eitzen, "The Atrophy of Social Life," *Society* 41, no. 6 (2004): 641–48.

3. Quoted in Lisa Trei, "New Study Yields Instructive Results on How Mindset Affects Learning," Stanford Report, February 7, 2007, https://news.stanford.edu/news/2007/february7/dweck-020707.html.

4. Karina Schumann, Jamil Zaki, and Carol S. Dweck, "Addressing the Empathy Deficit: Beliefs about the Malleability of Empathy Predict Effortful Responses When Empathy Is Challenging," *Journal of Personality and Social Psychology* 107 (2014): 475–93, https://doi.org/10.1037/a0036738.

5. Kevin J. Swick and Nancy K. Freeman, "Nurturing Peaceful Children to Create a Caring World: The Role of Families and Communities," *Journal of Childhood Education* 81, no. 1 (2004): 8, https://doi.org/10.1080/00094056.2004.10521284.

6. Gwen Dewar, "The Case for Teaching Empathy: Why Empathy Doesn't 'Just Happen,'" *Parenting Science*, 2009–2013, https://www.parentingscience.com/teaching-empathy.html.

7. Susanne Ayers Denham, Hideko Hamada Bassett, and Todd Wyatt, "The Socialization of Emotional Competence," in *Handbook of Socialization: Theory and Research*, ed. Joan E. Grusec and Paul D. Hastings (New York: Guilford Press, 2015), https://www.researchgate.net/publication/232535707_The_Socialization_of_Emotional_Competence.

8. David A. Levine, *Teaching Empathy: A Blueprint for Caring, Compassion, and Community* (Bloomington, IN: Solution Tree, 2005).

9. John Gottman and Joan DeClaire, *The Heart of Parenting: How to Raise an Emotionally Intelligent Child* (London: Bloomsbury Publishing, 1997), 161–62.

10. Helen Riess, *The Empathy Effect: 7 Neuroscience-Based Keys for Transforming the Way We Live, Love, Work, and Connect across Differences* (Boulder, CO: Sounds True, 2018).

11. Quoted in Jane Brody, "How to Foster Empathy in Children," *New York Times*, December 10, 2018, https://www.nytimes.com/2018/12/10/well/live/how-to-foster-empathy-in-children.html.

12. Steve Mueller, "Developing Empathy: Walk a Mile in Someone's Shoes," *Planet of Success* (blog), March 31, 2017, http://www.planetofsuccess.com/blog/2011/developing-empathy-walk-a-mile-in-someone%E2%80%99s-shoes/.

Chapter 7. Teaching Empathy: Infant to Three Years

1. Claudia M. Gold, "Adverse Childhood Experiences (ACE) Study: Beyond Screening in Pediatrics," *Child in Mind* (blog), December 14, 2017, http://claudiamgoldmd.blogspot.com/2017/.

2. Abraham Sagi and Martin L. Hoffman, "Empathic Distress in the Newborn," *Developmental Psychology* 12, no. 2 (1976): 175–76, https://doi.org/10.1037/0012-1649.12.2.175.

3. Tia Murphy and Deborah Laible, "Attachment and Empathy: The Mediating Role of Emotion Regulation," *Merrill-Palmer Quarterly* 58 (2012): 1–21, https://www.researchgate.net/publication/236670743_Attachment_and_empathy_The_mediating_role_of_emotion_regulation.

4. I highly recommend the academy's website. For its recommendations, see "American Academy of Pediatrics Announces New Recommendations for Children's Media Use," October 21, 2016, https://www.aap.org/en-us/about-the-aap/aap-press-room/Pages/American-Academy-of-Pediatrics-Announces-New-Recommendations-for-Childrens-Media-Use.aspx.

5. Ibid.

6. Michael Orlans and Terry M. Levy, *Healing Parents: Helping Wounded Children Learn to Trust and Love* (Washington, DC: CWLA Press, 2006).

7. Ibid.

8. Laura K. Certain and Robert S. Kahn, "Prevalence, Correlates, and Trajectory of Television Viewing among Infants and Toddlers," *Pediatrics* 109, no. 4 (2002): 634–42, https://www.ncbi.nlm.nih.gov/pubmed/11927708.

9. Mark H. Davis, *Empathy: Social Psychology Approach* (Boulder, CO: Westview Press, 2018), 74–75.

10. Adam Grant, *Originals: How Non-Conformists Move the World* (New York: Viking, 2016), 165.

11. Adam Grant, "Raising a Moral Child," *New York Times,* April 11, 2014, https://www.nytimes.com/2014/04/12/opinion/sunday/raising-a-moral-child.html.

12. Ibid.

13. Grant, *Originals,* 169.

14. Cited in Malia Wollan, "How to Get Preschoolers to Share," *New York Times Magazine,* January 3, 2019.

Chapter 8. Teaching Empathy: Three to Six Years

1. Go to https://rangerrick.org/ for your own dose of Ranger Rick.

2. Elizabeth Erickson, "Effects of Storytelling on Emotional Development," Masters of Arts in Education Action Research Papers (St. Paul, MN: St. Catherine University, 2018), 5, https://sophia.stkate.edu/cgi/viewcontent.cgi?article=1258&context=maed.

3. Leah Shafer, "Summertime, Playtime," *Usable Knowledge Blog*, Harvard Graduate School of Education, 2018, https://www.gse.harvard.edu/news/uk/18/06/summertime-playtime.

4. Maia Szalavitz and Bruce D. Perry, "Born for Love," *Psychology Today*, May 28, 2010.

5. Carla Poole, Susan A. Miller, and Ellen Booth Church, "How Empathy Develops: Effective Responses to Children Help Set the Foundation for Empathy," *Scholastic Early Childhood Today* 20, no. 2 (2005): 21–25.

6. Elisabeth Stitt, "Building the Consistency Muscle: An Introduction," *Joyful Parenting Coaching* (blog), November 2, 2014, http://www.elisabethstitt.com/past-newsletters-and-other-musings/joyful-musings-a-weekly-blog/2014/11/2/november-newsletter-building-the-consistency-muscle.

7. Mary VanClay, "The Caring Child: How to Teach Empathy (Ages 3 to 4)," Babycenter, March 2017, https://www.babycenter.com/0_the-caring-child-how-to-teach-empathy-ages-3-to-4_65717.bc.

8. Miki Tesh, "How to Teach Self-Compassion to Children," National Institute for Trauma and Loss in Children, January 6, 2012, https://tlcinstitute.wordpress.com/2012/01/06/mindful-self-compassion-for-kids/.

9. Erika Christakis, "The New Preschool Is Crushing Kids," *Atlantic*, January/February 2016, https://www.theatlantic.com/magazine/archive/2016/01/the-new-preschool-is-crushing-kids/419139/.

Chapter 9. Teaching Empathy: Elementary Years

1. Quoted in Anndee Hochman, "How Do You Celebrate 'Day of the Dead' and Other Questions N.J. Classroom Asks Kids around the World," Inquirer. com, March 26, 2019, https://www.inquirer.com/news/empatico-web-cam-wedgwood-elementary-classroom-kind-kathi-kersznowski-20190326. html. Also, I encourage teachers to visit Empatico's website at https://why. empatico.org/ for more information on how they can get this free tool. Empatico's goal is "creating a global movement to spread kindness and empathy around the world." It doesn't get better than that.

2. Quoted in Hochman, "How Do You Celebrate 'Day of the Dead.'"

3. Ibid.

4. David Gelles, "Mindfulness for Children," *New York Times*, n.d., https://www. nytimes.com/guides/well/mindfulness-for-children.

5. Adam Grant, "How to Create a Creative Child; Step One: Back Off," *New York Times*, January 30, 2016, https://www.nytimes.com/2016/01/31/opin-ion/sunday/how-to-raise-a-creative-child-step-one-back-off.html.

6. Claire Cain Miller, "How to Be More Empathetic," *New York Times*, n.d., https://www.nytimes.com/guides/year-of-living-better/how-to-be-more-empathetic.

7. He is also one of the founders of the Collaborative for Academic, Social, and Emotional Learning (CASEL). For more information, visit https://casel. org/.

8. Visit www.sel4us.com for more information.

9. See Maurice Elias, "Developing Empathy in Kids Ages 8–11," *Parent Toolkit* (blog), n.d., https://www.parenttoolkit.com/social-and-emotional-develop-ment/advice/social-awareness/developing-empathy-in-kids-ages-8-11.

10. Quoted in Mari-Jane Williams, "6 Ways Parents Can Help Kids Strike a Balance between Screen Time and the Real World," *Washington Post*, February 11, 2019, https://www.washingtonpost.com/lifestyle/on-parenting/6-ways-parents-can-help-kids-strike-a-balance-between-screen-time-and-the-real-world/2019/02/11/09e941f8-1a87-11e9-88fe-f9f77a3bcb6c_story.html?noredirect=on&utm_term=.9f1e8c7d967d.

11. Quoted in Leigh Anderson, "Bullying: Can Schools Teach Kids Empathy?" *Newsweek*, December 15, 2010, https://www.newsweek.com/bullying-can-schools-teach-kids-empathy-68795.

12. Quoted in ibid.

13. Gail Gross, "Violence on TV and How It Can Affect Your Children," *The Blog, HuffPost,* updated October 15, 2013, https://www.huffpost.com/entry/violence-on-tv-children_n_3734764.

14. Amy I. Nathanson and Joanne Cantor, "Reducing the Aggression-Promoting Effect of Violent Cartoons by Increasing Children's Fictional Involvement with the Victim: A Study of Active Mediation," *Journal of Broadcasting & Electronic Media* 44, no. 1 (2000): 125–42, https://doi.org/10.1207/s15506878jobem4401_9.

15. Scholastic, *Kids & Family Report,* 7th ed., 2019, https://www.scholastic.com/readingreport/home.html.

16. Mari-Jane Williams, "A New Report Shows Reading for Fun Declines between Ages 8 and 9. How Can We Stem the Tide?" *Washington Post,* March 20, 2019, https://www.washingtonpost.com/lifestyle/2019/03/20/new-report-shows-reading-fun-declines-between-ages-how-can-we-stem-tide/?utm_term=.0e17a5e81599.

17. Sandra L. Bosacki, Zopito A. Marini, and Andrew V. Dane, "Voices from the Classroom: Pictorial and Narrative Representations of Children's Bullying Experiences," *Journal of Moral Education* 35, no. 2 (2006): 231–45, https://doi.org/10.1080/03057240600681769; and Debra Linesch, "Art Therapy at the Museum of Tolerance: Responses to the Life and Work of Friedl Dicker-Brandeis," *Arts in Psychotherapy* 31, no. 2 (2004): 57–66, http://dx.doi.org/10.1016/j.aip.2004.02.004.

Chapter 10. Teaching Empathy: Middle School Years

1. Jessica Alexander and Iben Sandahl, *The Danish Way of Parenting: What the Happiest People in the World Know about Raising Confident, Capable Kids* (New York: TarcherPerigee, 2016), xviii.

2. Ibid., 141.

3. Ibid., 141–42.

4. Anne Williford et al., "The Effect of Bullying and Victimization on Cognitive Empathy Development during the Transition to Middle School," *Child & Youth Care Forum* 45, no. 4 (2016): 525–41.

5. See Catherine Gewertz, "Principals Dealing with Hostility and Division in the Age of Trump, Survey Shows," *Education Week,* March 13, 2019, https://blogs.edweek.org/edweek/high_school_and_beyond/2019/03/hostility_and_division_schools_in_the_age_of_trump.html.

6. Thomas R. Hoerr, "Steps and Strategies for Developing Empathy," *Learning with Empathy* 13, no. 1 (2017), http://www.ascd.org/ascd-express/vol13/1301-hoerr.aspx.

7. Ibid.

8. Ibid.

9. Here are a couple of books that are geared toward educators, although parents may find them useful, too. *Building Cultural Competence: Innovative Activities and Models*, by Kate Berardo and Darla K. Deardorff (Sterling, VA: Stylus Publishing, 2012), is a real train-the-trainers book. It provides educators and others with a collection of more than fifty ready-to-use tools and activities to help develop understanding about the cultures of others. *Diversity Programming for Digital Youth: Promoting Cultural Competence in the Children's Library*, by Jamie Campbell Naidoo (Santa Barbara, CA: Libraries Unlimited, 2014), provides recommendations for print and digital media.

10. "Food Taboos: It's All a Matter of Taste," *National Geographic News*, April 19, 2004, reprinted at Digital Chalkboard, https://www.mydigitalchalkboard.org/portal/default/Resources/Viewer/ResourceViewer;jsessionid=2gUm-2FLZUEY61Ilg37CacA**?action=2&resid=35179&discussion.ascdesc=descending&discussion.listtype=chronological.

11. Amanda Holpuch, "Alaskan Village Threatened by Rising Sea Levels Votes for Costly Relocation," *Guardian*, August 18, 2016, https://www.theguardian.com/us-news/2016/aug/18/alaska-shishmaref-vote-move-coastal-erosion-rising-sea-levels.

12. Ibid.

13. Maggie Astor, "Dove Drops an Ad Accused of Racism," *New York Times*, October 8, 2017, https://www.nytimes.com/2017/10/08/business/dove-ad-racist.html.

14. Emily Long, "3 Ways to Teach Empathy with Media Literacy," *Huffington Post*, June 29, 2016, https://www.huffpost.com/entry/3-ways-to-teach-empathy-w_b_10595740.

15. Kenneth R. Ginsburg and Martha M. Jablow, *Building Resilience in Children and Teens: Giving Kids Roots and Wings* (Elk Grove, IL: American Academy of Pediatrics, 2011), 126.

16. Ibid.

17. Sarah Lynne Bowman, *The Functions of Role-Playing Games: How Participants Create Community, Solve Problems and Explore Identity* (Jefferson, NC: McFarland, 2010), 47.

18. Ibid., 183–84.

19. Amanda Morin, "8 Social Situations to Role-Play with Your Middle-Schooler," Understood, n.d., https://www.understood.org/en/friends-feelings/common-challenges/following-social-rules/social-situations-to-role-play-with-your-middle-schooler.

20. Center for Parenting Education, "Freeing Your Child from Disabling Labels," n.d., https://centerforparentingeducation.org/library-of-articles/self-esteem/freeing-your-children-from-disabling-labels/.

21. Erin Reiney and Susan P. Limber, "Why We Don't Use the Word 'Bully' to Label Kids," October 23, 2013, https://www.stopbullying.gov/blog/2013/10/23/why-we-dont-use-word-bully-label-kids.html.

22. Adam Bryant, "How to Be a Better Listener," *New York Times*, n.d., https://www.nytimes.com/guides/smarterliving/be-a-better-listener.

Chapter 11. Teaching Empathy: High School Years

1. D. Stanley Eitzen, "The Atrophy of Social Life," *Society*, 41, no. 6 (2004): 12–16.

2. Jennifer L. DePaoli et al., *Respected: Perspectives of Youth on High School & Social and Emotional Learning* (Chicago: Collaborative for Academic, Social, and Emotional Learning, 2018), 48, https://casel.org/wp-content/uploads/2018/11/Respected.pdf.

3. Quoted in Sara Goudarzi, "Study: Why Teens Don't Care," *Live Science*, September 7, 2006, https://www.livescience.com/7151-study-teens-care.html.

4. Ibid.

5. Ugo Uche, "Empathy Promotes Emotional Resiliency," *Psychology Today*, May 18, 2010, https://www.psychologytoday.com/us/blog/promoting-empathy-your-teen/201005/empathy-promotes-emotional-resiliency.

6. Ibid.

7. Adena M. Klem and James P. Connell, "Linking Teacher Support to Student Engagement and Achievement," *Journal of School Health* 74, no. 7 (2004): 262, https://onlinelibrary.wiley.com/doi/10.1111/j.1746-1561.2004.tb08283.x.

8. Sue Klebold, *A Mother's Reckoning: Living in the Aftermath of Tragedy* (New York: Broadway Books, 2017), xxiv.

9. Monica Arkin, "School-Based Mindfulness Programs Can Help Students Cope with Stress," *Child Trends* (blog), April 16, 2019, https://www.childtrends.org/school-based-mindfulness-programs-help-students-cope-with-.

10. See the International Space Hall of Fame website, http://www.nmspacemuseum.org/halloffame/detail.php?id=19.

11. Kristin Neff and Christopher Germer, *The Mindful Self-Compassion Workbook: A Proven Way to Accept Yourself, Build Inner Strength and Thrive* (New York: Guilford Press, 2018), 139.

12. Po Bronson and Ashley Merryman, "Even Babies Discriminate: A NurtureShock Excerpt," *Newsweek*, September 4, 2009, https://www.newsweek.com/even-babies-discriminate-nurtureshock-excerpt-79233.

13. Reported in ibid.

14. Claire Cain Miller, "How to Be More Empathetic," *New York Times*, n.d. https://www.nytimes.com/guides/year-of-living-better/how-to-be-more-empathetic.

15. Bronson and Merriman, "Even Babies Discriminate."

16. Zero to Three, "Talking to Toddlers about Differences," n.d., https://www.zerotothree.org/resources/1539-talking-to-toddlers-about-differences.

17. Miller, "How to Be More Empathetic."

18. Discussed in ibid.

19. Brenda L. Lundy, "Service Learning in Life-Span Developmental Psychology: Higher Exam Scores and Increased Empathy," *Teaching of Psychology* 34, no. 1 (2007), https://doi.org/10.1080/00986280709336644.

20. Ryan Maxwell, "When Character Is Center Stage, Teens Rise Up," *Schools Teens Need* 14, no. 26 (2019), http://www.ascd.org/ascd-express/vol14/num26/when-character-is-center-stage-teens-rise-up.aspx?utm_source=ascdexpress&utm_medium=email&utm_campaign=Express%2014-26.

21. Winnie Hu, "Learning Empathy by Looking Beyond Disabilities," *New York Times*, June 21, 2011, https://www.nytimes.com/2011/06/22/nyregion/at-nj-school-learning-not-to-look-away-from-the-disabled.html.

22. Ibid.

23. Sarah Holding, "Sarah Holdings Top 10 Cli-Fi Books," *Guardian*, April 23, 2015, https://www.theguardian.com/childrens-books-site/2015/apr/23/sarah-holdings-top-10-cli-fi-books.

24. See Centers for Disease Control, "Understanding Teen Dating Violence," fact sheet, 2014, https://www.cdc.gov/violenceprevention/pdf/teen-dating-violence-2014-a.pdf.

25. See the National Institute of Justice website for more information at https://www.nij.gov/topics/crime/intimate-partner-violence/teen-dating-violence/Pages/prevention-intervention.aspx.

26. Sylvia A. Morelli et al., "Empathy and Well-Being Correlate with Centrality in Different Social Networks," *PNAS* 114, no. 37 (2017): 9843–47, https://www.pnas.org/content/114/37/9843.

Chapter 12. Empathy: Critical for Bullying Prevention

1. Noreen Gillespie, "Mother Receives Suspended Sentence in Son's Suicide," Associated Press, May 14, 2004, http://www.nbcnews.com/id/4979447/ns/us_news-crime_and_courts/t/mother-gets-suspended-sentence-sons-suicide/#.XsgzsGhKjIU; see also Deborah Serani, "Bullycide" (blog), *Psychology Today*, June 2, 2018, https://www.psychologytoday.com/us/blog/two-takes-depression/201806/bullycide.

2. See Southern Poverty Law Center, "The Trump Effect: The Impact of the 2016 Presidential Election on Our Nation's Schools," November 28, 2016, https://www.splcenter.org/20161128/trump-effect-impact-2016-presidential-election-our-nations-schools.

3. See Institute for Social Policy and Understanding, *American Muslim Poll 2017*, https://www.ispu.org/american-muslim-poll-2017/.

4. Public Religion Research Institute, prod., *PRRI Survey, February 2017*, US-PRRI.031017.R07C (Ithaca, NY: Cornell University; Roper Center for Public Opinion Research, iPOLL, distrib.2017).

5. For the full text of the New Jersey law, see https://www.njleg.state.nj.us/2010/Bills/PL10/122_.PDF.

6. Ken Rigby, "What Parents Can Do to Prevent Their Child from Being Involved in Bullying at School?" *What Parents Can Do* (blog), n.d., http://www.kenrigby.net/12-Prevention.

7. See www.healthychildren.org for ideas like these and others.

8. For more, see PACER's National Bullying Prevention Center, *Cyberbullying* (blog), n.d., https://www.pacer.org/bullying/resources/cyberbullying/.

9. "How to Encourage Empathy," PREVNet, n.d., https://www.prevnet.ca/bullying/parents/how-to-encourage-empathy.

10. Ibid.

11. Ibid.

12. Ibid.

13. Ken Rigby, "What If Your Child Is Being Bullied at School?" *What Parents Can Do* (blog), n.d., http://www.kenrigby.net/13-If-your-child-is-bullied.

14. Quoted in Dan Jones, "The Power of Mind," *New Scientist* (March 12, 2016), 30–33.

15. PACER, *Cyberbullying*.

16. Paul Bischoff, "Almost 60 Percent of Parents with Children Aged 14 to 18 Reported Them Being Bullied," *VPN & Privacy* (blog), May 8, 2019, https://www.comparitech.com/blog/vpn-privacy/boundless-bullies/.

17. Tchiki Davis, "6 Tips for Decoding Emotions in Text Messages," *Psychology Today*, October 11, 2017, https://www.psychologytoday.com/us/blog/click-here-happiness/201710/6-tips-decoding-emotions-in-text-messages.

Chapter 13. What Parents Want

1. Kim Parker, "Families May Differ, But They Share Common Values on Parenting," *FactTank* (blog), Pew Research Center, September 18, 2014, http://www.pewresearch.org/fact-tank/2014/09/18/families-may-differ-but-they-share-common-values-on-parenting/.

2. Ibid.

3. Ibid.

4. Ibid.

5. "Dear Reader: Would You Rather Raise a Child to Be . . . ?" *New York Times Magazine*, January 6, 2019.

6. Hart Research Associates, *Public School Parents on the Value of Public Education* (Washington, DC: Hart Research Associates, September 2017), https://www.aft.org/sites/default/files/parentpoll2017_memo.pdf.

7. See Jennifer Kotler Clarke, "Diversity: Brought to You by the Letter E, Exposure & Empathy" (blog), July 11, 2017, Joan Ganz Cooney Center, Sesame Workshop, https://joanganzcooneycenter.org/2017/07/11/diversity-brought-to-you-by-the-letter-e-exposure-empathy/.

8. Take the survey at http://kindness.sesamestreet.org/parent-survey/.

Chapter 14. Self-Compassion and Self-Empathy

1. Quoted in Clemmie Moodie, "Rihanna Receiving 'Confidence Counselling' and Help from a Life Coach to Combat Low Self-Esteem Issues," *Daily Mirror*, May 13, 2014, https://www.mirror.co.uk/3am/celebrity-news/rihanna-getting-confidence-counselling-help-3537117.

2. Kristin Neff and Christopher Germer, *The Mindful Self-Compassion Workbook: A Proven Way to Accept Yourself, Build Inner Strength and Thrive* (New York: Guilford Press, 2018).

3. Cited in Deborah Farmer Kris, *How Self-Compassion Supports Academic Motivation and Emotional Wellness*, KQED News, MindShift, January 14, 2019, https://www.kqed.org/mindshift/52854/how-self-compassion-supports-academic-motivation-and-emotional-wellness.

4. I highly urge you to go online hear more from Neff. View her TED talk, "The Space between Self-Esteem and Self Compassion: Kristin Neff at TEDxCentennialParkWomen," February 6, 2013, https://www.youtube.com/watch?v=IvtZBUSplr4, or her interview with empathy expert Edwin Rutsch, https://www.youtube.com/watch?v=5hchn9KMRNM. Also, this great cartoony video on self-compassion has six steps and outlines a peaceful, compassionate exercise with (spoiler alert) a slightly inappropriate use of bubbles at the end: "Self Compassion," February 1, 2016, https://www.youtube.com/watch?v=-kfUE41-JFw&feature=youtu.be.

5. Kristin D. Neff, "The Development and Validation of a Scale to Measure Self-Compassion," *Self and Identity* 2 (2003), 223.

6. Marina Krakovsky, "Self-Compassion Fosters Mental Health," *Scientific American*, July 1, 2012, https://www.scientificamerican.com/article/self-compassion-fosters-mental-health/?redirect=1.

7. Ibid.

8. Hooria Jazaieri, "Compassionate Education from Preschool to Graduate School: Bringing a Culture of Compassion into the Classroom," *Journal of Research in Innovative Teaching & Learning* 11, no. 1 (2018), https://www.emeraldinsight.com/doi/full/10.1108/JRIT-08-2017-0017.

9. See "Karen Gerdes & Edwin Rutsch: Dialogs on How to Build a Culture of Empathy," Center for Building a Culture of Empathy, n.d., http://culture-ofempathy.com/References/Experts/Karen-Gerdes.htm.

10. Peter Funt, "Does Anyone Collect Old Email?" *New York Times*, April 5, 2019, https://www.nytimes.com/2019/04/05/opinion/memory-collections.html.

11. Ibid.

Chapter 15. Active Listening

1. "Prince William and Kate Middleton Are the New Faces of This Parenting Technique," *Time*, September 26, 2016, http://time.com/4507607/kate-middleton-prince-william-active-listening/.

2. Erin Hill, "Why Every Parent Should Copy Prince William's Special Dad Move with Prince George," *People*, July 21, 2016, https://people.com/royals/prince-williams-special-dad-move-with-prince-george/.

3. Gill Connell and Cheryl McCarthy, *A Moving Child Is a Learning Child* (Minneapolis, MN: Free Spirit Publishing, 2014), 148.

4. David A. Levine, *Teaching Empathy: A Blueprint for Caring, Compassion, and Community* (Bloomington, IN: Solution Tree, 2005), 63.

5. Ibid.

6. Adam Bryant, "How to Be a Better Listener," *New York Times*, n.d., https://www.nytimes.com/guides/smarterliving/be-a-better-listener.

7. Ibid.

8. See https://therelationshipfoundation.org/ for more from this group.

9. See "Empathy: The Art of Listening," n.d., https://therelationshipfoundation.org/images/pdfs/empathy-art-of-listening.pdf.

10. Ibid.

11. Henrik Edberg, "How to Become a Better Listener: 10 Simple Steps," *The Positivity Blog*, updated March 4, 2019, https://www.positivityblog.com/better-listener.

12. Tali Shenfield, "How to Communicate with Your Teen through Active Listening" (blog), October 16, 2017, http://www.psy-ed.com/wpblog/communicate-with-teen/.

Chapter 16. Empathy and Gender

1. See "New Girl Scouts Research Exposes the Impact of Reality TV on Girls," *gsblog*, October 13, 2011, http://blog.girlscouts.org/2011/10/new-girl-scouts-research-exposes-impact.html.

2. Ibid.

3. Claire Cain Miller, "Many Ways to Be a Girl, But One Way to Be a Boy: The New Gender Rules," *New York Times*, September 14, 2018, https://www.nytimes.com/2018/09/14/upshot/gender-stereotypes-survey-girls-boys.html.

4. Ibid.

5. Cited in Moises Velasquez-Manoff, "Real Men Get Rejected, Too," *New York Times*, February 24, 2018, https://www.nytimes.com/2018/02/24/opinion/sunday/real-men-masculinity-rejected.html?smid=tw-nytopinion&smtyp=cur.

6. Ibid.

7. Miller, "Many Ways to Be a Girl."

8. Jessica Zack, "Penny Orenstein Wants You to Talk with Your Boys about Sex," *San Francisco Chronicle*, January 17, 2020, https://datebook.sfchronicle.com/books/peggy-orenstein-wants-you-to-talk-about-sex-with-your-boys.

9. Gwen Dewar, "The Case for Teaching Empathy: Why Empathy Doesn't 'Just Happen,'" *Parenting Science*, 2009–2013, https://www.parentingscience.com/teaching-empathy.html.

10. Frans de Waal, *The Age of Empathy: Nature's Lessons for a Kinder Society* (New York: Harmony, 2009), 214.

11. Ibid.

12. Ibid., 67–68.

13. Jolien Van der Graaff et al., "Perspective Taking and Empathic Concern in Adolescence: Gender Differences in Developmental Changes," *Developmental Psychology* 50, no. 3 (2014): 881–88, http://dx.doi.org/10.1037/a0034325.

14. Karla McLaren, *The Art of Empathy: A Complete Guide to Life's Most Essential Skills* (Boulder, CO: Sounds True, 2013), 230.

15. Ibid.

16. Ibid.

Chapter 17. Empathy's Cousins: Social-Emotional Skills

1. Joseph A. Durlak et al., "The Impact of Enhancing Students' Social and Emotional Learning: A Meta-Analysis of School-Based Universal Interventions," *Child Development* 82, no. 1 (2011): 405–32, https://www.casel.org/wp-content/uploads/2016/01/meta-analysis-child-development-1.pdf.

2. Rebecca D. Taylor et al., "Promoting Positive Youth Development through School-Based Social and Emotional Learning Interventions: A Meta-Analysis of Follow-Up Effects," *Child Development* 88, no. 4 (2017), https://doi.org/10.1111/cdev.12864.

3. See CASEL, "What Is SEL?" n.d., https://casel.org/what-is-sel/.

4. Walter Mischel, *The Marshmallow Test: Mastering Self-Control* (New York: Little, Brown, 2014).

5. Ibid.

6. Sarah Ramirez, "5 Easy Ways to Teach Kids Self-Control and Delayed Gratification," *A Fine Parent* (blog), n.d., https://afineparent.com/emotional-intelligence/delayed-gratification.html.

7. Cited in Jennifer Breheny Wallace, "How to Raise More Grateful Children," *Wall Street Journal*, February 23, 2018, https://www.wsj.com/articles/how-to-raise-more-grateful-children-1519398748.

8. John Gottman and Joan DeClaire, *The Heart of Parenting: How to Raise an Emotionally Intelligent Child* (London: Bloomsbury Publishing, 1997), 41.

9. Ibid., 20.

Chapter 18. Teaching Empathy through Documentary Films, Storytelling, and Photos

1. Visit https://nj.pbslearningmedia.org/ to find their wonderful videos, categorized by grade.

2. Karla McLaren, *The Art of Empathy: A Complete Guide to Life's Most Essential Skills* (Boulder, CO: Sounds True, 2013), 217, 277.

3. Ibid., 276.

4. Joan Skolnick, Nancy Dulberg, and Thea Maestre, *Through Other Eyes: Developing Empathy and Multicultural Perspectives in the Social Studies* (New York: Pippin Publishing, 2004), 23.

5. Ibid.

Chapter 19. Pets and Empathy

1. Quoted in Stephanie Larratt, "1 Year after Parkland School Shooting, Therapy Dogs Get Special Yearbook Honors," *Today*, May 17, 2019, https://www.today.com/pets/marjory-stoneman-douglas-honors-its-therapy-dogs-yearbook-photos-t154344.

2. Denise Daniels, "Want to Raise Empathetic Kids? Get Them a Dog," *Washington Post*, April 14, 2015, https://www.washingtonpost.com/posteverything/wp/2015/04/14/want-to-raise-empathetic-kids-get-them-a-dog/?noredirect=on&utm_term=.7454002585a3.

3. Ibid.

4. Marguerite E. O'Haire et al., "Social Behaviors Increase in Children with Autism in the Presence of Animals Compared to Toys," *PLOS ONE*, February 27, 2013, https://doi.org/10.1371/journal.pone.0057010.

5. Charles Siebert, "What Does a Parrot Know about PTSD?" *New York Times*, January 28, 2016, https://www.nytimes.com/2016/01/31/magazine/what-does-a-parrot-know-about-ptsd.html.

6. Daniels, "Want to Raise Empathetic Kids?"

7. Rebecca Purewal et al., "Companion Animals and Child/Adolescent Development: A Systematic Review of the Evidence," *International Journal of Environmental Research and Public Health* 14, no. 3 (2017): 34, https://dx.doi.org/10.3390/ijerph14030234.

8. Andrea Beetz et al., "Psychosocial and Psychophysiological Effects of Human-Animal Interactions: The Possible Role of Oxytocin," *Frontiers in Psychology* 3 (2012), https://doi.org/10.3389/fpsyg.2012.00234.

Chapter 20. Heroes and More Heroes

1. Quoted in P. Kim Bui, "The Empathetic Newsroom: How Journalists Can Better Cover Neglected Communities," American Press Institute, April 26, 2018, https://www.americanpressinstitute.org/publications/reports/strategy-studies/empathetic-newsroom/single-page/.

2. Robert Mackey, "Jailed Chinese Dissident's 'Final Statement,'" *New York Times*, October 8, 2010, https://thelede.blogs.nytimes.com/2010/10/08/jailed-chinese-dissidents-final-statement/.

Chapter 21. Empathy and Paying It Forward

1. Jason Hanna, "Suicides under Age 13: One Every 5 Days," CNN, August 14, 2017, https://www.cnn.com/2017/08/14/health/child-suicides/index.html.

2. Peter Gray, "The Decline of Play and Rise in Children's Mental Disorders," *Psychology Today*, January 26, 2010, https://www.psychologytoday.com/us/blog/freedom-learn/201001/the-decline-play-and-rise-in-childrens-mental-disorders.

3. Jean M. Twenge et al., "Age, Period, and Cohort Trends in Mood Disorder Indicators and Suicide-Related Outcomes in a Nationally Representative Dataset, 2005–2017," *Journal of Abnormal Psychology* 128, no. 3 (2019): 185–99, http://dx.doi.org/10.1037/abn0000410.

4. Sarah Schwartz, "Teachers Support Social-Emotional Learning, But Say Students in Distress Strain Their Skills," *Education Week*, July 16, 2019, https://www.edweek.org/ew/articles/2019/07/17/teachers-support-social-emotional-learning-but-say-students.html.

5. Dan Rather and Elliot Kirschner, *What Unites Us: Reflections on Patriotism* (New York: Algonquin Books, 2017), 101.

6. Ibid., 91, 95.

7. Ibid., 98, 102.

8. David Sloan Wilson, *This View of Life: Completing the Darwinian Revolution* (New York, Pantheon, 2019), 153, 193, 197.

9. Ibid., 222.

10. Joel Westheimer, "What Kind of Citizens Do We Need?" in "Citizens in the Making," special issue, *Educational Leadership* 75, no. 3 (2017): 12–18, http://www.ascd.org/publications/educational-leadership/nov17/vol75/num03/What-Kind-of-Citizens-Do-We-Need%C2%A2.aspx?utm_source=ascdexpress&utm_medium=email&utm_campaign=Express%2014-29.

11. Ibid.

Last Thoughts

1. Jamil Zaki, *The War for Kindness: Building Empathy in a Fractured World* (New York: Crown, 2019), 169.

appendices

Appendix A: Lynne's Online Resources for Empathy Development for Youth

For those looking for great resources to help teach empathy to a child, here are my favorites.

Best General Empathy Websites

- Books That Teach Empathy (https://www. commonsensemedia.org/lists/books-that-teach-empathy) A great compilation of books for all ages that celebrate friendship, difference, and the importance of caring for one another.

- Brightly (https://www.readbrightly.com/) Provides information on books to get kids reading, including plenty that build empathy. Do yourself a favor and look up the book list "How to Talk to Kids about Race: Books and Resources That Can Help."

- The Collaborative for Academic, Social and Emotional Learning (https://casel.org)
  Resources from leading experts for everyone from researchers to teachers to parents.

- Empathy Library (https://www.empathylibrary.com)
  Connects you to inspiring books and films.

- Empathy Museum (http://www.empathymuseum.com/)
  Created in the United Kingdom, this organization creates pop-up museum exhibits that travel around the world. Visit the site for great podcasts where you can walk in others' shoes.

- goodcharacter.com (https://www.goodcharacter.com/)
  A great site with curriculum, lesson plans, activities, programs, and resources for learning more about social emotional skills.

- Joel Sartore's Photo Ark (https://www.joelsartore.com/photo-ark/)
  A few minutes on this exotic animal-filled site will generate tons of empathy for our planet and its live treasures.

- A Mighty Girl (https://www.amightygirl.com/)
  Provides books and resources for girls, including about indigenous girls.

- Social-Emotional and Character Development Lab (www.secdlab.org)
  The SECD lab's website has excellent resources on social-emotional skills.

- Start Empathy (https://startempathy.org/)
  An initiative of Ashoka, a community dedicated to building children's empathy, designed to encourage youth to be problem solvers and changemakers.

- Teaching Tolerance (https://www.tolerance.org/)
  A mainstay for educators and others passionate about tolerance.

Media Literacy

- Common Sense Education
  (https://www.commonsense.org/education/)
  Go to the Digital Citizenship section for resources on
  information literacy in the digital age.

- National Association for Media Literacy
  (https://namle.net/)
  The go-to site for academics and practitioners.

- Media Literacy Now (https://medialiteracynow.org)
  Plenty of materials to help prepare young people to be
  thoughtful, safe, and effective consumers and creators of
  media.

Parenting

- The Bully Project (http://www.thebullyproject.com/parents)
  Provides tips for parents on how to deal with their kids
  getting bullied.

- The Center for Parenting Education (https://
  centerforparentingeducation.org/)
  Lots of articles and resources to help families create a warm,
  caring home environment.

- Fred Rogers Center, near Pittsburgh (https://www.
  fredrogerscenter.org/)
  Fred Rogers's work carries on at the Fred Rogers Center;
  check out the archive!

- Parenting Science (https://www.parentingscience.com/)
  Helpful tips from evolutionary anthropologist Gwen Dewar
  on parenting.

Assessment/Evaluation: Empathy Surveys for Parents and Teachers

- Eckerd College's Interpersonal Reactivity Index survey
  (https://www.eckerd.edu/psychology/iri/)
  Taps into various facets of empathy, including perspective taking, empathic concern, and personal distress.

- The Empathy Questionnaire
  (https://www.focusonemotions.nl/empathy-questionnaire)
  A twenty-item questionnaire filled out by parents on how much empathy their child shows.

- K Is for Kind: A National Survey on Kindness and Kids
  (http://kindness.sesamestreet.org/parent-survey)
  Take this survey to help Sesame Street build a community of kindness.

Appendix B: Lynne's Top Ten Most Empathy-Triggering Moments

Here are the top ten events that generated empathy in me that I've read about or lived through.

1. 1861: Harriet Beecher Stowe publishes Uncle Tom's Cabin about the cruelty of slavery, helping to lay the groundwork for the Civil War and emancipation.

2. 1911: The Triangle Shirtwaist Factory fire results in the deaths of 146 mostly immigrant young women and girls. The tragedy fuels the Progressive social movement.

3. 1932: The baby of famed aviator Charles Lindbergh is kidnapped and later found murdered.

4. 1963: President John F. Kennedy is slain using a high-powered rifle while riding in a convertible in Dallas. I was in fifth grade. I remember my teacher telling us what happened and crying.

5. 1964: Kitty Genovese is stabbed to death in Queens, New York. The New York Times reported that thirty-eight bystanders heard her scream but did nothing. I could only wonder what would have happened if one person had gone to her rescue. (Note: Many years later, the claim that there were numerous witnesses was debunked.)

6. 1964–1973: The Vietnam War is full of horrific moments, especially the dropping of napalm on innocent Vietnamese citizens, including children; the slaughter of innocents by American soldiers in the My Lai massacre; and the killing of four college students at Kent State by members of the Ohio National Guard. I personally took part in protests on my college campus against Nixon's escalation of the war.

7. 1999: Two high schoolers go on a rampage at Columbine High School, killing more than twelve fellow students and one teacher. We need to remember the victims. However, we also need to keep in mind that the perpetrators were bullied and excluded for years. This can be prevented.

8. 2001: Four planes are hijacked by terrorists, including two that slammed into the World Trade Center towers, killing nearly three thousand. I knew a father of four who perished.

9. 2005: Hurricane Katrina strikes New Orleans. Dead bodies are seen on TV and in newspaper photos floating in the water. How could this happen in the United States?

10. 2015: A three-year-old Syrian boy's dead body washes up on the beach in Turkey amid a massive refugee crisis. One of the hashtags is "humanity washed ashore."

Can you think of events that have evoked empathy in you during your lifetime? What are your moments? What are your kids' moments? Suggest to your kids that they research one of these events and discuss it as a family. Did these events create more empathy for others? Why or why not? Did they result in anything positive? Negative? Consider making an empathy scrapbook.

Appendix C: Empathy Trivia FAQ Quiz

Here's a quiz to test your empathy knowledge. The answers are on the next page. No peeking!

Questions (True or False)

1. Since the 1970s, empathy has been improving.

2. Females are born with more empathy than males are.

3. People cannot increase the level of empathy they are born with.

4. Video games decrease empathy, especially violent video games.

5. Sympathy is the same as empathy.

6. The motivation to connect with a human being is the primary driver in language learning.

7. Cyberbullying victims experience lower levels of depression than "standard" bullying victims.

8. Two out of three American children say that their parents limit the amount of TV they watch.

9. A child's own emotional needs must be met before he or she can show empathy for others.

10. Empathy is not an essential life skill.

Answers

1. False
2. True (research says probably)
3. False
4. True
5. False
6. True
7. False (higher levels)
8. False (fewer than one out of three parents limit TV)
9. True
10. False

Appendix D: Lynne's Top Ten Empathy Builders

Refresh what you have learned with these handy top ten empathy builders; complete as many as you can. Remember, the earlier you start in your child's life, the better.

1. **Engage in active listening.** This is the most important skill you can practice. It will benefit you in many ways. Listen to your kids, your spouse or significant other, relatives, and coworkers. You will hear more and become more mindful and focused.

2. Make time each week to **schedule empathy activities and reading**, even if it's only fifteen minutes a week.

3. Don't overschedule kids. Make time for nature, creative play, and face-to-face time. Imagination is important, too.

4. **Establish "screen free" zones in your home.** Put screens away during meals, interpersonal time, and at night in the kids' bedrooms. For example, collect phones at bedtime. Consider a weekly "media fast" with your family. Do more with books, art projects, pets, and so on.

5. **Turn your own phone off.** Increase your face-to-face time with your family, relatives, and friends. Your family is watching you. Role model that you can exist without a cell phone as part of your day.

6. **Role model empathy, compassion, and respect for others.**

7. **Discipline, don't punish.** Be consistent. Search for teachable moments, engage in conversations, and discuss making better choices when your kids fall short. Punishment doesn't teach anything. Build a lifelong relationship with your youngsters.

8. **Look for teachable moments.** Be on the lookout in the mall, sports events, food store, and community events to role model prosocial behavior. Discuss better choices that others could have made.

9. **Volunteer.** Look for ways to expose your children to those in the community who have less than you. Visit a senior center, soup kitchen, or charity with which your child is familiar. As we have learned, community service on its own does not make for empathy. Research informs us that discussions that examine "walking in the shoes" of, for example, a poor person, an elderly person, or someone in pain are the necessary empathy builders before or after community-service activities.

10. **Have some fun.** Kids learn better when they are having fun. Can you think of a fun empathy activity that I haven't suggested yet? An empathy game? An empathy challenge? Be inventive!

CPSIA information can be obtained
at www.ICGtesting.com
Printed in the USA
LVHW092235220322
714156LV00015B/293

9 781956 450101